GEORGE GRAHAM
The Wonder Years

JEFF KING lives in Barcelona and writes for a number of Spanish newspapers and magazines on English football and youth culture. He also contributes to *90 Minutes* on European soccer. He has been an Arsenal fan for twenty years.

TONY WILLIS was born in Highbury. In 1986 he founded the irreverent Arsenal fanzine *One-Nil Down, Two-One Up*, which he still edits. He also writes for *Time Out* magazine.

NICK HORNBY is author of the best-selling *Fever Pitch*, which has been successfully transferred to the stage. He also writes for a host of national magazines and newspapers.

MICHAEL COLLINS is a freelance writer who contributes regularly to *Time Out* and *The Big Issue*. He also co-edits *One-Nil Down, Two-One Up* with Tony Willis.

HENRY WINTER, formerly the football diary writer on *The Independent*, is the football correspondent at *The Daily Telegraph*.

TOM WATT is an actor, broadcaster and writer. His last book, *The End*, chronicles eighty years of life on Arsenal's North Bank, and *A Passion for the Game* is published later this year.

PAUL HAWKSBEE is the editor of *90 Minutes* and executive editor of *World Soccer* magazine.

BRIAN GLANVILLE is one of Britain's best-known football writers; formerly at *The Sunday Times*, he is now at *The People*. With a number of books to his credit, Brian also writes for *World Soccer* magazine.

'AL FRESCO' is the pseudonym of the enigmatic author of the George Graham column in *One-Nil Down, Two-One Up*.

GEORGE GRAHAM
The Wonder Years

★ ★ ★

JEFF KING *and* TONY WILLIS

First published in Great Britain in 1995 by
Virgin Books
an imprint of Virgin Publishing Ltd
332 Ladbroke Grove
London W10 5AH

A catalogue record for this book is available from the British
Library

ISBN 1 85227 580 4

Text designed by Roger Kohn
Typeset by TW Typesetting, Plymouth, Devon
Printed and bound in Great Britain by
Mackays of Chatham, Lordswood, Chatham, Kent

*Dedicated to our dads for taking us and our mums
for indulging the obsession*

Contents

Illustrations

Acknowledgements

We would like to thank Lee Dixon, Alan Smith, Brian Marwood, Charlie Nicholas, Paul Davis, David Court, Pat Rice, Terry Murphy, Terry Neill and Alf Fields for their invaluable help in writing this book.

Thanks also to Lesley Trachy; Matthew at Colorsport; Doug Poole; John Cross at the *Islington Gazette*; Linda Willis; Paul Hawksbee, Dave Cottrell, Adam Boyle and everyone at *90 Minutes*; Antoni Closa and everybody at *Sport*, Barcelona; Silvia Roig Felius, Andrew Allerton and Steve Ford for their support, enthusiasm and contributions.

To Mal Peachey, Paul Forty and Hannah MacDonald at Virgin Publishing – sorry about some of the deadlines!

To Mike, Ian, Sarah, Chas, Al and the rest of the crowd at *One-Nil Down* – keep the faith.

Finally, thanks to Tom Watt, Henry Winter, Brian Glanville, Paul Hawksbee, Mike Collins and Nick Hornby. As they say at the Oscars, without you none of this would have been possible.

The last word is for Brad and Mark, fellow sufferers in the bad old days and *real* Arsenal fans.

Foreword

When George Graham arrived at Highbury in May 1986, Arsenal had won only one trophy since he himself formed part of the famous Double-winning side fifteen years earlier. Since then Arsenal have collected six major trophies in eight seasons, a remarkable record which has seen Graham's reign dubbed 'the second golden era' in the club's history – the wonder years.

This book does not attempt to make 'odious comparisons' (in the words of Brian Glanville) with Herbert Chapman's original golden era of the 30s. When Chapman came to Highbury in 1925 Arsenal had won nothing in their forty-year history. From 1930 to 1939 they won five league titles and the FA Cup twice, and in the process became the most famous club side in the world.

Graham's trophy haul bears comparison with Chapman's but his teams have never come close to dominating an era in the way Chapman's Arsenal dominated the 30s.

Off the pitch, no manager could hope to influence the game in the way that Herbert Chapman did. Chapman was responsible for the introduction of the numbering of players' shirts and the 45-minute clock, and was one of the first figures within the game to recommend a solitary manager of the England team. Most famously, in 1932 he persuaded London Electric Railway (forerunner to London Underground) to change the name of the station near Highbury from Gillespie Road to simply Arsenal.

On the other hand, Chapman did not have to contend with saturation TV coverage, a rabid tabloid Press, prima donna millionaire players, fanzines and a clutch of club chairmen with bottomless pockets in a spiralling transfer market.

Today, football is big business where the merchandising and marketing boys call the shots. Graham, like many other modern managers of big clubs, is part of a senior management team, but has clearly defined responsibilities. At Highbury the business side is dealt with by vice-chairman David Dein and managing director Ken Friar.

This book therefore sets out to chronicle and analyse Graham's wonder years purely in a modern context, concentrating on what's taken place on the pitch. Graham's tenure as manager has coincided with a number of social upheavals within the game; the Taylor Report and the move toward all-seater stadia, in general, and the infamous Arsenal Bond Scheme in particular. The story of the social re-engineering of football, however, is for another time and another place.

This is a book of two halves.

The first is an eclectic set of essays which try to capture some of the broader themes of the wonder years. In his introduction, Nick Hornby provides his own inimitable insight into Graham's managerial machinations. Jeff King follows with an analysis of the 'Cult of the Manager', a phenomenon fuelled by the media, which has seen football managers assume a cult status and profile to match pop stars and politicians. Don't believe the hype, King argues.

Next, I spoke to some of the key players to find out what kind of man George Graham is to work for, probing for the secrets of Arsenal's remarkable success under 'the gaffer'.

Mike Collins takes aim from the terraces (or should that be the seats?), assessing Graham's image with the fans. Most Gooners display a superficial respect for Graham's achievements, but he is not revered like a Busby or a Shankly. Why?

In his chapter 'No One Likes Us', Henry Winter examines Arsenal's relationship with the media under Graham. It is a poorly kept secret that the inner sanctum at Highbury feel slighted by the lack of respect shown by the media for the achievements of the last eight years. Winter, a prominent member of the fourth estate, assesses the mood of Fleet Street in an attempt to get to the bottom of the 'boring Arsenal' tag.

Much of Graham's success has come from building a team with a mixture of astute buys from lesser clubs blended with a clutch of home-grown youngsters. Paul Merson, Tony Adams, Paul Davis, Kevin Campbell and Michael Thomas are all products of Arsenal's remarkable youth system. Tom Watt charts the development of this football factory and analyses the contribution it has made to Graham's reign.

If all of this sounds like one-way traffic from N5, to create some balance we invited Paul Hawksbee, editor of *90 Minutes*, to put the wonder years into perspective from the other end of Tottenham High Road. Hawksbee, a lifelong Spurs fan, has watched his team struggle while Arsenal have collected the silverware under Graham. Is it really a third of a century since Spurs last won the title? It surely is, so what do our cousins from N17 make of the recent success of their more famous and glamorous rivals? Hawksbee, through gritted teeth, tries to explain.

Finally we look to Brian Glanville, the doyen of English football writers, for his own impressionistic view of life at Highbury under Graham the manager. Glanville and Graham are seasoned protagonists and this chapter sees the Fleet Street veteran strike a crucial psychological blow just before half-time.

The second half of the book is a season-by-season history of the wonder years, from 1987, when Charlie Nicholas ruined Ian Rush's record in the Littlewoods Cup Final at Wembley, to the Parken Stadium, Copenhagen, in May 1994, when Alan Smith's half-volley saw Arsenal defeat Parma, the aristocrats from Serie A, in the European Cup-Winners' Cup Final.

These two events emphasise how little has changed at Highbury during the wonder years. George Graham's underdog Arsenal are always at their best when called on to thwart more flamboyant and creative opponents. A second golden era, surely, but one founded on a blue-collar ethos and formidable team spirit.

Graham has said that he would like his teams to play with more flair but his actions often belie his words. In an attempt to maintain the momentum of almost a trophy every season, Graham seems to have lost all contact with the soul of the beautiful game.

Arsenal under Graham have been almost the exact opposite of the Ugly Duckling. In 1989 and 1991 the Championship sides were free scoring spirits inspired by Marwood, Rocastle, Thomas, Davis and Limpar. Since then they have mutated into a predictable robotic unit. Effective, but ugly to watch, the young guns of 89 have been replaced by John Jensen. Graham's failure to construct a dynasty to replace the Liverpool model of the 70s and 80s has left him exposed. In the harsh world of modern football the marketing men, the kit manufacturers, the sponsors, the board and the fans, of course, demand success.

But even that, it seems now, is not enough.

During eight years George Graham has restored Arsenal to former glories and given us a catalogue of experiences and memories unparalleled in the club's modern history. For the price of a Paul Warhurst he has built two Championship-winning sides, while Kenny Dalglish has spent £27 million and won nothing. Pretty is as pretty does. Just ask Ossie Ardiles.

Yet still there is a question mark over George Graham. Is he about to mastermind an extension to the second golden era or will the Highbury crown turn out to be from Ratner's? Has the manager who uncannily knows when to offload players reached his own sell-by date? And how is it that a man who has brought such success to their club is disliked by so many Arsenal fans?

Therein lies the enigma of George Graham. An enigma that this book seeks to explain.

Tony Willis

Part One
The Man

Introduction

by Nick Hornby

I n those few farcical weeks between Graham Taylor's resignation and
Terry Venables' appointment, there was a lot of loose, undoubtedly
preposterous talk in the tabloids about George Graham getting the
England job. Three or four years ago, rumours like these would have
plunged me into deep gloom: then, life without George was unthinkable.
Who wanted to go back to the bad old days of a half-empty Highbury,
perennial seventh place in the League and a side full of overpaid, under-
achieving ex-internationals who seemed to be allergic to anything made of
silver?

In the winter of 93/94, however, I caught myself thinking, well, maybe
it would be for the best if he went now. Like most Arsenal fans, I hadn't
enjoyed myself much at Highbury for a good season and a half; even the
double Cup-winning year had provided very little in the way of excitement.
The goals had dried up, the Championship apparently conceded before the
end of August, and everyone, apart from the manager, felt the need for a
new striker and at least one, possibly two or three, new midfielders. Maybe
I did want to see someone else take over, someone to build a new team,
one that did something other than grind the opposition down week after
week. For the first time ever, winning trophies no longer seemed to be
enough. I wanted to see some football, even if it meant an end to the
endless Wembley trips and open-topped buses around Islington.

The defeat against Bolton in the FA Cup intensified the air of depression.
A boring winning team is one thing; a boring losing team quite another. I
booed, and I was glad I booed, too, despite an article the next day in the
Evening Standard accusing me and my fellow booers of unforgivable fickleness. (Journalists, eh? They watch a team half-a-dozen times a season and
then tell you what you should be thinking.)

A few weeks later, I travelled to Copenhagen for the Cup-Winners' Cup
Final. After the win, and the magnificent, gut-busting performance, I sang
'Georgie Graham is magic/He wears a magic hat' over and over and over

3

again, and I meant every word of it, every time. I don't know what I want from football any more, and George is the source of this confusion.

Do you remember the Big Five? In the 80s, the Big Five were the teams that ran the First Division. They had things carved up between them, and nobody else was allowed a look-in: that was the way the game had gone, and there was nothing anyone could do about it. And yet, in the 93/94 season, Everton and Spurs, two of the Big Five, were coming to resemble the Shrinking Two. And what about Leeds? Or Blackburn? Or Newcastle? Or Villa? My point is simply that it is actually very easy for a healthy club to become a sick club – look at the histories of Wolves and Sunderland – and for ailing giants to get better. Nothing is fixed, provided you have a few million quid to spare and, more importantly, a manager who knows what to do with the money.

In the 1985/86 season, the year before George's arrival, Arsenal were sick, and the fact that we were big and rich only served to remind us just how empty the place was, and how much money had been wasted. If nobody regarded the club as a serious candidate for relegation, then certainly nobody expected it to be challenging for the Championship for the next few decades. It would be easy to interpret history differently – you know, top manager takes over big club, wins a few trophies, so what? – but anyone who watched Arsenal in the mid-80s knows that it wasn't like that. We were in trouble, going nowhere, and Highbury was a haunt only for people who could remember (or whose dads could remember) happier times, so it was a feat of major managerial brilliance to swing all that around. 'They'll be there or thereabouts,' someone says about Arsenal at the beginning of each season; they weren't saying that ten years ago.

How did it all happen? In his first season, George sold half the first-team squad, bought Perry Groves, and won the Littlewoods Cup; in his eighth season, he bought Eddie McGoldrick, dropped him, and won the Cup-Winners' Cup. In between there were two League titles and another couple of cups – the first title for the price of a couple of Stoke defenders, a Wimbledon full-back and a number nine from Leicester City. Only Terry Venables, who sold Maradona, bought Steve Archibald and won the Championship for Barcelona, has pulled off an equivalent trick in modern football history, and he only did it once. (Actually, the Spanish club had already decided to offload Maradona before Venables arrived, but as they say: If the myth's more interesting than the truth, go with the myth.)

For me, the big difference between Arsenal pre- and post-George is that they turned into a team that looked like they wanted to win. If the low point of Don Howe's last year as Arsenal's manager was the dismal, gutless

3-0 Cup defeat at Luton in 1986, the high point of George's first year was the Littlewoods Cup Semi-Final tie against Spurs. Spurs, with Allen and Hoddle and Waddle and Richard Gough, were a better team than Luton; just between ourselves, they were a better team than Arsenal. But players who will do anything they can to avoid defeat (and I am talking about legitimate defiance, rather than illegitimate thuggery) are dangerous opponents indeed: as Parma discovered, all the talent in the world won't help you if you don't have the guts to go with it. Against Tottenham, an injury-hit, inexperienced Arsenal team clung on and clung on and clung on, and eventually delivered a couple of quick knock-out punches right near the end, when it really mattered. A lot had changed in a year.

For the first few years, this sort of tenacity could, against the right kind of soft-bellied opposition produce goals, too. A characteristic of the first half of George's reign was the ability to score threes and fours and fives, sixes even, *sevens* even, in a short burst. The score at half-time v. Austria Vienna was one-nil; the final score was six-one. A few months later, we scored six second-half goals against Sheffield Wednesday. There were four second-half goals in less than twenty minutes against Norwich and Chelsea, five against Southampton . . . once they had wounded their opponents, they wouldn't stand back and wait for them to bleed to death, like previous Arsenal teams. They would tear them to pieces, and it was thrilling to watch. For the first time, I understood the thrill of hunting in packs.

That era officially ended on the final day of the 91/92 season, when George had been in charge for exactly five seasons; in Ian Wright, who scored two-thirds of a hat-trick in injury time that afternoon, we now had the best goal-scorer any of us under forty had ever seen in Arsenal colours, and yet we could no longer score to save our lives. One-nil to the Arsenal became both a song and a philosophy, and it was much more fun singing the song than watching the team.

It is not difficult to see why the goals dried up. As the Arsenal fanzine, *One-Nil Down, Two-One Up* pointed out recently, Brian Moore's memorable Thomas, charging through the midfield on *that night* was only possible because we possessed someone capable of charging through the midfield; John Jensen, much as we love him, isn't much of a charger. Marwood scored, Rocky scored, Micky scored, Limpar scored, Davis scored. In the old days. Schwarz, Jensen, Parlour, Selley, McGoldrick and Hillier have scored half-a-dozen times between them, ever. None of them, however, has had a row with the manager, and nowadays, sadly, that seems to be the point.

And yet we win things . . . the new, low-scoring Arsenal have won three trophies, as many as the old, high-scoring Arsenal (although the clunking Jensen model hasn't come close to winning the League yet). So what does it matter whether they play football or not, if the end result is the same? To me it matters – more so now, I guess, simply because we have won so much recently, and therefore I feel sated. In the last two years, I have spent nearly £500 on season tickets, and in return I have seen Arsenal score one or nil approximately 35 times. Thirty-five times in two seasons! Some of those – two or three, maybe – were memorable games, but the vast majority were not, and I would happily forgo another trophy for a few years if I could watch something that kept me warm on a Saturday afternoon – someone like Rocky or Micky or Anders, for example.

Is this heretical? Judging from the moans and groans and snarls emanating from the seats around me in the Lower East Stand, it's not a minority view. I would have liked us to sign Klinsmann, or Dumitrescu, or Cantona (whom George once memorably described as a 'cry-baby' in an interview) or Brolin, or . . . actually, I have just come back from another nil-nil draw, against Blackburn, and I would weep with relief if we signed Ian Ormondroyd. But George has his idiosyncrasies, and one of them is his mistrust of forwards: in eight years, he has signed only two strikers, Wright and Smith, but we seem to sign a new central defender every other week.

In a sense, the tenacity that Graham has bred in his players has worked against us. If it is possible to win trophies without talented players, simply by making the grafters work harder than footballers have ever worked before (Stephen Morrow is not, one feels, ever going to attract an offer from an Italian club, but he gave an extraordinary performance against Parma), then why bother with the likes of Limpar and Charlie Nicholas? They only get in the way of the coaching. Over the last couple of years, George has turned Arsenal into a table football team. All the players look the same, and he seems to control every kick from the sidelines. But during the Cup-Winners' Cup Final, as Brolin and Asprilla and Zola and the rest slowly got tangled up in Arsenal's constricting webs, you couldn't help but feel proud of a team that seems to be able to beat anyone, however superior on paper. And there it is, the old dilemma: would you rather support a team that thrills, or a team that wins things?

For four of five years, we had a team that did both. My fondest memories of the George Graham years will always be, I think, the teams that he turned out at the end of the 80s, with Rocastle creating havoc down the right, Williams and Davis, and later Thomas, strutting and biting through the middle, Smudge knocking them in, and huge crowds, 50,000 and more on quite a few occasions, squashed into Highbury to watch. I would guess that those are George's favourite years too, when it was still new to him but he was realising that he could do it, that he could break the Merseyside grip, that he could maybe become the best ever manager in Arsenal's history. Those must have been exciting times for him; they were certainly exciting times for us.

The most characteristic George Graham moment was at Anfield, that night. The final whistle blows; the players on the bench, Quinn and Bould and Merse and Miller, all go mad; George, the man who has just won Arsenal's first Championship for nearly two decades in the most dramatic way possible, comes over to them ... and tells them to calm down and stop being so silly. George doesn't make me smile very often – that's not his function in life. But I can never resist a grin when I see that on the video. What a guy! What, one wonders, would make him run like a demented deer across the pitch, *à la* David Pleat? A European Champions' Cup win, Arsenal having come back from 3-0 down to beat Milan 4-3 with Jensen dribbling round Baresi before dummying the keeper and sticking the ball into an empty net? Nah. George would straighten his tie, offer his congratulations to his opposite number, and stroll out on to the pitch to shake Tony's hand. That's how he is. If he were any different, Arsenal wouldn't be where they are, and he wouldn't be where he is, and nobody would have wanted to write a whole book about him, because there wouldn't be anything to say.

The Cult of the Manager

by Jeff King

'*The best team always wins. The rest is only gossip.*'

Jimmy Sirrel

'*I'm not in the entertainment business.*'

Jack Charlton

'*If war is too important to be left to generals, is football too important to leave to football managers?*'

Brian Glanville

'*Fucking hell's bells!*'

Graham Taylor

'*George knows.*'

Banner in the West Stand at Highbury

The all-pervading influence of the manager; his pivotal role in the success or failure of his club and his ability to make decisions that will have a real bearing on the outcome, not just of one-off matches, but whole seasons, is now taken for granted. Three decades on from its TV-assisted birth, the cult of the manager is alive and well and it takes a brave soul to suggest that maybe, just maybe, the influence of the man-at-the-top is not all it's cracked up to be.

For those within the game there is simply too much self-preservation involved to encourage dissenting voices. The managers themselves are part of an exclusive and self-perpetuating clique that is duty-bound to play along with the myth of managerial absolutism: in the case of those at the top of the pile, in order to justify their prestige and salaries; for the less fortunate, simply to hang on to their jobs. As for club directors, so long as an opportune change of manager offers a convenient panacea every time the team's fortunes are at a low ebb, why should they embrace the role of scapegoat by admitting *mea culpa*? Although sometimes an unwilling accomplice, the Press completes this incestuous triangle. Relations between journalists and managers are often strained, but always symbiotic; the manager as god-like figure is a convenient peg on which to hang newspaper articles and TV features; these, in turn, reinforce the mystique of the profession in general – the notion that managers really do make a difference, even if their influence is, at times, barely visible to the untrained eye.

But how much control does the football manager really wield? Why attribute so much influence to a figure who, after all, is but a peripheral character when it really matters? Footballers win and lose matches; for those all-important 90 minutes the manager is a mere bystander. Parallels can be drawn between the question marks over the real extent of managerial influence and the debate about the role of the director in the film-making process, an argument that has raged ever since the 50s when the French New Wave coined the term *auteur* to describe the more personal vision of a few select directors. The case against is not altogether dissimilar. When film-making is so obviously a collective process, one that demands scores of indispensable contributions – the screenwriter's, the cinematographer's, the editor's, the designer's, and a long etc. – is it not ridiculous to talk about a movie purely as the work of such and such a director? *Schindler's List* may well have been a labour of love for Steven Spielberg – though that hardly explains why he sat on the rights for a whole decade, during which time he offered the film to several other directors, including Martin Scorsese and Sydney Pollack – but it was hardly *his* in the exclusive sense of the word. The screenplay was written by Steven Zaillian; the very un-Spielbergesque *cinema verité* look was courtesy of the director of photography, Janusz Kaminski; and the stunning production design was the work of Allan Starski – and they were just three of the many vital collaborators. What is more, the film was based on Thomas Keneally's Booker Prize winner about a real person, Oskar Schindler. Yet people still talk about it as 'Spielberg's *Schindler's List*'. Admittedly, there may be a few directors like Woody Allen and Martin Scorsese who do impose a more personal vision on their films, but they are exceptions. As an enraged scriptwriter once said to the legendary director Frank Capra after handing him a blank page: 'Put the famous Capra touch to that!'

The average Hollywood journeyman may be a glorified lackey at the whims of the star, the producer and the studio, but even the directors without the clout of a Spielberg or Coppola have meaningful control on the set, the cinematic equivalent of the football pitch. If an actor fluffs his lines the director can always call a halt to the proceedings and roll the cameras anew. If a centre-forward blasts the ball over the bar from five yards, the manager – even one of the big shots – can hardly scream cut, rush on the pitch and get his erring striker to try again. However highly you rate the influence of the manager in the wider scheme of things, the fact remains that for those critical 90 minutes he is just another spectator. As Graham Taylor put it, 'Once the players have crossed that touchline they really are on their own.'

In an equally rare display of humility amongst managers, another ex-England boss, the late Don Revie, once insisted that 'the game is all about players'; an observation that saw him scratched off the Christmas card list of many a fellow boss, methinks. Jorge Valdano, Real Madrid's coach and World Cup winner with Argentina, is even more scathing about the cult of the manager: 'The figure of the coach is assuming far greater importance than it merits. It's the curse of a new age. I have to accept it, but it's not a trend I agree with. When I'm watching a game on television and the producer flashes us a shot of the coach, it strikes me as an absurd and irritating interruption. Even if I'm the coach in question.'

As with film directors though, there are exceptions to the rule, managers who clearly do make a difference. Herbert Chapman, Matt Busby, Bill Shankly and, despite his protestations, Don Revie, all imposed their character and style on one club *and* left some kind of legacy to the game in general. More recently, Brian Clough's clout was undeniable. You might argue the case for a couple more, but beyond them what is left? Quite simply, an insecure mass that in most cases can only whistle along to the sound of managerial musical chairs. Most managers, however competent and knowledgeable, are simply unable to impose themselves on situations governed by so many extraneous (and overwhelmingly adverse) circumstances.

Consider the handicaps the average boss has to deal with. There are the playing staff – if he's lucky, a couple of inconsistent prima donnas surrounded by the mediocre, gutless, hungover, homesick and past-it (and as the cupboard is invariably bare, he can forget about buying anything better). There are the vastly superior opponents (or simply slightly more motivated and/or marginally less incompetent). There are the wildly unrealistic expectations of the fans (and not only the ones who still turn up to hurl abuse from the stands – there's the butcher, the baker and his uncle too). There is a board which demand instant success but are unable or unwilling to provide the raw material. And then there are the sundry whims of Lady Luck: injuries and suspensions; bad refereeing decisions and blind linesmen; posts and crossbars; a bad bounce or an unkind deflection; and an interminable list of other potential problems. These imponderables haunt all teams and are quite simply *beyond any manager's control*.

On top of all these mitigating circumstances, the manager has to do battle with the most unwavering enemy of all – the law of averages. In a game that demands end-of-term results from each manager (at least from those who get that far) only a tiny minority can actually win; after all, there is only one Champion and a handful of consolation prizes. In which other walk of life is the man at the top given so much credit for success, or blame for failure, when so much is out of his hands? Even the Prime Minister rides out successive government cock-ups by fobbing the blame off on hapless subordinates (cabinet ministers and football managers are currently running neck and neck in the job security stakes). As Jorge Valdano put it on taking over at the desperate-for-success Spanish giants in 1994: 'No coach can guarantee results, you can only guarantee a style of playing. Results fall in the hands of fate. It is ridiculous to pin the etiquette of success or failure on a coach, just because a coin comes up heads or tails.'

Even the manager who gets it right on the night is likely to miss his curtain call tomorrow. Ron Saunders, Terry Neill, Dave Mackay, Tommy Docherty and Malcolm Allison were all well-known managers who enjoyed success at the highest level – winning League Championships and FA Cups. They have another thing in common; they all experienced the ignominy of failure: sackings, relegations and the realisation that top clubs were no longer interested in them. More recently, Howard Kendall, Graeme Souness, Ossie Ardiles, Graham Taylor and Ron Atkinson have all run the gamut of footballing fortunes from popular acclaim to disdain, and in some cases, back again. So what happens to the once-successful managers, the men who at the time of their triumphs – aided and abetted by the media – would have us believe that yes, they had discovered the magic ingredients, and yes, of course they were the principal reason for the team's success? The answer is really quite simple. When they were kings of the castle they were by no means the gods of popular myth, and their subsequent failure doesn't make them worthless charlatans either. Like most managers, their influence never approached the levels of conventional myth and eventually they succumbed to a destiny that was largely out of their hands. And these were men who were working at clubs that could provide the money and resources that most managers can only dream about. Lower down the scale it simply doesn't matter how many times you change the boss, it won't change a thing (ask any Hartlepool or Torquay fan).

If each generation throws up its exceptions to the rule, whither the 90s equivalents of the Quentin Tarantinos and Spike Lees in the footballing world? Alex Ferguson is currently riding on the crest of a wave at Old Trafford, but it sure was a long hard struggle before he got there. Only the untypical and admirable patience of the United board enabled Ferguson to weather regular Press campaigns to get rid of him (particularly during a period of frenzied attacks in the winter of 89/90) before he finally won the Championship at the seventh attempt in 1993. 'The backing of the board was vital for Alex,' says George Graham, 'because he inherited a situation fraught with danger at United, and came in for a hell of a lot of criticism. It took him three seasons to turn things around, but he has repaid the loyalty.' Apart from precious time, Ferguson had that other salient asset on his side – money. Given the way he spent it in his first few years at the club (he got no change from £3 million for Danny Wallace, Mike Phelan and the already ancient Mal Donaghy), United must surely be with the 'listening bank'; the 1994 Double side alone cost £23 million in transfer fees.

A year before the 1993 Championship triumph, Manchester United handed the title on a platter to Leeds with the fat lady at Old Trafford already rehearsing for the celebrations. Ferguson, who visibly buckled under pressure, was largely blamed. The United players were thrown out of gear by his constant tinkering with team selection in the run-in and a doubting and disorientated team succumbed to three defeats in the last ten days of the season. Even the triumphant Double campaign of 93/94 was tarnished by the early European debacle when Ferguson's expensively assembled outfit snatched defeat from the jaws of victory against the modest and mediocre Turkish side, Galatasary, at Old Trafford. As the still fallible manager later admitted, 'I made a pig's ear out of that one.'

David Pleat once said 'Four out of five ex-internationals don't do that well as managers. But one in five gets some money to spend and does.' Kenny Dalglish is one of the lucky ones. In his first two years at Blackburn Rovers, Dalglish spent some £27 million in the transfer market – until recently, the kind of silly money that only Italian managers got to throw around. If Rovers eventually win the League, the Scot will have achieved the rare feat of managing two different clubs to the Championship and talk of Dalglish the great manager will become common currency. But whatever his merits as a coach, the real motives behind Blackburn's rapid rise from anonymity to glory are quite patently economic. Of course, money doesn't guarantee silverware, but barring the emergence of a local sugar-daddy *à la* Jack Walker, it really is difficult to imagine an Ipswich Town, Derby County, Nottingham Forest, or even an Aston Villa (all sides that *won* rather than *bought* the Championship in the not-so-distant past), emerging through the big-money pack to sneak the League.

Another manager poised to write his name in the history books is Kevin Keegan. After an extended sojourn on the Costa del Sol (odd kind of managerial breeding ground, that) Keegan has worked miracles in a couple of years on Tyneside but again, it must be said, with considerable resources. Not surprisingly, Keegan has been heralded as a Messiah in the football-crazy North-East, where you've got to be getting on a bit to remember anything but the barren years, and he does seem to carry an aura of invincibility around him – Geordies say that if he fell in the Tyne he'd come up with a salmon in his mouth. Some great raids on the transfer market (Cole and Beardsley were bargains in any language) and an undeniable gift for man-management make Keegan a solid contender in the managerial legend stakes although it's perhaps a bit early to make sweeping judgements. It will certainly be interesting to see how an essentially intuitive and manifestly impatient personality deals with the inevitable troughs of management.

Howard Wilkinson is another manager who has plenty of admirers. In his first three-and-a-half years at Elland Road, 'Sergeant Wilko' transformed Leeds from a side struggling to avoid relegation to the Third Division into First Division champions (albeit courtesy of the wobbles of a superior United side). But the last couple of years have seen him unable to build on that success and his recent forays into the transfer market, in search of defenders and forwards to complement that enviable midfield, have been markedly unsuccessful.

As for Bobby Robson, surely anything England achieved under his misguided tutelage was in spite of his efforts? But even then, Robson's Italian swansong saw England just a couple of 'if only's . . .' short of a place in the World Cup Final itself: if only Chris Waddle's shot against Germany had not come back off the post; if only Andreas Brehme's on-the-road-to-nowhere free-kick hadn't taken a wicked deflection off Paul Parker; if only Waddle and Stuart Pearce hadn't missed those penalties. If England had come through that match and overcome a mediocre Argentina in the Final, Bobby Robson – despite years of blunders and ill-conceived tactics – would have written his name in the history books as the most successful England manager of all time (bearing in mind that Sir Alf's team triumphed on home turf). Who then would have dared to question his competence? Back in club football, Robson may be more relaxed, but he is still prone to the most inexplicable decisions. In what must rate as one of the all-time managerial howlers, the 1994 European Cup Semi-Final between Barcelona and

Oporto saw Robson assign a not particularly swift centre-back, the ageing Brazilian Aloisio, to mark Hristo Stoichkov down the flanks. The result? The bemused Aloisio with a very sore bum as the Bulgarian, just about the most explosively quick forward in world football, led him a merry dance and inspired Barça to a three-nil win (he scored twice and created the other goal). Sitting in the Press box at Camp Nou that night, I recalled Brian Glanville's comments about the fallibility of coaches: 'What is it that makes managers and coaches commit so many crass, basic tactical errors, flying in the face of common sense?'

After a spell that saw his star in danger of waning, the media's (and Fred's) favourite son, Terry Venables, is back in the limelight as England manager, even if it is by default (if it hadn't been for the fiasco at Tottenham he wouldn't have been available). Venables is a highly-rated coach, but his reputation has always gone hand-in-hand with his ability to court the media. When he came back to England after his spell in Spain he was greeted like a returning saviour – the fact that Camp Nou attendances had fallen to an all-time low, given the absolute sterility of Barcelona's football, was conveniently overlooked. And what exactly is a typical Venables side? Average with a nasty streak and/or a dodgy pitch (Crystal Palace and Queens Park Rangers), boring but effective (a Bernd Schuster-inspired Barcelona in 'El Tel's' first year in Spain), boring and ineffective (Barça with an out-of-sorts and eventually sidelined Schuster in the next three years), shapeless and spineless (Spurs before the off-field turmoil)? Despite the hype about the so-called Christmas tree formation, the early signs with England were not that promising either. If the most basic of coaching tenets suggests that a manager should shape his team around the available players rather than let a pre-ordained formation do the talking, how could Venables possibly justify using a system with only one out-and-out forward at a time when English football enjoys such an embarrassment of riches up front? As the World Cup confirmed, there is *no* country in the world with an array of strikers as potent as Shearer, Wright, Cole, Beardsley, Sutton, Ferdinand et al. Given that kind of potential, England should start as favourites to win the European Championship on home soil in 1996 and, if Venables can harness such abundant talent effectively, they could well break their duck in the competition. If that happens, the manager will get a large share of the credit and the Press will assail us with headlines about 'El Tel's England'. The Venables cult will be unstoppable. But with the kind of raw material at his disposal, should we expect anything less?

These days, nobody would rate Graham Taylor's chances of entering the pantheon of managerial greats, but with even a reasonable roll of the dice things could have been very different and the tactical gaffes aggravated by a touching but absurd faith in off-form players would be long forgotten. What if injuries hadn't robbed Taylor of so many key players when it mattered? Make no mistake, any country would miss an on-his-game Paul Gascoigne and a front-man as vigorous and incisive as Alan Shearer. And what if a certain man in black from Germany had sent off Ronald Koeman as he was duty-bound to do? Given the depressingly mediocre fare on offer in America, who knows what England might have done if they had qualified? If Lady Luck had smiled on Taylor, 'Do I not like that' might never have entered popular folklore and we might be looking at a derided character in a totally different light.

In reality, there is only one contemporary manager who is seriously threatening to forge himself a place in the annals of football legends alongside the Chapmans, Busbys and Shanklys; and like him or loathe him, that man is George Graham. The single-minded and unwaveringly ambitious Scot made an immediate impact on arriving at Highbury in 1986 and his Arsenal side have been the most consistently successful force in the English game ever since. Like Jorge Valdano, a budding legend himself in Spain, Graham concedes that 'you can never guarantee titles', but he quickly adds, 'you can make sure you are there and thereabouts'. And thereabouts Arsenal have most certainly been: two League Championships, the FA Cup, two League Cups and the European Cup-Winners' Cup, a testament to steadfast achievement. And before anybody gets blasé about this kind of success, or claims that it is par for the course at a club of Arsenal's stature, suffice to say that the Gunners won more Championships in Graham's first five years than in the previous three decades! Outside Highbury, the Scot may remain something of an enigma, but the results are there for all to see: he has imposed his personality and ideas on the club in a way that has no equal amongst his managerial peers and, in doing so, he has established such high standards and levels of consistency that it is unthinkable that Arsenal will slip out of the running for major honours whilst he remains at the helm. And Arsenal most certainly have a style. In cinematic terms, there is no clearer 'genre' in the footballing world than Arsenal's. There is not a football supporter in the country who can't sum up in a short sentence how Arsenal play and few would balk at the sobriquet, 'George Graham's Arsenal'. He, in turn, has no doubts about the managerial sway: 'You have a big influence because all your ideas and philosophy get through to the team and the way it plays. And the things you believe in affect the way the whole club is run.' If there is such a thing as a footballing *auteur*, Graham is it.

But what is the secret? What exactly is George Graham doing that his rivals aren't? Given that his own public pronouncements on management rarely extend beyond a self-serving line in sardonic platitudes – the 'you wouldn't understand even if I tried to explain' school of thinking – we can only guess. There is a lot of talk about hard work, not least from Graham himself, an argument that always strikes me as exceedingly dubious. Surely hard work is the least you can expect from such highly-paid professionals? I would have thought that even at struggling clubs a lack of effort is rarely the problem. What are we supposed to believe: that Swindon conceded 100 goals in the 93/94 Premier League because their management team and players weren't trying? When asked about the difficulties of having to work so hard in such stifling heat at the 1994 World Cup, the Spanish coach, Javier Clemente, replied: 'Hard work? This isn't hard work; working in a factory or a mine is what you call hard work.' Oops! Another manager on the Christmas card blacklist. The next time boss X, Y or Z starts to lecture self-servingly on the virtues of hard work, how about drowning him out with a chorus of 'and at more readies in a year than most of us will see in a lifetime – bloody right and all!'

It has become something of a cliché, but as a team Arsenal are very definitely more than the sum of their individual parts, a characteristic born of a high level of organisation and a system in which each player assumes a clearly defined role. Alex Ferguson, Graham's only contemporary rival in the trophy-winning stakes, lords it over a team that is still less than the sum total of its parts (Milan are probably the only other club side in the world with the kind of competition for places comparable to that which produces the eternal Ryan Giggs, Andrei Kanchelskis, Lee Sharpe dilemma) but Arsenal's success is based on no such embarrassment of riches. This probably has something to do with Graham's inherent distrust of what he always refers to as 'the so-called stars'. Despite all the collective achievements in Graham's first eight seasons, not one Arsenal player has been chosen as either the Footballer of the Year by the football writers or as PFA Player of the Year by his fellow players, and England sides have not exactly been crowded with players from Highbury either (see the statistics section on pages 278–86). Perhaps unfair, but surely no coincidence. If you accept the fact that Arsenal have rarely had the best footballers – something even the playing stalwarts of the wonder years readily admit – is Graham's success based on tactical acumen?

The Scot is obviously a good coach and he is certainly a dedicated one. He himself argues that his real power-base is Arsenal's training ground at London Colney and in his first eight years at the club you could count the number of times he didn't personally take control of training on one hand. As far as Graham is concerned, his time with the players every morning is sacrosanct. He is certainly adept enough at shuffling his pieces, and the daily meetings with the rest of the coaching staff before training gets under-way ensure a continuity of ideas throughout the club. But is there evidence of an innovative coach at work?

Graham believes that his experiment with the sweeper system in the 1989 Championship run-in didn't earn him the credit he deserved. But although that shift in emphasis had a positive short-term effect on Arsenal's title bid and was perhaps unusual in the context of the English game, it was hardly anything new, just a bastardised version of a system played elsewhere for years. Subsequently, Arsenal have rarely abandoned the flat back-four. Then again, few coaches have really changed the way football is played. And are there really any secrets still waiting to be discovered? In this respect a lot of rubbish is churned out: on the Continent, Arrigo Sacchi was greeted as some kind of tactical wizard for his supposedly new-fangled tactics at Milan in the late 80s. In fact, Sacchi simply borrowed the 4-4-2 system that has held sway in England ever since Alf Ramsey decided to abandon wingers back in 1966 (the same formation, incidentally, that Brazil used in most of their 1994 World Cup winning campaign). Milan's football under Sacchi and his successor, Fabio Capello, tends to be played in a reduced area in the centre of the park and is characterised by the rapid closing down of opponents whenever and wherever they enjoy possession. The key defensive trait is a liberal use of the offside trap (Franco Baresi must be the only man in Europe who spends more time than Tony Adams with his arm raised in the air like he just don't care!) Sounds familiar right? Sacchi may deserve credit for initiating a long-overdue rebellion against the stifling *catenaccio* of more classic Italian stock, but the essential difference between the European aristocrats of Lombardy and practically any English side you care to mention, was and is the players, i.e. *gracie* to Gullit, Van Basten, Savicevic, Desailly et al. If you still don't get the picture, that's *gracie* to Silvio Berlusconi's chequebook scrawl, not the etchings on Sacchi's blackboard. Lester Piggott once said that the best jockey is the one who wins when he is riding the best horse – Sacchi's merit was that he got the best out of the best players, nothing more.

Of the most prestigious European coaches, only Johan Cruyff has con-sistently experimented in recent years, often fielding a team that contains no more than a couple of nominal defenders and with an innovative verte-bral column of three attacking pivots – normally Ronald Koeman at the back, Pep Guardiola just ahead of him, and José Mari Bakero tucked in behind the forwards. But the most striking features of Cruyff's Barcelona are an absolute commitment to attacking in numbers, an enviable degree of technical ability throughout the team and the sheer flexibility of players who rarely spend a whole match in the same position. And, of course, these are all characteristics reminiscent of the Dutch side that pioneered the concept of 'total football' some two decades ago when Cruyff himself was a player. Even the Dutchman, never slow to blow his own trumpet, admits in more reflective moments that Barcelona's success is thanks to the players: 'My job is to look for good players and put together the best possible squad. If your players are better than your opponents 90 per cent of the time you will win.' As for the last time an English coach came up with something new (barring Alf Ramsey's purge of wingers), you'd probably have to go back to the days of the 'push and run' style of Arthur Rowe's Championship-winning Tottenham in 1951!

Innovative coaches at a macro-level may be something of a mythical and/or historical breed – again, a concept happily perpetuated by managers themselves, because after all they have to be seen to be doing something – but the role of the coach in planning for specific matches is less contentious and, in this respect many would argue that George Graham has few peers. His admirers argue that he possesses an uncommon flexibility on the tactical front and that this enables him to respond to varying situations – different opponents, competitions or playing conditions – by putting out sides designed to do a job on a given day. Depending on the circumstances, this might involve switching from a flat back four to the sweeper system, the singular use of a two-man axis in a nominal 4-2-4 system, the occasional deployment of Lee Dixon as an out-and-out midfielder, asking David Hillier or Martin Keown to assume the role of a man-to-man marker or the constant shifting around of Paul Merson. Nothing revolutionary, perhaps, but at least it shows something is going on upstairs.

On the debit side, Graham's sides have had an increasingly unbalanced look about them in recent seasons as his meddling leads to the habit of playing people out of position. Terry Venables once said that coaching was all about putting players in the area of the field where they would be most effective. I'm sure that Paul Merson – a player who in recent seasons has played virtually everywhere but in his natural position alongside the main striker – wishes Graham subscribed to the same theory. And the Scot's treatment of the once so promising Kevin Campbell seems almost sadistic. Campbell's sheer physical presence and eye for a goal (presuming it has not disappeared for ever) perhaps make him a valid option in and around the penalty area, but to exile a player of such limited touch and seeming lack of footballing nous out wide or in deeper positions appears odd. Other injured parties include John Jensen and Kevin Richardson – both asked at some stage to assume creative duties in midfield; an absolute nonsense given the distinct lack of verticality in their game. As for asking Michael Thomas to mark Paul Gascoigne in the 1991 FA Cup Semi-Final, that was a piece of strategic thinking worthy of General Custer.

Yet Graham does possess the knack of learning from Arsenal's rare set-backs. The successful Euro-campaign in 93/94 was forged out of the ashes of the European Cup defeat against Benfica in 1991 – on that occasion, Arsenal paid a heavy price for giving the Portugese too much space in midfield. In the 93/94 Cup-Winners' Cup, Graham's ploy of playing only a solitary forward up-front with two nominal wide-men tucking in to cramp the opposition's attacks at source ensured that Torino, Paris Saint-Germain and Parma enjoyed no such concession. And in the run-up to the Final, John Jensen was an exceedingly effective defensive foil positioned just in front of the Arsenal back four. The attention to detail was also prominent in the European campaign: Graham knew that dead-ball specialists like Ginola and Valdo in the semis, or Zola, Asprilla and Brolin in the Final, could well make Arsenal rue giving away free-kicks within reasonable shooting range. At his general HQ at London Colney, Graham incessantly drilled this fact into his players. Out on the pitch, they responded to his warnings and showed enormous discipline when competing in danger areas. And in Copenhagen, it was absolutely no coincidence that Bould, Adams, Winterburn et al., gave each Parma dangerman a healthy kick early on; just to let them know who they were dealing with, but always in the most innocuous of places (on the pitch, that is!).

Some critics argued that Graham's side played a more sophisticated passing game in Europe, too. Perhaps Arsenal did knock the ball around more than was normally the case in the Premiership, but that was surely a result of the less frantic nature of the opposition. Claims that Arsenal's approach in Paris was far more positive than in Turin were also unfounded. The line was that Graham realised his side needed at least one away-goal against a French side which would be far more dangerous on the counter-attack back in London, and changed his plans accordingly. But as some of the players later admitted, Arsenal's approach was the same – it was the nature of the opposition that was different. It may seem churlish to deny the attention to detail but, as many of Graham's senior players argue, the core of the side has been together so long now that things practically run themselves. Equally, Lee Dixon points out elsewhere that Graham's *modus operandi* on the training ground has barely changed in all his time at the club:

repetition, more repetition and yet more repetition is the motto of a man-ager who insists on the constant grilling of the basics. 'Innovative', however, is not the word that springs to mind.

Likewise, Arsenal have never threatened to keep anyone on the edge of their seat with imaginative set-pieces, although over the years they have scored their fair share of goals from corners and free-kicks simply by sending the big guns forward from the back. When you've got the likes of Adams, Smith, Bould (the Marwood corner, Bould flick at the near post, was especially effective in its day)and Linighan to get on the end of it, there is arguably no more effective ploy in football than the high ball into the box. But it hardly requires tactical genius. That aside, there has been little on offer in the dead-ball stakes.

On an aesthetic level, Graham has been criticised for building sides that are effective but dull; and clearly Arsenal make absolutely no concessions to the gallery. It would indeed take a distortion of the truth of Big Brother proportions to argue the case for Arsenal as an attractive side. In the last couple of seasons in particular, Graham's team have tended to grind their opponents into submission by sheer brute force rather than by anything more subtle, and most Arsenal fans would concede (in private, and only amongst fellow devotees, of course) that the 'Boring! Boring! Arsenal!' tag has been more than justified of late. Graham is not unaware of this repu-tation and, despite his ostensibly haughty demeanour in the face of criticism, he is not insensitive to the barbs: Paul Hawksbee, the editor of *90 Minutes*, recently commented that 'one of George's more endearing qualities is that after so long and after so much success, and despite his own protestations to the contrary, he still really *cares* what people write about him and Arsenal.'

He may care, but the bottom line is that Graham simply doesn't accept the terms of reference of the aesthetic debate. Martina Navratilova once said 'Winning is all that matters. They don't put an asterisk beside your name saying "she won the title but didn't play well" ', an attitude Graham would second wholeheartedly. As far as the head-most-definitely-not-in-the-clouds Scot is concerned, his job is to win honours for Arsenal, not accumulate Brownie points for painting pretty pictures. And if this means subduing his own natural footballing instincts, then so be it. And make no mistake, George enjoys his dose of pure skill as much as the next man. Get him talking about football in general and his musings are those of a purist spectacularly at odds with the signed-up member of the results-orientated and percentage-based-football Neanderthal fraternity. Graham has been known to bemoan the lack of defenders with skills on the ball, complain about the excessive speed of the English game and point out the inherent contradictions between excitement and quality. In sticking up for what he believes is good for the game in general, he is even capable of momentarily forgetting the loyalties involved in his day job.

He recently had this to say on the overload of games in England: 'The more games that are played, the bigger squads you need. This is good for the wealthier clubs, but not for smaller clubs that can't carry injuries or suspensions. If the Premier League was smaller in number or the season shorter, they might have a better chance.' Graham's obsession with getting results at Arsenal reflects nothing if not hard-headed realism. He knows life can be tough (his father died when he was barely out of the cradle) and this is one Scot who needs few lessons in self-preservation. In a conversation with David Pleat, shortly after the two managers had taken over on either side of the North London footballing divide, Graham commented, 'Success in this job will be returning here in five years' time as managers of the clubs.'

No one would deny that Arsenal's success has been based on a parsimonious defence, but clearly you don't win so much silverware without scoring the odd goal or two: in 88/89 and 91/92 Arsenal were top scorers in the top flight and in 90/91 only Liverpool scored more. Both Alan Smith (twice) and Ian Wright won the 'Golden Boot' during George Graham's first eight seasons at the helm, and only Liverpool's tally of 546 League goals bettered Arsenal's 491. Graham's supposedly 'boring' side outscored both Manchester United (478) and Tottenham (445) – sides that are generally perceived to be more attractive. However, it is undeniable that the less successful campaigns have been characterised by a drying up of goals rather than by a haemorrhage at the other end. In the 92/93 and 93/94 campaigns in particular, Graham seemed to follow the theory of the ex-France manager, Michel Hidalgo – 'In defence you prepare, in attack you improvise' – rather too closely for comfort. All too often, Arsenal's only offensive plot seemed to be 'give the ball to Ian Wright, he'll come up with something'. The ace striker invariably did but, however impressive Wright's scoring exploits, no team can rely on just one man for its goals. While happy to acknowledge Wright's phenomenal goal-scoring return, some of the senior players at Arsenal are privately critical of Graham's disavowal of a more democratic attacking policy in the wake of the arrival of the South London goal-machine. They argue that Arsenal's Championship successes were the fruit of an attacking policy that was based on penetration down the flanks (first from Brian Marwood, then by Anders Limpar) and that the team is desperately lacking effective wide-men. Indeed, Lee Dixon argues that with a Sharpe or a Giggs out wide, Arsenal would have won the League in the last couple of seasons.

In 1992/93, Arsenal earned the dubious honour of being lowest scorers in the inaugural Premier League (with their lowest goals tally since 1912/13 when they were relegated to Division Two) and the following season they were again outscored by half the Division. An appalling dearth of creativity in midfield has posed a major problem at Arsenal for several years now and though Graham has often conceded this, he has consistently failed to do anything about it. He often argues in his own defence that the players are simply not available, and the fact that his most recent midfield acquisitions have been imported from Scandinavia reflects his scepticism about what is on offer at home.

The helter-skelter of the English game may not breed as many technically gifted players as it once did but nonetheless, Graham's failure to solve a problem of such unrelenting importance borders on the negligent. Graham's fans would counter that the Premiership is hardly flowing over with budding Liam Bradys or Glenn Hoddles but, as the Scot is so fond of telling us, he wouldn't be interested anyway. He says a young Graeme Souness, Peter Reid or Bryan Robson is what he would really like – fair enough, but did he never see Brady play? Now there was a player who combined rare class with true grit. Of the top British midfielders who have moved around in recent seasons, David Platt and Paul Gascoigne were out of any English club's price range, while Andy Townsend and Roy Keane found the grass greener (sic) elsewhere. You do wonder, however, why didn't Arsenal bid for Paul Ince when West Ham decided to let him go? A player straight from the Graham mould who was reasonably cheap and is a Londoner to boot. Most recently, the Bulgarian, Krasimir Balakov – one of the best end-to-end midfielders on show in the 1994 World Cup and a man who scored an impressive fifteen League goals for Sporting Lisbon in the 93/94 season – turned down the chance to join Arsenal because he wasn't prepared to take a £2,000 a week drop in wages. And Graham feigns surprise when players turn him down!

Referring to his strictly defensive role in the Cup-Winners' Cup Final, the young Arsenal defender-cum-midfielder Steve Morrow said, 'It was a bit restricting. I do like to get forward, unfortunately, someone's got to do the job. I knew exactly what to do. I had to be very disciplined. It was a question of: do you want to be pretty or do you want to win things?' You suspect that George Graham actually prefers working with unspectacular but wholehearted footballers like Morrow, players who will carry out his orders to the letter without dissent. The problem with creative players as opposed to competitive ones (the dichotomy is not always cut and dried, but you get my drift) is that the former tend to be more inconsistent and therefore more difficult to programme – and Graham is nothing if not a control freak.

In his days as a philosophising football journalist before taking over at Real Madrid, Jorge Valdano once said of the erstwhile boy-genius of Spanish football, Emilio Butragueño (a player whose inconsistency became a matter for national debate in Spain in the late 80s): 'No genius can possibly be inspired without the occasional hiatus.' Closer to home, Glenn Hoddle reacted to being hustled out of his stride by Coventry's Lloyd McGrath in the 1987 Cup Final by saying, 'It is easier to destroy a painting than create one'. Somewhat paradoxically, Graham himself was an elegant midfielder of genuinely attacking instincts, but as a coach he has never managed to either nurture or buy a player with similar characteristics. Arsenal could do with a 90s version of 'Stroller', a midfielder who could ghost forward from deep and notch a dozen or so goals every season. Mind you, Graham the coach would never have put up with George the player in other respects. Bertie Mee admits that George was a bit of a Jack the Lad when he first arrived at the club, and that he had to be motivated on a stick-and-carrot basis – even if that did mean the occasional spell in the reserves.

Whatever his inclinations as an Arsenal player, when he was back at his happiest hunting-ground as manager, Graham immediately concentrated on building solid if less engaging foundations. In his early days at the club, he was fond of saying 'Getting the side right means getting the defence in order.' He inherited a very good defence – Anderson, O'Leary, Adams and Sansom – and arguably, created an even better one – Dixon, Bould, Adams and Winterburn. But defending is not just about the back four's capabilities, it's about what kind of wall you throw up in front of them. To the eternal gratitude of his defenders, Graham has consistently opted for the kind of midfield player who is happier ripping down pictures than putting them up, to borrow Hoddle's analogy. This invariably means sacrificing something elsewhere. Despite all the talk about balanced sides, assembling a team involves making choices: opting for one thing, discarding another. As the ever-expressive Valdano puts it: 'Football is like a short blanket – however much you shift it about you are always going to leave something exposed. The place of the coach is to choose what.' Graham's choice has been clear from day one and his tunnel vision (the only thing at Arsenal more obdurate than the defence is the boss himself) has been the bane of forwards (and the purists) ever since.

Nowadays – with the defence practically running itself – Graham tends to concentrate on the forwards in training and Arsenal's critics would be surprised to learn that ball-work takes up the vast majority of Graham's sessions at Colney. He subscribes to the famous Liverpool boot-room philosophy, i.e. you work with the ball in training and two tough matches a week will keep you fit. He is also a meticulous planner – the opposition, especially unknown quantities like European sides, are analysed in exhaustive fashion on video and the strengths and weaknesses of both opposing teams and individuals are drummed into his own players in the build-up to games. But this attention to detail would be so much wasted time without Graham's ability to explain clearly and concisely to every player what is expected of him. As Alan Smith puts it: 'Everybody knows exactly what they are doing. The boss always makes players understand what he wants from them.' Arsenal's team-spirit and camaraderie are much-heralded, but equally important is Graham's ability to coax the best out of individuals, to convince each player of both his ability and his importance to the unit. It's often said that football is a simple game made complicated by managers. You doubt somehow if Graham falls into the trap of over-elaborating with his players – after all, we are talking about a manager who often alludes to the frustratingly disparate attention-span of his pupils, sorry, players and, in case we don't get the picture, compares his role to that of a schoolteacher.

Only players meticulously prepared, and with an unwavering belief in what they are doing, could produce the kind of runs that Graham's Arsenal have regularly churned out: in the 86/87 season there was a run of 25 unbeaten games; in 87/88 there were 15 wins on the trot; in the 90/91 Title triumph, only one defeat all season; in 91/92 there was a run of 17 unbeaten games to end the season; and in 93/94, on paper a highly disappointing League season, only the two defeats at the death when minds were understandably on Copenhagen prevented Arsenal being unbeaten during the entire second half of the season. This belief is also reflected in Arsenal's ability to claw their way back from adverse situations: the 86/87 League Cup Semi-Final against Spurs; the Final in the same year against Liverpool; Anfield 1989; just the most obvious examples. The victories in Europe against Parma and Paris Saint-Germain were the latest example of the triumph of superior willpower over, as George Graham himself has coined it, 'superior skill-levels'. The French sports daily *L'Equipe* got it about right with their front-page headline on the day of the game in Paris: 'Tonight is a night for men!'

No player represents Arsenal's will-to-win better than Tony Adams. This is how Bob Wilson described the demeanour of Arsenal's captain when he came down to the dining-room for breakfast on the morning of the Cup-Winners' Cup Final: 'He strolled in like John Wayne. His face was fixed like a mask and it never broke again until the final whistle. You could see him thinking, "This is the day of the battle".' Away from the fray, the taciturn Adams seems anything but eloquent. However, in the close-knit Arsenal dressing-room he is a noisy and influential presence and Graham is happy to let his captain do the last-minute psyching-up of the troops. Adams' role is not dissimilar to that of the Double-winning skipper, Frank McLintock, some twenty years earlier. As his coach, Don Howe, put it at the time: 'I am beginning to feel obsolete in the dressing-room. Frank is doing as much talking as I am – and working wonders with his words. He lifts players up and makes them feel inches taller and he continues to inspire them on the pitch.'

As a captain, Adams is respected both by Graham and his fellow players. But sticking with the Western analogies, Adams remains a trusted and well-liked subordinate (rather like a Ward Bond or a Victor McLaglen to John Wayne), rather than an equal to be consulted when it comes to making the really big decisions. George Graham rarely consults any of his senior players, and even the captain is more of a go-between than conspirator. The fact that Adams is the kind of skipper who is reluctant to run to his manager every five minutes suits the autocratic Graham down to the ground. In this sense, Adams' role is manifestly different to that of the more outspoken McLintock (during Graham's reign at Highbury, players like Marwood and Richardson who felt uncomfortable in the strait-jacket have invariably fallen out with the boss in the end). On the positive side, the kind of dressing-room cliques that ruled the roost at Highbury in the days of Terry Neill and Don Howe have never been allowed to thrive since Graham's arrival. Paul Davis has said that one of the problems he had as a youngster trying to find his way in the first-team back in the early 80s was the lack of support from the senior players. Graham's persistent use of young players could never have borne such fruit without an open and egalitarian dressing-room. And it's this team-spirit that breeds the famous resilience.

Graham's critics have often latched on to Arsenal's formidable resilience as if it were somehow a despicable quality. During the 1994 World Cup, Javier Clemente, the Spanish coach, was quick to defend Italy from similar accusations: 'The Italian side knows how to compete and never flinches when faced by adversity. *Really* knowing how to compete is not something any old team can do and it's one of the most important characteristics of a winning side.' He could have been talking about Graham's team. Like

Clemente, the Italians never underestimate resolve and Arsenal's victories against Torino and Parma produced only praise in Italy.

Graham, of course, does his best to use the widespread criticism to his own ends; he is not averse to pinning up negative press-cuttings around the club in the hope of motivating his players. Bob Wilson reckons he learnt the trick of turning criticism on its head from Bertie Mee: 'Everyone attacked us during the Double season, saying we were negative, and boring, the draw specialists. Bertie used that to fire us up. We were determined to show them what we could do. George has done the same. He's used adversity – like Tony Adams' jailing and the brawl at Manchester United in the 1991 Championship-winning season – to increase team-spirit, one thing the present side has in abundance. It reminds me of the feeling in our 1971 side.'

George Graham's career has seen him coincide with some heavyweight characters in the coaching stakes, but he insists that no single manager or coach has been an overriding influence. As a player, Graham's move from Chelsea to Arsenal was motivated largely by the desire to continue working under Dave Sexton. Much later, as a coach, he did his initial apprenticeship under the auspices of Terry Venables at Crystal Palace and Queens Park Rangers. Graham admits this was a valuable learning process and a period when he learnt the managerial lessons he would then put into practice as his own man at Millwall: 'It was Terry who encouraged me to take up coaching and there are a lot of elements in the way that I manage that come from him. He's very strong and thought-provoking; when you leave Terry after lunch or a few drinks, which I do often as he's a good friend, your mind is full of thoughts and ideas. He has that effect on people.' Venables may well have been a healthy influence, but more has been made of Graham's debt to his playing days at Highbury and few would argue that the current Arsenal set-up bears at least a superficial resemblance to the framework that spawned the famous Double team.

It is well known that George Graham has a keen sense of the club's history and he is fond of citing the 'Arsenal way of doing things'. Quite what this means exactly is more difficult to establish. There is regular talk of adhering to the principles established by Herbert Chapman in the 30s and perpetuated by Bertie Mee at the turn of the 70s. Field-Marshall Graham defines these principles as 'Discipline, organisation and camaraderie', but that explains very little. You would assume that any successful team boasts these same qualities, would you not? Nevertheless, the best Graham sides do have obvious things in common with the Mee vintage. Both the Double side and the 1989 Championship winning outfit were more renowned for their defensive parsimony than their attacking flair (the last four League victories in the Double year were by one-nil!); both were formed around players reared at Highbury (for Tony Adams read Peter Simpson; for David Rocastle, George Armstrong; for Paul Merson, Charlie George, etc.); and both were characterised by their enormous resilience which was never better than when their backs were against the wall. Graham would argue that resilience and adversity are inextricably linked. This belief is well chronicled elsewhere with regard to the Graham years, but it was just as apparent under Mee. The nucleus of the Double-winning side was practically written off at birth. After the Wembley debacle against Third Division Swindon in the 1969 League Cup Final, the critics said Mee's team would never win a thing. 'I truly believe that the rise of the Double side stemmed from that afternoon at Wembley,' says Bob Wilson. 'We came home to headlines about the "Shame of Arsenal" and a lot of us were determined that it would never happen again.'

The very next season, Mee's team brought the first major trophy to Highbury in seventeen years by winning the Fairs Cup (a victory that started with a touch of that indispensable 'Arsenal luck' – they only quali-fied for the competition because UEFA had refused entry to their Third Division conquerors). In the Double-winning season, a potentially cata-strophic 5-0 defeat at Stoke was not allowed to undermine morale: Arsenal's next League game produced a 4-0 win over Nottingham Forest and a couple of games later, the still-reigning champions, Everton, were dispatched by the same score. Later on in the season, Arsenal's resilience saw them come back from two down against their early-season tormentors, Stoke, in the FA Cup Semi-Final, thanks to Peter Storey's last-gasp penalty (the replay only had one winner after a text-book header from Graham powered past Gordon Banks in the thirteenth minute). In fact, Mee's team swam against the tide all season and the smart money for the title remained on Don Revie's formidable Leeds side right until the death. Needless to say, having to travel to Tottenham of all places and secure a result to guarantee the first League title since 1953 was a massive test of will for George Graham and company.

Graham has often commented that the Mee regime taught him profes-sional standards and how to organise his life. At the same time, working under coaches like Dave Sexton and the young Don Howe must have been an immensely rewarding experience for the manager-to-be, however self-taught he may claim to be. But while the experience may have served Graham well, it still doesn't explain his own success as a manager. Playing in a good side and under a good manager doesn't necessarily rub off on you. In theory, all the players in that Double-winning outfit would have received the same 'education' and had the same good habits instilled into them, but apart from Pat Rice and George Armstrong – both members of Graham's present coaching staff at Highbury – no other member of that team works in the professional game full-time. Even Frank McLintock, the man whose leadership qualities saw him pencilled in as prime management material, failed to make a go of it at Leicester, Millwall and Brentford. Graham was, in fact, the darkest horse of all. As McLintock admits, 'George never looked management material; he was the last person you'd pick. He was so laidback, always taking the mickey. Everything was light-hearted about George.'

A further refutation of the good player-good manager equation is provided by England's World Cup winning side. Nobody can achieve more than that as a player, but the less said about the managerial records of Geoff Hurst, Martin Peters, Nobby Stiles, Bobby Charlton and the late Bobby Moore, the better. Only Jack Charlton, very much a bit-player in that side, saves the day and his success confirms that other managerial norm: nobody gets it right all the time. Charlton has enjoyed a wonderful Indian (or maybe that should be Irish) summer of a career at international level, but there were plenty of less glorious episodes in the past. His record at Middlesbrough and Sheffield Wednesday was respectable enough if not spectacular, but he appeared to have turned his back on football for good when he walked out on Newcastle United after a spell on Tyneside that was as brief as it was unhappy. When a pre-season game in 1985 was played out against a backdrop of 'Jack out' chants, the immensely proud (and financially comfortable) Charlton decided he could live without the hassle. What if Ireland hadn't come calling? Of the rest of Charlton's World Cup teammates, only Alan Ball survives as a moderately successful club manager.

George Graham is a signed-up member of what Brian Glanville has described as the school of football insiders (professional players, managers, coaches) who contend that outsiders (essentially the Press and fans) have no right to an opinion. Having been a top player obviously can't do a manager any harm when it comes to earning the respect of his players, but it is hardly a prerequisite. For every Franz Beckenbauer, Johan Cruyff and Michel Platini, there is a Carlos Parreira, Arrigo Sacchi and Roy Hodgson. For every Kevin Keegan and Glenn Hoddle, there is a Graham Taylor and David Pleat. And what does George Graham the footballer really represent to his players? Even the most veteran of his present squad was barely out of nappies when Arsenal did the Double. To his young charges, Graham the player is at best a fleeting glance on a video.

If we are talking about successful football managers who never made it as players, there is a very pertinent example in Graham's own much-quoted mentor, Bertie Mee. During the war, Mee was a part-time player with Mansfield and Derby but, as he himself admits, he would have struggled to make the grade even if an injury hadn't forced him into early retirement. After six years in the Royal Army Medical Corps and a long spell running courses in the treatment of injuries for the Football Association, Mee eventually joined Arsenal as club physiotherapist in 1960. When Billy Wright was given the sack in 1966 (being England's most capped player of all time didn't help him very much in the management stakes, either!), his erstwhile assistant was given the job. The reaction outside Highbury was one of general stupor given Mee's apparent lack of pedigree and at best, the appointment was seen as a stop-gap measure. But the new manager quickly imposed an almost military discipline at Highbury and the results soon silenced the doubters. The Arsenal chairman of the time, Denis Hill-Wood, said of Mee, 'Bertie is a hard, shrewd little man, full of character and pride. He's nobody's fool and a man-manager of the highest class'. Difference in physical stature aside, this could be his son, Peter, talking about Graham twenty years on.

George Graham was Bertie Mee's first-ever signing and the disciple admits the influence of Mee's demanding personality: 'It took me a couple of years to get used to the professionalism at Arsenal, and I'll admit that some of Bertie's restrictions irritated us, but in retrospect his efforts taught me a lot about the job.' Ironic, then, that a manager who sets so much store by 'football people' learnt so much from a man whom he would probably exclude from that category. Given the presence of Dave Sexton and then Don Howe, Mee's tactical input was always minimal and in this crucial sense, the current Highbury set-up bears no relationship at all with the Double year regime. Delving even further back into Arsenal's history, Tom Whittaker was another man who joined the club as a physio and went on to become a Championship-winning manager. Neither Theo Foley or Stewart Houston, Graham's two first-team assistants during the wonder years, were ever responsible for a major input in the coaching. They may have been willing foils, but their job has basically been to keep the players fit and happy.

Whatever the contradictions, Graham's merit is to have taken the lessons he learned in his playing days at Highbury and apply them in his own single-minded way. Bertie Mee may have handed the coaching reins over to others but his authority and motivating powers were legend. Graham also excels in the psychological aspect of the job and he has even described himself as an 'amateur psychologist'. His naked ambition and commitment to Arsenal rubs off on people. The writer, Hunter Davies, describes the fickleness of the typical manager like this: 'Look at managers. Swear it's for ever, swear they really care, swear they're doing it for the community, but we all know that, like players, half of them don't know what town they're in. Just feel the wage packet.' But even Graham's enemies wouldn't accuse him of geographical confusion, and his awareness of Arsenal's history and traditions is irrefutable. Davies was probably being a little harsh on men who themselves are constantly exposed to the fickleness of fans, players and boards, but as a Tottenham fan he would probably second the opinion of the club's former chairman, Irving Scholar: 'You know why I admire George Graham? Because he loves Arsenal.' Spoken at a time in 1991 when Scholar was falling out with Terry Venables, this could only be interpreted as an implicit dig at the then Spurs boss (when full-blown hostilities were later declared, Scholar described Venables as 'the man with the silver tongue').

Beyond all the smoke-screens, one of the indisputable keys to successful football management is the ability of the manager to get the best out of his players. A manager who is as committed to his club as George Graham undoubtedly has a head start in this respect. After all, the players who don't like Graham, or don't agree with his methods, can hardly console themselves with the daydreams of disgruntled footballers at most other clubs – 'The boss will get the sack eventually. It's just a case of hanging in there and then it'll be a fresh start all round.' With Graham so firmly entrenched at Fortress Highbury, it's a case of knuckle down or on your bike!

In a tribute to the late Matt Busby, the broadcaster Cliff Morgan said: 'When you met him he made you feel you were the only person he wanted to see and that his life had been a desert since the last time he saw you.' In a similar vein, Mike Hazard had this to say about Ossie Ardiles: 'His strength is that if you talk to him you feel that he's your very best friend – the most special in the world to you. That means that each and every one of his players will feel a special person to him. They will go out on to the park and think: I'm going to show him what I can do, I'm going to do the business for him.'

Although neither Morgan or Hazard actually use the word, what they are talking about here is charisma. I doubt somehow that Graham's players view him as their best friend, or any kind of friend at all for that matter, but his overwhelming strength of personality does get through to them. Graham dominates his club in the same way as a Busby or a Shankly did:

his confidence (if he ever wavers in his belief, he certainly doesn't let on) and his burning ambition (he won't rest until he becomes the first Arsenal manager to win three Championships) sweeps all before him. That strength of personality has always been there. Nobody who played with or coached Graham claims to have sensed his management potential, but equally, everybody recognises his sheer presence: even in the early days at Stamford Bridge, the other Chelsea players called their cocksure team-mate 'big fry'. When the former Millwall chairman Alan Thorne interviewed Graham for the managerial vacancy at the Den, he was taken aback when the rookie-coach accepted his initial salary offer without the slightest haggle. When he expressed his surprise, Graham answered, 'Don't worry. When I'm success-ful, I'll be very expensive!'

Graham's relationship with the Arsenal players (they might call him 'big' something, but I doubt if it's 'big fry') was firmly established from his very first day at the club. Kenny Sansom was already on cordial terms with the new manager, but as Graham's first captain explains: 'When I arrived at the training ground on the first day he greeted me and I said "Hello, George". The reply was quick and to the point. "Don't call me George, it's boss from now on." ' Away from football, Graham may be nothing like the dour and hard-faced bugger of folklore and quite possibly he dislikes having to put up a wall between himself and the players, but it is the way he has chosen to do things and no one can argue with the results. The legendary Scottish manager, Jock Stein, once said 'The secret of being a good manager is to keep the five players who hate you away from the half-dozen who are undecided.' In Graham's case the numbers may be even less flattering, but the Highbury Don knows he is not in a popularity con-test. 'The players at Arsenal may not like me, but they respect me and they want to be associated with success.' Indeed, there is almost a hint of regret when he says, 'I don't get too close to the players. I love my coaching but I keep my distance. It is difficult to socialise when you know you've got to wield the axe, to drop players or release them.' Graham acknowledges that the role of buffer between manager and players must fall to his assistants: first, the jovial Theo Foley and, more recently, Stewart Houston (with the inestimable help of physio, Gary Lewin, one of Highbury's unsung heroes). 'It's the coach's job to be the players' ear,' says Graham. And many of his stalwarts on the playing staff are perfectly happy that the boss keeps his distance, maintaining, 'It wouldn't be Arsenal otherwise.' It's all well and good for a Dave Bassett or a Joe Kinnear to be one of the lads at Bramall Lane or Selhurst Park, but around the marble halls a little more decorum is expected. When he was asked about the rough and ready dress-sense of his Wimbledon players, Kinnear replied 'I do draw the line at stockings and suspenders . . . on the pitch, that is!' Suffice to say that George Graham's men will be sticking to their more elegant club suits and ties and that not just the players, but the etiquette-obsessed Highbury board as well, approve wholeheartedly of their manager's more patrician bearing.

Graham earns considerable respect at Arsenal through (a) treating all the players equally (he belongs to the 'stars should shine on Saturday but during the week everybody is the same' school of thought) and (b) being extraordinarily positive about his players in public. The errant Swede, Anders Limpar, was virtually the only player he criticised publicly in his first eight years at the club and that was probably only in a desperate attempt to motivate the infuriatingly inconsistent winger. The Arsenal players may be in awe of the boss, but any shouting goes on behind firmly closed doors. And if Graham is unhappy with a player, he generally prefers to speak to them in private – 'I'll lie rather than slag off my players in public,' he says. Not that Graham is a slacker in the high-decibel stakes: success doesn't seem to have mellowed him and any of his players will tell you that he still gets as hyped-up on match days as ever (his half-time outbursts in the dressing-room if things are not going well are legend). In public, though, Graham is enormously protective of his charges – again, this suggests an almost patriarchal relationship – and as one current Arsenal player expresses it, 'a word of praise from the boss makes you feel ten feet tall.' Indeed, when a character as demanding as Graham goes on record to sing the praises of an Alan Smith or a Paul Davis, refers to Tony Adams as 'my hero', or sticks up for Ian Wright when he is under the media hammer, it must be hugely motivating for all concerned.

There is no doubt that this approach earns Graham the respect of his players; one of the reasons it is extremely rare to hear public criticism of him, even from those who left Arsenal under a cloud. Actually, it is difficult to find anybody in the game who will bad-mouth Graham. He is revered by ex-team-mates, respected by fellow managers and his ex-charges stay tight-lipped. Mind you, we are talking about a tough Scot who was raised in a mining village on the outskirts of post-war Glasgow; a man capable of offering a dissenting journalist 'outside'. It's also fair to say that ex-Arsenal players are not exactly queuing up to sing his praises. 'The biggest compliment a footballer can pay a manager is to say he has learnt something from him when he leaves the club,' said Graham. By this criteria, he himself is struggling to make the grade.

When the occasion demands it, Graham is not averse to rallying his troops in almost military fashion. On his very first day at Highbury, he sat all the players down and explained at length his philosophy, his demands and his expectations. And famously, after the docked points incident in the 1991 season and amidst fierce attacks on himself and his team from the media, he got all the players together for a let's-show-the-bastards-what-we-are-made-of, backs-against-the-wall consciousness-raising session. This bears comparison with a famous moment two decades earlier. In February 1971, Bertie Mee called together his poised-for-glory squad and said, 'Now is the time for you to be really ambitious and aim for the success which may never be possible for you as players again in your lifetimes.'

Whatever emotions Graham engenders amongst his players – respect, awe, fear – the desired effect is what you get; they go out on to the park wanting to prove something to him. Much has been made of Graham's disciplinarian streak and the problems that it causes with big-name players. He strenuously denies any such prejudices on his part, claiming, 'I don't have personality clashes with any players. I just pick people on ability, on performance.' After the departure of Charlie Nicholas – a sad day for most Arsenal fans, even though with the passing of time few would argue with Graham's decision – the manager observed: 'I like performing stars and Charlie wasn't performing. I don't like so-called stars, social stars who are not doing it on the pitch.' The clichés about George not liking big person-alities have been buried to some extent by the success of Ian Wright at Highbury, although personality-wise the South-London goal-machine is a case apart. Stars certainly don't come much bigger, but footballers don't come any more motivated either – and doesn't George just love him!

What is clear is that nobody in the Highbury set-up questions the man-ager's authority and sticks around long to tell the tale. The only possible exception is Paul Davis and, even then, being an Arsenal loyalist and one of George Graham's favourite players didn't save the graceful midfielder from spending a long period on the sidelines in 91/92 after he had dared to challenge the Scot's authority, and subsequently he has been used spar-ingly. Ostensibly, Graham sets great store by discipline, but it must be said that his particular brand only goes so far. He is fond of talking about 'standards', but he has demonstrated a decidedly equivocal attitude to the less savoury off-the-park adventures of Tony Adams, Steve Bould, Paul Merson, Ray 'Pizza' Parlour et al. Contradictory noises aside, Graham has probably got it about right on this one. He has often referred to the press-ure on young boys who are expected to act like men and he is not blind to the possible consequences of such high demands. Young footballers are occasionally going to let off steam in ways not markedly different from their peers and if some of them overstep the mark occasionally, well, so be it. That's not to say Graham doesn't get angry when the good name of Arsenal is damaged, but he never takes it as a personal slight or harbours a grudge. The fact that in his own playing days as a youngster at Stamford Bridge he was involved in the infamous 'Blackpool Eight' after-hours escapade with a bunch of Chelsea cronies that included Terry Venables and John Hollins ensures that George knows the score.

The occasional nocturnal peccadillo aside, the 'in-with-the-workaholics, out-with-the-prima-donnas' form of motivation clearly works better with a certain type of player. Graham's Arsenal have laid their reputation on the altar of home-grown products and the trust engendered in Adams, Merson, Thomas, Rocastle and all the others reflects the Scot's preference for working with players who have made their way through the ranks. His experience in the Double side with the likes of Pat Rice, Charlie George, Peter Storey, Peter Simpson and John Radford is an obvious reference point, as is his experience in coaching the youngsters at Palace and QPR. But Graham's exposure to what a good youth policy can achieve goes back even further.

As an impressionable youngster from Bargeddie, he chose to come south to England and join Aston Villa in the face of considerable competition, chiefly because of the good impression Villa boss Joe Mercer made on his family and because of the excellent way the youth scheme was set up at Villa Park. Thus a valuable lesson was learnt early on – before you can turn promising raw material into the finished article you've got to get them through the door. Graham eventually left Villa for Chelsea, and at Stamford Bridge he was a member of a successful young side which included the equally fresh-faced Terry Venables, Ron Harris, Charlie Cook and co. Again, this provided him with an early example of youth thriving on responsibility.

It's not only that a strong youth policy can save clubs a fortune in the transfer market (and at Arsenal it most certainly has) – it also breeds an attitude. Graham is convinced that Arsenal's home-grown players identify more deeply with the club and what it represents. When he arrived at Highbury the first thing he did was to get rid of big-name 'outsiders' like Tony Woodcock and Paul Mariner whose performances on the pitch no longer justified their large salaries. Others who initially stayed, but dared to challenge his authority and/or lacked the requisite commitment – Charlie Nicholas, Steve Williams, Kenny Sansom – were packed off at the first available opportunity. The only established members of the team that Graham inherited from Don Howe who would win Championship medals in both 1989 and 1991 were David O'Leary and Paul Davis, both Arsenal 'born-and-bred'.

What must be conceded, however, is that with the notable exception of Tony Adams, none of the players lauded as stars in the making have made the transition from promising youngster to established figures, which is one of the reasons the much-heralded Graham dynasty has never happened. After the exceptional achievements of 1991 there was considerable talk of Arsenal lording it over English football in the 90s in a similar fashion to that of the Chapman era of the 30s. In the event, however praiseworthy the Cup-winning efforts might be, this is palpably not the case.

On the other hand, the players who have left Highbury have not managed to prove Graham wrong either. Even the younger outcasts like Stewart Robson, David Rocastle, Michael Thomas, Martin Hayes and Niall Quinn have not managed to surpass or even match their Highbury form in fresh pastures. John Lukic may have shown why Arsenal fans were reluctant to see him go by winning a Championship medal with Leeds, but given the extraordinary form of David Seaman only the vindictive would deny that Graham got that one right too. And though Kevin Richardson won a belated England call-up in 1994 at the age of 31 (the kind of eleventh-hour arrival in the big time you would expect from a player once described as 'the most consistently high-class ordinary player in the country') he has hardly been sorely missed at Highbury.

When Graham lets people go he drives an extraordinarily hard bargain: Rocastle, Thomas, Robson, Quinn and Hayes earned Arsenal an astonishing £5,600,000 in transfer fees, yet they are all players who didn't cost the club a penny. Perry Groves, Graham's very first buy at just £65,000 from Colchester, went to Southampton six years later at £750,000, and despite Anders Limpar's diminishing returns at Highbury, in 1994 Graham got over half a million more than he had paid for him three years earlier. Even Alan Miller, Neil Heaney and Pat Scully (products of the Highbury conveyor-belt who failed to make an impression on the first-team scene) earned Arsenal just some loose change short of a cool million. Of course, if a manager stays long enough at a club, especially a big one like Arsenal where the competition for places is so fierce, there is bound to be the odd mistake. Unfortunately for Graham, his *bête noir* goes by the name of Andy Cole, and the Scot could certainly be excused for praying that the youngster's 40-goal first season in the top flight was a fluke! But nobody is infallible when it comes to the notoriously difficult job of judging young players: in the 88/89 South-East Counties League, Andy Cole scored 21 goals in 26 games for Arsenal. Not a bad return, but it was one goal short of his team-mate Kwame Ampadu who played one game less. And where is Ampadu now? Who could have predicted five years ago the disparate fortunes of the young striking duo? In the end, Andy Cole's attitude helped force Graham's hand – even as a teenager Cole's self-confidence was such that he was convinced he should have been a first-choice. When Ian Wright arrived in September 1991 and effectively shut off Cole's route to the first-team, the youngster was vocal in his protests. Cole is a player who thrives on being the centre of attention and, confined to the fringes at Highbury, he made it clear he wanted out. The fact that George Graham pays little attention to players outside the first-team (a player who has been at the club for several years admitted recently that getting dropped by Graham is tanta-mount to being sent to Coventry) was a further irritant to the ambitious Cole. After his successful period on loan to Bristol City at the end of the 91/92 season – his eight goals in twelve games effectively saved the West Country side from the drop to the Third Division – Graham accepted the club's £500,000 bid to make the move permanent. Arsenal did get a percen-tage of the fee when Cole quickly moved on to Newcastle, but given what he is worth now it was still an exceedingly bad piece of business. Still, I insist, there is always one who gets away – just ask Manchester United (David Platt), Tottenham (Graham Souness famously, Des Walker more recently) or almost every club in South London (Ian Wright! Wright! Wright!).

Even so, no other major club has saved so much money in the transfer stakes through a productive youth scheme as Arsenal, and Graham's sides are always bolstered by a considerable degree of home-grown talent: three or four on a bad day, but often more. Of the six who played a part at Anfield 89, only Tony Adams and Paul Merson took the field for the 1994 Cup-Winners' Cup Final, but in Copenhagen they were joined by four others. Compare that to Arsenal's major rivals: Leeds won the title in 1992 with just David Batty and Gary Speed from the Elland Road ranks and their successors, Manchester United, could boast Ryan Giggs – after that you can stop counting. But as a club, Arsenal have always placed far more emphasis than their major rivals on producing their own players. This is a philosophy that Graham has inherited rather than instigated (see Tom Watt's chapter): no less than ten members of the 1971 Double-winning squad were players nurtured at Highbury and, more recently, the likes of Liam Brady, Graham Rix and Frank Stapleton were all illustrious servants who emerged from the ranks. However, nobody can deny George Graham's willingness to give youth a fling and, like a chef with a recipe or a scientist with a formula, it isn't only about a list of ingredients; it's how, when and in what quantity you use them.

Mind you, Graham's faith in the 'made in London Colney' brigade has had its occasional downside. Gus Caesar had already made a couple of brief appearances when George Graham arrived at Arsenal (when he came on as substitute for his first game at Highbury in 1985, the tannoy announced his entry as 'and number 12 for Arsenal, Augustus Caesar', to which a wit in the crowd near me observed, ''ere, he don't look Italian, does he?'). When Graham finally let the hapless Gus go, his career nose-dived through Cambridge, Bristol City, Airdrie and Colchester in record time. The rise and fall of Caesar demonstrates that even the best judges of players – and Graham is not bad, despite the myopia over creative midfielders and his obsession with collecting centre-halves – can get it wrong.

Graham's eye for a bargain in his early days at Arsenal was exemplary, but his more recent forays into the market have veered between the misguided and the genuinely incomprehensible. Steve Bould, Lee Dixon and Nigel Winterburn, three-quarters of the most unbreachable defence in English football history, all arrived in Graham's first couple of seasons and, at a combined price of barely £1 million, have given new meaning to the expression 'value for money' (Gary Pallister alone cost twice as much as Arsenal's whole double-Championship-winning back four). Like Brian Marwood and Perry Groves they arrived from less glamorous surroundings or from the lower divisions. None were household names (in most cases not even in their own house, as the saying goes) but they all arrived with everything to prove and anxious to grasp their opportunity. The fact that they weren't big-name stars, and therefore were less likely to challenge Graham's autocratic ways, was another plus for the boss. That all these players were unqualified successes goes without saying. Yes, even the much-maligned Groves, a more than useful twelfth man for several seasons and a match-winner at Wembley. Don't forget that Charlie Nicholas may have scored the goal that won Graham his first trophy, but it was 'El Pel's' dainty jink past Gillespie that made it. In picking up the likes of Dixon and Bould, Graham showed a fine eye for players that he would have come across personally in his time at Millwall. In more recent seasons, with Graham inevitably less in control of things outside the top flight, his scouts have not proved anywhere near as adept at talent-spotting.

When it came to spending larger sums of money, Graham's bigger signings early on were cheap by the reigning standards and even cheaper in the light of their payback. Alan Smith has been a fine servant at Highbury; his goals were decisive in the 1989 and 1991 Championship-winning campaigns and more recently in the 1994 Cup-Winners' Cup Final; David Seaman, despite having failed to reproduce his Arsenal form for England, has been a 'colossus'; and Anders Limpar was a key figure in the 1991 Championship team before his disappointing fall from grace. And what can you say about Ian Wright, except thank God Ron Noades never went to charm school and thank George for signing him.

With the notable exception of Wright, Graham struggled to get it right in the wake of the 1991 Championship success. The fundamental principle of his management may be the squad system (he insists that 'when you put your name to a long-term contract, you're not signing for the first team, you're signing for the club') but in the 92/93 and 93/94 seasons Arsenal's squad sure could have done with some replenishing from the top to complement the bits and pieces. Not that the bit-players have come cheap. Andy Linighan and Eddie McGoldrick each cost over £1 million. The verdict is still out on John Jensen despite those sterling performances in the 93/94 European campaign. Colin Pates cost £350,000 and made a grand total of fifteen starts in four seasons before finally being off-loaded on a free-transfer. As for Jimmy Carter, whatever can have possessed Graham to spend £500,000 on such an average player? Presumably the same thing that made Kenny Dalglish splash out £800,000 on him just nine months earlier. Is there something about young Jimmy (or George and Kenny?) that we should be told? That two such highly-rated managers can spend so much money so easily is a stunning example of how even the most experienced professionals can get it spectacularly wrong.

Which leads us to the strange case of Martin Keown. Now Keown is a decent enough defender, and if Steve Bould ever gives up the ghost (George keeps buying centre-halves but 'Bouldie' just keeps on getting better and better) he could well enjoy some belated good times at Highbury, but was he really worth so much money? Maybe buying a player for £2 million whom he had earlier let go for just £200,000 was Graham's own perverse way of saying, 'Up yours, Jimmy, I'm my own man, and totally beyond criticism'. It was certainly a bizarre decision and one that left Graham wide open to the snipers, especially given Keown's oft-repeated motive for leaving Highbury: 'I left because George and I could not agree over money. I wanted £50 a week more and he didn't think I was worth it. It seemed crazy that we couldn't agree, and though I didn't want to leave and Arsenal didn't want me to go it became a matter of principle.' Not that Graham could seriously be accused of profligacy – before getting their respective marching orders, Graeme Souness spent over £9 million and Terry Venables £5.1 million! And Kenny Dalglish's £22 million net outlay since the start of the 90/91 season and, to a lesser extent Alex Ferguson's £7.4 million, leave George standing in the cheque-writing stakes (see *Four Four Two*, September 94 edition).

Graham's caution in the transfer market is legend, and in his first eight years at Arsenal he signed only eighteen players; the odd signing short of what a Dalglish, Keegan, Ardiles or Atkinson gets through in a couple of close seasons. Lee Dixon claims that Graham, Steve Burtenshaw, Stewart Houston and Pat Rice all watched him several times, both home and away, over a period of more than six months before Arsenal finally made the plunge for him at a princely £350,000 – heaven knows for how long more expensive signings are kept under tabs! It is pointless speculating over the number of players Arsenal have missed out on because of Graham's reluctance to compete with the admittedly silly money that other clubs are prepared to offer, although one can reasonably assume that the likes of Andy Townsend and Scott Minto didn't go to Chelsea because they were hungry for trophies. What can be argued without fear of contradiction is that Graham has been incredibly lucky in being turned down by a number of players who subsequently flopped. His most spectacular let-off was Geoff Thomas – he actually offered Crystal Palace £2.5 million before Ron Noades upped the ante – but Terry Fenwick, Kerry Dixon, Frank McAvennie, Andy Sinton and Tony Cottee are other players that George was damned lucky not to get. But did he really pass over the chance to sign John Barnes?

Bertie Mee's biggest mistake during his Arsenal career lay in his failure to rebuild after winning the Double and, by the time he resigned at the end of the 75/76 season which witnessed an embarrassing flirtation with relegation, the Gunners had fallen from grace in spectacular fashion. The rot was deep-set – Arsenal's seventeenth-place finish that year (the lowest since Herbert Chapman arrived at the club way back in 1925) followed the sixteenth-place finish in 74/75 and tenth place in 73/74. The feeling remains that George Graham forged the nucleus of a great side in his first couple of years at Highbury but has failed to build on it. The 1994 victory against Parma was definitely a triumph for the old guard of Smith, Dixon, Bould, Winterburn and Davis. Graham's ability to find adequate replacements for this thirtysomething core (plus Ian Wright, of course) in the next couple of seasons will determine whether he avoids the fate of his mentor.

Chris Sutton was the last big name to forego the challenge of Highbury in favour of fool's dust (Walker's millions, that is), or so the Press would have us believe. Given Graham's strained relationship with the tabloids in particular, it's not always easy to sift through the malicious gossip and get to the truth about life *chez* George. He admits that 'I'm no good at public relations' and he invariably comes across as aloof and arrogant; he is certainly not media-friendly in the style of a 'Big Ron' or an 'El Tel'. Hugh McIlvanney once said of the latter that 'where other coaches might deal in generalisations clothed in cult jargon, he has the clarity of mind and the confidence to be constantly specific'. However you rate Venables' merits as a coach, there is no denying that his transparency is in stark contrast to Graham's stock line in smoke-screens.

Graham invariably struggles to hide his contempt for journalists behind an unconvincing smarm and when he spits 'it's a pleasure' after another monosyllabic interview with Richard Keys or Martin Tyler, he makes it sound uncannily like a death threat. His attitude to the popular Press borders on the paranoid – though given some of the treatment dished out to Arsenal, perhaps understandably. This persecution complex is best demonstrated by the now familiar and pathetic images of Graham's behaviour during games that are broadcast live from Highbury. He generally prefers to take in the first 45 minutes from a seat in the East Stand from where he transmits any relevant orders to the bench by telephone. Nothing unusual about that, of course, *but is it really necessary to cover your mouth when you are talking, George?* Even in Arsenal's official and presumably George-friendly video magazines, he palpably fails to disguise his distaste for the PR side of things. Graham would struggle to make a go of it if he ever went abroad to one of the high-profile European Leagues simply because he would never be able to cope with the incessant demands of the daily sports papers and of the football-crazy radio and TV stations. (If he thinks our journalists are dishonest and rapacious, he should try hacking it with the vultures in Rome or Madrid on a daily basis!)

Still, being able to handle the PR side of things may help, but it is hardly a prerequisite for successful managers. The bumptious Brian Clough was always good for a colourful quote, but he was unpredictable to a fault with the gentlemen of the Press. Alf Ramsey, England's most successful manager of all time, treated the Press like pariahs, whilst Bob Paisley, the most successful club manager in English history, was amiable enough but hardly had a way with words (something he obviously passed on to Kenny Dalglish). And Graham's contemporary rival in the history-making stakes, Alex Ferguson, shares the same sense of paranoia and what-is-in-it-for-me? attitude of his fellow Scot. Of course, one of the dangers implicit in the cult of the manager is that it so easily translates into the cult of the personality, i.e. the boss ends up being judged on his character and not on what really counts – his results. This might explain why George Graham still has so many detractors amongst the Highbury die-hards. Put another way, few Arsenal fans question Graham's enormous achievements, but even fewer really warm to him.

Not that Graham has ever gone out of his way to court the club's supporters. The average football fan positively fumes at being talked down to: given his less-than-diplomatic 'the fans don't understand' attitude (the Arsenal fans, that is) Graham either doesn't grasp that fact or simply doesn't consider the plebs worthy of even the merest show of diplomacy. Contrast this attitude to that of Terry Venables, albeit in very special circumstances, when he courted the Spurs fans so effectively during the Alan Sugar conflict. If there is one thing other than good results guaranteed to help make a manager popular, it is going out of his way to make the fans feel important.

George Graham may not be popular, but in his own terms he's damn successful, although if you really pushed him I'm not sure even he could tell you why. As for the notion that the best football managers, like the few genuine *auteurs* in the cinema, bring to their teams a vision of their own, then Graham would surely be better off if we considered him a mere craftsman, given Arsenal's unflattering physiognomy. The Scot's routine and philosophy certainly don't throw up an obvious recipe for his own managerial success, let alone present us with a wider role-model. An examination of the Graham commandments merely produces contradictions. To wit, George Graham is successful because:

(a) *He works hard* Graham himself maintains that he has won things because of hard graft. By the same token, it must follow that the leaner times were a result of taking the foot off the accelerator. Did he ask the board to dock his wages after the 'terrible' (his words, not mine) showings in the 92/93 and 93/94 League campaigns?
(b) *He is a good coach* Like his mentor, Bertie Mee?
(c) *His sides carry out his orders to the letter* Does that mean the midfield players are not allowed to score?
(d) *His sides are highly disciplined* The Battle of Old Trafford?
(e) *He played in the Double side* So did Peter Storey.
(f) *He was a good player* So were the other 99 per cent of good players who played with Graham and now run pubs or sell insurance.
(g) *He is a good judge of players* Andy Cole? Gus Caesar?
(h) *He drives a hard bargain in the transfer stakes* Martin Keown?
(i) *He is a great motivator* Anders Limpar? Charlie Nicholas?
(j) *He shows his players how to 'organise their lives'* Tony Adams? Paul Merson?
(k) *He's got the gift of the gab* No comment!
(l) *His sides are consistent* Top scorers in 91/92 ... lowest scorers in 92/93 ...
and a very long etc.

Maybe Arsenal's achievements as a team reflect Graham's success as a manager – the sum of the parts and all that? Then again, why expect logic from such an illogical game? In the end, there is only one hard and fast rule in the game of football – you may be a budding myth *à la* Alfred Hitchcock (Herbert Chapman) and John Ford (Bill Shankly), but without a dash of good fortune you'll never hear the legend 'And the winner is . . .'

Even a manager as single-minded and ambitious as George Graham needs to be in the right place at the right time. When he arrived at Highbury in 1986, he inherited a bunch of promising youngsters who were either in, or on the fringes of, the first team, the likes of Tony Adams, David Rocastle, Martin Hayes, Michael Thomas and Paul Merson all played a major role in helping Graham get off to a positive start. Peter Hill-Wood has since revealed that Graham had also been among the candidates when Terry Neill was sacked three years earlier. At that time the youngsters in or on the fringe of the first team were the likes of Brian McDermott, Colin Hill, David Cork and Paul Gorman. As their subsequent careers have proved, it would have been difficult to build a Championship-winning side around that lot. It doesn't matter how good a coach you are or how much onus you put on youth, you need the raw material.

What is more, Graham only got into coaching in the first place by sheer coincidence. As he was winding down his playing career at Selhurst Park and with injuries starting to take their toll, Terry Venables, the then Palace boss and Graham's good friend, said to him, 'What are you going to do when you pack up?', to which Graham replied, 'I've not really thought about it'. Somewhat surprised at this lack of foresight, Venables suggested that he have a go at coaching Palace's youth team. In Venables' words, 'George took to it like a duck to water, he was keen, conscientious and worked hard'. But it was hardly a case of the best-laid plans, was it? However much Graham has made his own luck ever since, it still begs a pertinent question; what if the enquiry about the future had been raised by a different friend and the offer had been 'Come and work for my insurance company' or 'You've got a great future in car-haulage, George'? On such shaky foundations are great careers forged.

George Graham has always been surrounded by an aura of good fortune, even as a player. His career at Arsenal didn't really take off until he was converted from a journeyman centre-forward into an attacking midfielder, but again, the shift was anything but calculated. It started when Arsenal's left-half, David Court, was injured and Don Howe was forced to turn to Graham as a stop-gap. He did well and there he stayed. But if it hadn't been for that twist of fate, who knows where his career might have gone? And if Graham had not made such an impact at Highbury as a player, he probably never would have been offered the manager's job. In a rare moment off his guard, Graham once recognised his good fortune: 'I've had two great careers. I'm very happy. I'm a very lucky and fortunate person.' None the less, his achievements at Highbury are obviously too wide-ranging and durable to be purely down to luck and Graham himself has always insisted that 'you make your own luck'.

All things being equal, better a single-minded, generally efficient and committed manager like Graham than some bungling misfit. However, in the normal run of things (a) everything is not equal and (b) even if they were, the aforementioned whims of Lady Luck are always lurking just around the corner to wreck the best-laid plans. He would be loath to admit it, but even a control freak like George Graham is at the mercy of the vagaries of fortune or, to be more precise, other people's fortune. When things go wrong at Arsenal, Graham's stock response is to claim that 'you can't legislate for individual errors'. This is tantamount to admitting that things are *always* out of the manager's hands, for when things go right, surely the opposite applies? A film director may rely on the inspiration of his players (the actors) but at least he can choose from myriad takes in the editing suite. The football manager enjoys no such luxury; sitting on the sidelines for those crucial 90 minutes, he has to take the good with the bad. While the director can influence what the cinema-goer eventually sees on screen before *and* after the shooting stage, for the football manager there is no way of rewriting football history once the final whistle goes. At 3 o'clock on a Saturday afternoon, Graham can only shut his eyes and hope the gods are on his side, just like every other manager.

Arsenal's most famous manager of them all, Herbert Chapman, had no problem in admitting that good luck was crucial. Discussing the possibility of a team winning the Double, three decades before Spurs first achieved a feat which in his day was still thought to be nigh on impossible, he said, 'All you need is a team of eleven very good players that are also very lucky!'

It is irrefutable that George Graham enjoyed the roll of the dice early on that afforded him the luxury all managers need and so few actually get – time. In 1989 Arsenal were just seconds and one charmed ricochet away from being the side that surrendered a seemingly unassailable eighteen-point lead at the top of the First Division. Take that away, and a winner scored at Wembley in 1987 with a shot that dribbled home after a fortu-itous deflection, and George Graham could well have stumbled into his fourth or fifth year at Highbury still looking for his first silverware and with a board beginning to lose patience at the continuing lack of success. Even for budding legends, the margin between success and failure is wafer-thin.

The Gaffer

by Tony Willis
*in conversation with Lee Dixon, Brian Marwood, Charlie Nicholas and
Alan Smith*

*'It is a terrible thing seeing Benny. He is a bit like Busby. The great thing
about Busby was that you would go in there fighting and full of
demands. And he would give you nothing at all. He might even take a
tenner off your wages. And you would come out thinking – what a great
guy! I remember going in there once absolutely livid. And ten minutes later
I came out, no better off, walking on air. Delighted!'*

Eamon Dunphy on the love-hate relationship between
player and manager – 'Only a Game', 1976

'Football is a simple game, made difficult by players.'

Jock Stein

To get an authoritative insight into the management style of George
Graham is not easy. For many seasons he has actively discouraged
(and in some cases banned) his players from talking to the Press.
There is often talk of a 'bunker mentality' in football and Highbury is a particularly well-defended fortress. But no account of the wonder
years would be complete without the ultimate insider's view of the chosen
ones entrusted with putting the manager's best-laid plans into action – the
players.

What kind of manager is George Graham? What are his motivations?
How does he inspire his players? What is he like to work for? And, most
important of all, what has been the key to Arsenal's success over the last
eight years and who should take the credit? The manager or the team he
built?

To find the answer to these questions I approached four players who
have played key, if different, roles during the wonder years.

The first two, Alan Smith and Lee Dixon, were signed by Graham in
March 1987 and January 1988 respectively. Their signings, plus those of

Steve Bould and Nigel Winterburn, must rank as four of the most inspired acquisitions in modern football history. Combined, they cost Graham less than £2 million and helped to form the backbone of the wonder years.

Lee Dixon came to Highbury after spells at lowly Burnley, Chester City, Bury and Stoke. As a Manchester City fan in his youth, Dixon confesses to 'hating Arsenal. I don't know what it is about them but everyone up north saw them as southern softies.'

Graham quickly moulded Dixon into the quintessential modern attacking full-back and he has been almost ever present since making his debut in 1988. He has also been England's right-back for much of the 90s, making 21 appearances between 1990 and 1994.

Alan Smith arrived from Leicester City having established a reputation as Gary Lineker's striking partner. Like Dixon, Smith was excited at the prospect of joining a club of Arsenal's stature. 'I remember playing against Arsenal at Filbert Street and at the end of the game David O'Leary said "I'll see you soon". I rushed back to my wife Penny and said, "David O'Leary said 'see you soon'". I could hardly contain myself.'

This was clever psychology on Graham's part – something for which he is given little credit. Alan Smith was the most expensive signing of the early years, yet even his fee was hardly exorbitant at £850,000.

The one thing that Smith, Dixon, Bould and Winterburn had in common was a hunger to better themselves at a top club. Graham sublimely moulded this blue-collar ethos into a formidable team-spirit which was to underpin the wonder years from Anfield 89 to Copenhagen 94.

Smith also featured in the England team while playing for Graham, claiming thirteen caps, although the 'beaky behemoth' never became an England regular and is perhaps most famous for ending the career of Gary Lineker, his erstwhile partner, at the European Championships in 1992, when Graham Taylor inexplicably decided to commit tabloid hara-kiri.

The third player I contacted was Brian Marwood, arguably the best short-term buy in the club's history. At 28, Marwood had played all his football for Hull City and Sheffield Wednesday, latterly under the tutelage of hard-man manager Howard Wilkinson.

Few at Highbury could understand why Graham had paid £600,000 for this journeyman winger, and Marwood made a quiet start to his Arsenal career at the back end of the 87/88 campaign. The following year he was a revelation, scoring in the first four games of the 88/89 season and providing endless assists for Alan Smith. More than anything, Marwood's infectious enthusiasm transmitted itself to the fans who adopted 'Brian Marwood on the wing' as one of their own and began to believe that this diminutive Geordie might be the catalyst needed to turn Arsenal into a Championship-winning unit. They were right, as Marwood helped Arsenal to an eighteen-point lead over Liverpool by the turn of the year. Unfortunately, injury forced him out of much of the second half of the season. However, when Arsenal fans think back to 1989 they generally remember two things: That Night at Anfield and the early-season contribution of Brian Marwood.

Marwood eventually left for Sheffield United in September 1990 after a short-lived Arsenal career during which he gained a solitary England cap against Saudi Arabia in Riyadh, coming on as substitute for his team-mate Michael Thomas. Brian has recently retired from professional football to work full-time as commercial director for the Professional Footballers' Association.

I spoke to Smith, Marwood and Dixon in the summer of 1994, a few weeks after the victory against Parma. For the fourth conversation we need to go back to 1987 and a pleasant evening spent with Charlie Nicholas, where else but in a pub in Highgate, North London. At the time, Bonnie Prince Charlie had graced Highbury for four years, since signing in a blaze of publicity from Celtic in the summer of 1983. For Arsenal fans still mourning the departure of Liam Brady and Frank Stapleton, Charlie was something of a rarity. He was a flair player with charisma, bought to replace the lumbering Lee Chapman.

When George Graham arrived in May 1986, however, Charlie's days were numbered. His fellow Scot was as suspicious of the consistent value of virtuosity then as he would be of Nicholas's heir-apparent, Anders Limpar, eight years later. Nicholas scored the goals at Wembley that clinched Graham's first trophy as Arsenal manager in 1987, but within the year he was gone.

Nicholas may have lacked the pace and work-rate demanded by Graham of his new-look Arsenal side, yet the plaintive cries of 'Charlie Charlie' could still be heard on the North Bank months after his departure.

Each of the players I spoke to have had different relationships with George Graham but I wanted to start with a common question: 'How do you go about signing for Arsenal?'

Lee Dixon:

I'd done the rounds in the lower divisions and ended up at Stoke for a season and a half. There were rumours that Arsenal were watching certain players over a period of about six months and it turned out it was me they were watching and perhaps Steve Bould as well.

They alternated who came to see me; a lot of times it was the gaffer. One time it was Pat Rice, then Stewart Houston and Steve Burtenshaw. They all came. They also watch you for so long, about six months, it's unbelievable.

We played Arsenal a few months before I signed, in the League Cup. They beat us 3-0 and Michael Thomas played really well at full-back so I thought the chance had gone, but a couple of weeks later we played Leicester and George Graham was talking to Mick Mills after the game and the next day I was down for talks.

Alan Smith:
I was training one day at Leicester and the manager said Arsenal had come in for me and agreed terms. I took the train down and Steve Burtenshaw picked me up from the station. At the time George Graham was in Portugal so I did the negotiations with Ken Friar at his house.

So you actually signed before you got to meet or talk to George?

Alan Smith:
Yes, I spoke to him on the phone just before I signed, but that was it.

Brian Marwood:
There was a lot of speculation in the Press for months leading up to me actually signing for Arsenal, which was very unsettling but also tremendously exciting because of the thought of joining a club like Arsenal. Sheffield Wednesday were a big club, but when you are linked with a club like Arsenal it's something different.

Charlie Nicholas:
Before I came to Arsenal I went to talk to Manchester United, a club I'd admired as a boy. I think if they had introduced me to Sir Matt Busby I would have signed on the spot because I respected him so much. But I didn't get to meet him and United handled it badly so I ended up coming to Arsenal.

Was there a big sales pitch from Arsenal before you signed?

Alan Smith:
Not really. Steve Burtenshaw and Ken Friar showed me around the ground but I didn't need much persuading because I'd turned Chelsea down a

month before. At the time I wasn't certain that Arsenal were going to make an offer for me. I just didn't like Chelsea, I never enjoyed going there. Ken Bates and John Hollins came up to Birmingham to speak to me. I just said, 'No I don't fancy it.'

Lee Dixon:

I met George Graham in a service station, sat in his car and had a cup of tea. He made me an offer and that was it. I didn't think it was good enough so I turned him down. I then went home and I was distraught. My wife and friends thought I was mad, so I called George Graham the next day and said, 'Can I come down to see you?'

I went, we had a chat, talked it around and I ended up signing that day.

We talked it through and the gaffer made the same offer but I stuck to my guns and forced his hand a little bit. There was a bit of give and take on both sides but if he'd looked at me first off and said that's my final offer, I'd have killed myself.

Brian Marwood:

When I signed, I dealt with George. To be honest it didn't take very long. I came down for the same salary I was on at Sheffield Wednesday. I've always put professional ambition in front of monetary considerations. I thought, 'Well I'm 28, I've got a chance to play for one of the biggest, if not the biggest club in the country', and I wasn't going to haggle over a few pounds here and there.

The circumstances surrounding the signings of Smith, Marwood and Dixon give a valuable insight into the psychology of George Graham's management style.

All three players were obviously extremely keen to sign for Arsenal as it represented a significant step up from their previous clubs (even for Marwood who was playing for Sheffield Wednesday). Graham has often spoken of the importance of desire and hunger in his teams and by purchasing most of his stock from lower divisions and lesser outfits Graham was certain to avoid the situation faced by his predecessors. Terry Neill and Don Howe had bought a number of 'star' players – Nicholas, Woodcock and Mariner – who had enjoyed success at other big clubs. As a consequence, playing for Arsenal may have been just another stepping stone for those seasoned internationals.

For Smith, Dixon, Marwood, Bould and Winterburn, *this* was their chance to make it in the big time. By buying the hungrier type of player

Graham also cleverly created a blue-collar, 'no-star' system which the players undoubtedly appreciated and is the single biggest factor in the forging of the formidable team-spirit which underpinned the successes of the wonder years. There is no room for prima donnas in the Arsenal dressing-room under George Graham. Significantly, though, none of the players cited Graham as a key factor in their wanting to move to Highbury. It is common to hear players refer to Hoddle, Dalglish, Venables or Keegan as one of the primary motivating factors when joining *their* clubs. At Arsenal it seems to be more of a team affair with Ken Friar and Steve Burtenshaw playing significant roles, and the players seemingly attracted to Arsenal and what the club represents rather than anything else.

This may seem an obvious point when discussing players from lesser clubs who *should* be impressed by the club's reputation and the lure of the marble halls. But what of the bigger stars, those less likely to be impressed by art deco stands and a bust of Herbert Chapman?

Graham's record of signing big names has been poor. Even the club's record signing of Ian Wright at £2.5 million was delivered by fate. An injudicious outburst by Crystal Palace chairman Ron Noades about black players saw Wright under pressure from his family and friends to leave Palace. Given that Wright would never fit into a club outside London and that Arsenal had an exemplary record with black players, Highbury was an obvious choice.

Graham's blue-collar ethos is supported by a wage structure which is based on competitive weekly salaries boosted by lucrative performance bonuses. Arsenal are now one of the top paymasters in the Premiership but at Highbury you have to earn it.

Other clubs are more likely to guarantee star signings a larger basic salary, which is cited as one of the major reasons why players of the calibre of Chris Sutton and Roy Keane rejected Arsenal's advances.

It is difficult to get the true picture in the murky world of football transfer dealings, but generally George Graham's forte has been identifying and attracting players from lesser clubs eager to step into the big time (1987–91) alongside some judicious Scandinavian signings as a result of diligent overseas scouting (1992–4).

However, even when George goes shopping on the Continent he is looking for the more English battling qualities of a Jensen or Schwarz. In eight years of management the one exception to the rule has been Anders Limpar, although judging by the way he was treated by George, you might think the manager had second thoughts about what he had done.

Uppermost in Graham's mind has always been the team rather than the individual. As Brian Marwood put it, 'George has been very concerned not to have the individuals before the team. If the team makes the individuals then fine, but the individuals shouldn't make the team.' So how important a factor is team-spirit in Arsenal's success over the last eight years?

Lee Dixon:
Individually we're not the most gifted players in the world but as a team we'd give anybody a go.

Brian Marwood:
It was a great team in every sense. We got on well with each other. There wasn't any feeling that one player is better than another which is a very big thing in a football club, especially these days. But in my opinion this incredible team-spirit was created by the players, not the manager. We all knitted together. There was no malice and no one person was better than the other, but it was a spirit created by the players.

What sort of individual relationship did you have with Graham?

Brian Marwood:
If there's one regret it's perhaps getting out the way I did. I should maybe have dug in and said 'I don't want to leave', but I think George had made his mind up that I was going. He never said it, but you can pick up the vibes. Don't get me wrong, I have enormous respect for George and now that I've finished my career I can say that, alongside Howard Wilkinson, he is the most organised and tactically aware manager I have ever worked with. I feel very fortunate to have worked with George Graham.

But that doesn't take away the bitter taste of how I felt I was treated. I felt that perhaps I deserved better. Fortunately I completed my soccer education with Dave Bassett.

My first trip with Sheffield United was away to Chelsea. I remember going down the M1 and the lads were stripping Dave naked and throwing his clothes out of the rooftop window of the coach.

I was thinking that I really couldn't see George doing this. And for me that's the difference. George is very tactically astute and gets respect that way. Dave is very much a man-manager. I thought if only you could combine the two, you would have the perfect manager.

With Dave, although we weren't successful I enjoyed every moment of it, whereas at Arsenal I was successful but didn't really enjoy it. You always felt you weren't allowed to enjoy it.

I don't know whether George did that intentionally but he never wanted us to get carried away. 'You've got training tomorrow, you have to work ultra-hard.' With Dave it was, we're all in this together, 'Win, draw or lose, let's hit the booze'.

I don't think I was a favourite with George. He liked me around because I was a dressing-room character. Every manager has their favourite players, maybe it's because they think that is the best way to get the most out of them.

I was disappointed when I left. I'd become involved in the PFA and that undermined my position with George. I know he'd never admit it but I think this had a part to play in my departure. George likes players that concentrate on playing football. He does not like them diversifying. And he thought I was diversifying and didn't appreciate it. That's my own opinion. Whether it's fair or not, it's how I read it. I look back now with great fondness but also with great sadness that I didn't finish my career at Arsenal Football Club. As for George, I wouldn't think of him as my best friend but I do think he will go down as one of the greatest football managers or coaches ever, and I used to work for him. So I'm fortunate in that.

We'll never be on each other's Christmas card lists but I've spoken to a lot of people who've played with him or had him as a player and they can't believe the things I say about him as a manager. I don't know whether he's had a bad experience and thought, 'That's it, I'm never going to get hurt again', but he's very similar to Howard Wilkinson in that you cannot get close to him.

Alan Smith:

George is one step removed from the players. He can be pally with the lads but he never socialises with the players and at a big club like Arsenal the players would rather it were like that. Gordon Milne at Leicester was very similar to George in that he kept his distance off the pitch.

From a personal viewpoint it's very rare that I meet formally with the gaffer. In the seven years I've been at Arsenal you can count the number of times I've been into his office on the fingers of one hand. Some players are knocking on his door the whole time but I've only really spoken to him about contracts or when I've really felt unsettled.

The gaffer doesn't really have any favourites, certainly not when it comes to dropping people. Tony Adams might be the only exception. He's got a special relationship with Tony. I think it's because he has got very strong leadership qualities. You can always count on Tony.

Lee Dixon:
I think he's got a good captain in Tony in that the lads love him, really respect him. Also he has the respect of the fans. I think Tony treats the gaffer as he should be treated. He doesn't really fight him.

When we've had cause to fight the gaffer as a team, Tony will do it but he won't always force his hand as much as he could. But I think the gaffer respects him for that.

Tony's not one of those people to go in saying, 'The lads want this, and the lads want that.' He's not one of those captains. But you couldn't do that anyway with the gaffer because he's so strong-willed and single-minded.

I don't think I would make a good captain under George because things would happen where I'd have to say something, then I would be out on my arse like Brian Marwood.

But I've learnt a lot about the game from the boss. He's an excellent coach. You cannot fault his record and he's brought me on as a defender. He's very conscious of his defence, as you've probably noticed over the years.

Charlie Nicholas:
George and I always got on fine. Sure, we've fallen out when I wasn't playing well – you always get that – but most of the time things were all right. However, when he left me out of a team that wasn't scoring goals I started to think it was a personal thing. I'd done nothing wrong for George to turn round and say I'm out of the team. I needed an explanation but never got one from George. It got to a stage where I had to book an appointment with his secretary to get to see him.

George Graham has a great reputation as a coach and tactician. Why?

Alan Smith:
George spends a lot of time on the training ground. It's very rare that he's not there. Stewart Houston will do the warm-up and will help, but the manager's there all the time.

Lee Dixon:
The gaffer does all the training. He's probably missed ten sessions in about eight years. He never misses training, very rarely. If he does, it means he's signing someone. Something's wrong if he's not there.

He doesn't bother with the reserves at all, just the first team. Now and then he'll take one of the young lads if he's short of numbers but Geordie Armstrong looks after the reserves. Pat Rice, the kids.

Brian Marwood:
Theo Foley used to take the warm-ups and I would say, 'Theo you must be the best-paid man in the world for putting out cones and handing out bibs.' Theo was a great character and provided a nice balance with George. When George was there you worked, when Theo was there you messed around. I was pleased I wasn't a defender because they were bombarded when I was there. He spent most of his time with the back four. I can never recall him saying to me this is where I want you, or that's what I want you to do. He was happy for us to develop in the final third of the pitch ourselves.

He was always much more concerned with his back four, the way they worked as a unit. He kept going over it to the point where, if I'd been a defender, I think it would have bored the pants off me. But it was so successful.

Alan Smith:
I think he prefers dealing with the strikers. He'll always say to us I want to come and join in with the skilful players rather than the defenders. He does enjoy working out with the defence and it is obviously very important at Arsenal but I think he prefers working with the strikers.

Lee Dixon:
The last couple of years he has really tightened us up at the back. We have always been good defensively but he wanted us tighter. It affected me and the way I like to go forward. He said, 'By all means go for it but you've been going too much recently – choose your time carefully.'

I didn't agree at the time but slowly it registered. You think, he's the manager and he's going to pick the team next week. I know I don't get forward as much as I used to but if it's for the benefit of the team then so be it.

As a senior player are you ever consulted by George?

Alan Smith:
Not really. The manager will talk to Tony about a few things but generally he does what he wants.

Lee Dixon:
We're very rarely consulted. He'll maybe say in training, 'What do you think?' Then you'll say this and that and he'll say, 'No, you're wrong'. He's his own man, he doesn't have to ask. He's achieved the lot, so he knows what he wants and we know what he wants.

The only reason he has to say anything is when we don't do it. That's the only time he says anything. The rest of the time it's repetitive. Doing it, doing it, doing it, to make sure you're doing it right on Saturday.

Arsenal are famous for their set-pieces under Graham. Do you spend a lot of time on dead-ball work?

Alan Smith:
Yes. Sometimes it drives the players mad. We'll work on a free-kick and the players will say 'the last time this worked was eight years ago'.

But we do work on set-pieces and corners quite a lot. On Friday we'll always work on them. Apart from that most of the work in training is ball-work, not physical training.

Brian Marwood:
We always used to work on set-pieces, free-kicks, corners. I can't remember the number of corners I took where Bouldy flicked it on and there was Tony Adams diving in amongst the flying boots and scoring.

Alan Smith:
If the opposition have got a good lad in the air we'll try and keep it away from him. But we've got so many good lads in the air, set-pieces have always been productive.

Does George use videos very much for training purposes?

Brian Marwood:
We'd do our homework, but then everyone does.

Lee Dixon:
On the coach to away games we'll always have the opposition's last game on the video. But you end up thinking, 'I only played against him a few months ago', plus there's so much football on television that you're seeing

the opposition every week. The boss will get very excited watching the video and say, 'Look, lads, come and watch this'. And we say 'righto, boss' and just carry on playing cards.

The consistent thread running through all the conversations was of a manager dedicated in training, a slave to preparation and attention to detail. Arsenal are probably the best-organised team in English football, the sum of the parts much more effective than the individual components could ever hope to be.

A criticism of Graham, however, is that the team has become too robotic, too predictable, some of the flair of the early years lost along the way as the Gunners have developed into football's ultimate mean-machine. Were the players conscious of a change in the emphasis or style of play, particularly over the last few seasons (92–4)? A period when Arsenal have not made a serious challenge for the title?

Lee Dixon:

Every season we set out to win the League and everything else is a bonus. Over the last few years we haven't challenged and I think I know what the reason is. Both times we won the League Alan Smith won the Golden Boot as top scorer. In 1989 Brian Marwood was supplying the crosses. In 1991 it was Anders Limpar, playing out of his skin.

We need a decent winger to put crosses in and the best striker to convert them. In the two seasons before he left, Anders had gone off the boil although the fans still loved him. If we'd had a Ryan Giggs or a Lee Sharpe we'd have won the League.

Alan Smith:

It's changed a lot in the last few years. We don't play with a wide-man anymore. If we do he's not a crosser of the ball whereas when Brian Marwood was here we could get the ball to him and he would always cross it in early. This suited my game. Now, if Kevin Campbell or Paul Merson play wide, they're not exactly wingers, are they?

As a result we play in straight lines sometimes. I'm just flicking it on which means I am out of the game and somebody else has to score. That's one reason why I personally haven't scored so many goals in the last few seasons.

Brian Marwood:

When I saw Arsenal play last season (93/94) they looked very predictable. I think George needs to bring in a John Sheridan type who is a visionary in midfield who can control the game. There's no one there who can do that. You look at Parlour, Hillier and Selley and they're all young players. That's an enormous burden for them. Perhaps Schwarz can do it.

If I were playing against Arsenal I would just try and stop Ian Wright. If you do that I cannot see Arsenal scoring.

Alan Smith is missing the service first I provided and later Anders. Since then, George has not got the best out of him.

Lee Dixon:
I don't want to criticise the boss because we've been so successful, even without winning the League. In the Cups we are very difficult to beat.

We can afford to be like that in Cup football – you'll always get a chance and as long as you don't concede a goal you will win 1-0. But over a period of 42 games you're not going to do that every week, which is why we drew so many games last year.

Since Ian Wright arrived at the club, he has scored ninety goals in two-and-a-half seasons and yet in the last two League campaigns Arsenal have been amongst the lowest scorers in the Premiership. What's the problem?

Lee Dixon:
Wrighty is a phenomenon you can't really explain. He's a goal-machine. But he's different to Alan Smith. Alan will never go over the top and chase balls and score from the edge of the box. Wrighty, on the other hand, will never hold the ball up for ten minutes when you need a breather at the back.

The gaffer is now in a dilemma about which way to play. He's said we need two more quality signings. I just hope one will be a top-quality winger.

We play two different games when Alan and Wrighty play together. If I get the ball when Wrighty's playing I look up, see him making a run and knock it over the top. With Alan, I look up and play it into feet.

When they play together the players tend to hit Alan and then Wrighty gets frustrated because he's not getting the ball. I enjoy playing with both of them but I don't know if they can play in the same team.

Brian Marwood:
It's the Gary Lineker syndrome. When Lineker went to Everton he was top goal-scorer, yet Everton finished second in the League. And I look at Kevin

Campbell and people like that, very much living in Wright's shadow. I think the whole scene at Arsenal has become focused on what Ian Wright's doing and not on what the rest of the team has been up to.

Alan Smith:
As I said before, I think we are missing a wide player. Ian has done superbly for Arsenal. He has become a legend in a couple of years at the club.

Much has been made of the sale of Andy Cole after making only one brief appearance as substitute for Arsenal under George Graham. With the benefit of hindsight it seems like George's biggest managerial mistake in the transfer market. Should he have persevered with Cole?

Brian Marwood:
I told George at the time it was the right thing to do. There was no way forward for Andy in the first team at Highbury. I played with him in the reserves and he was getting frustrated. Andy needs to be the centre of attention, to have the team built around him. At Arsenal there were too many strikers ahead of him. He would have been in and out of the first team. He went to Bristol City and that's where he grew up.

I think it's a great shame because Arsenal lost a rare talent. He's a super player but he needed a goal in life, a target. At Arsenal I don't think he felt he had a real chance of regular first-team football.

Lee Dixon:
If I ever became a manager of a big enough club to be able to send players out on loan then I would send every single young player out for three months to somewhere like Crewe. I did it and it made me. I came up the hard way. I was given a free-transfer. I moved for £3000 to Bury and thought I was a world-beater, because people were paying money to sign *me*. None of this does you any harm at all. And when you finally get somewhere you think, bloody hell, I've made it.

I can guarantee you there's never been a time since I've been at Arsenal, on a Saturday, where I've thought, 'I'm bored with this'.

You can see some players, though, Andy Cole is an example, who come up through the ranks, get within sight of the first team, then when it doesn't come immediately, pack it in. Maybe it's just bred in him but he didn't seem to give a damn. I've never taken it for granted so I can't relate to players like that.

Obviously neither could George, who dispensed with Cole's services after Kevin Campbell finished the 91/92 season firing on all cylinders.

The consensus among all the players that I have spoken to is that George Graham was right to sell Cole at that time. Graham has subsequently said that he never considered Cole a viable partner for Wright, which, when coupled with Cole's attitude problem and the emergence of Kevin Campbell as a genuinely exciting prospect, makes it difficult to question Graham's decision.

Turning again to tactics, can you point to some key games where the manager's preparation made the difference?

Alan Smith:
On the minus side there is the game against Spurs in 1991. We sat on the grass at the training ground and said, 'Shall we put a man on Gazza or not?' We decided we would and Mickey Thomas was to do it.

On the day, Gazza was going everywhere and Mickey tried to follow him but it just didn't work. After the game he was very conscious that Terry Venables had put one over on him.

Brian Marwood:
I always remember the night at Anfield in 1989. The players didn't really expect us to win and the manager got us nice and relaxed. I'll never forget George's team talk.

'Listen, you've got nothing to lose. If we don't win the title we've had a great season, the best season, the first season we've all been together. Think what it will be like next season.

'They'll be under pressure – Anfield will be packed, there's TV coverage.

'If it's 0-0 at half-time there'll be more pressure on them. We might nick a goal just after half-time and then there'll be even more pressure on them. Who knows what could happen then?'

It was a perfect forecast of what was about to happen. If I ever believed fate had a part to play then this was fate.

Lee Dixon:
Europe was great last year and nobody enjoyed it more than George Graham. He was in his element – he loved it. It has to go down as one of the highlights of his career as manager. He revelled in it, all the . . . 'what's he going to do, come and watch this video 'cos they play like this and we'll have to do this.'

We got the impression that he was on the verge of panicking before each game because he wasn't sure how we were going to cope.

Alan Smith:

Before the Torino game he was really building their players up to be world-beaters, saying 'you've got to stick to him or he'll destroy you' and that sort of thing. I think he likes that. He likes playing the tactical game. Tactics do come into it more in Europe than in the League. The lads sensed he really wanted to win in Europe last season. Even against Liege in the away-leg when we were about five up and I came off injured, he was still going mad on the bench. He gets very hyped-up on match days.

Lee Dixon:

Towards the end we took the pressure off him. We kept saying, 'Gaffer, we can handle it', and although we changed systems a few times throughout the competition we played more or less a similar way throughout the tournament. Near the end he thought, 'Well, I'll just let them get on with it'.

People say we played differently but in most games we played in a similar way. Even against Standard Liege. They were just crap. We got ten against them but you don't get ten against the top teams.

Are the players conscious that despite the Cup successes of recent years the fans are very concerned about the style of football at Highbury? Arsenal have been low scorers in the League for the past few seasons and played some dull football.

Alan Smith:

I think the fans have their own perception of what attractive football is. As long as we are winning, the manager is happy. However, he said in an interview after the Cup-Winners' Cup Final that he wanted to play with more flair, a bit more like Manchester United.

Charlie Nicholas:

Manager-wise, he always got me to fit into a pattern of play. I didn't mind that but I think you've got to give a player like me a bit of leeway to do his own type of thing in certain situations. Sure, when I've not got the ball I've got to work hard but I always try and judge what the crowd want. If the crowd appreciate me doing something, I carry on doing it. The manager might not like me doing certain things but I'd rather please the crowd than the manager. I think everybody's too worried about pleasing the manager nowadays. The game's becoming like a game of chess with everyone worrying about moving out of position.

Lee Dixon:
I take the point about entertainment but I know which way I'd rather have it. I'm not just saying that as a footballer but as a supporter as well. When I was a season-ticket holder at Maine Road I'd much rather have seen us win than entertain and lose. Whether that's because I enjoy winning, I don't know.

If you filled a stadium with 30,000 people and asked them individually what they'd like to see, I reckon most of them would want to see their team win.

Manchester United do both at the moment, but we haven't got the players to do both. Although Manchester United have flair players, exceptional players, like Giggs, Kanchelskis and Sharpe, you should watch them play. They work their nuts off for the team. The two midfield players do too. Hughes also tackles back and runs his legs off. Cantona's the only one who doesn't tackle back.

And that's why they're such a good side. Of course, they're tricky on the ball so they've got that as well.

I think our back four is better than theirs. I also think our midfield is on a par. Our midfield won't make as many runs as Keane, but you get something different from Stefan and J.J.

I think United are much better than us on the wing, no disrespect to Merse, and up front I think Wrighty is better than anything they've got although Hughesy is probably the best all-round centre-forward in England. Seaman is a better keeper than Schmeichel, so all round we're not far off.

Which brings us full-circle to Arsenal's recent record in the transfer market.

George Graham is always in the market for 'quality players', as he never tires of telling the press. Yet his inability to land a quality winger to replace Marwood and Limpar and the lack of a creative midfield player has seen Arsenal lose momentum after the Championship successes of 89 and 91.

Notwithstanding this loss of focus in the League, the wonder years have seen Graham and his team capture six trophies in eight seasons. What has been the key to that success? And who should take the credit? The manager or the players?

Alan Smith:
The key to success is having the players to start with, players with ability. Then you need a system of play and the players need to apply it on the pitch with the right attitude.

George is very organised, particularly on the pitch. Everybody knows what they've got to do. Plus we have a resilience which keeps us going for 90 minutes.

Brian Marwood:
We were very well-organised. George had us extremely well drilled from day one. We scored a high percentage of our goals from set-pieces. He also worked very hard on his back four. So we rarely conceded soft goals. As a consequence we became very hard to beat.

Charlie Nicholas:
George has done very well at Arsenal and I respect him for that. He's very well-organised and a strong character. George Graham deserves a lot of credit.

Lee Dixon:
The keys to Arsenal's success have been the manager, who has put together such a good team, and the team spirit within the club. If you look at the Anfield team of 89 there is still that nucleus of players who are at the club. We've done it all. It is something George Graham can take the credit for. He's brought new players in but based it around that core – built around defence – the defence that won the League in 89 and 91 and five years later triumphed in Copenhagen.

Alan Smith:
The players deserve a lot of the credit because there has not been a large turnover for seven years. It is the same nucleus that has won all those trophies. If it had been a different set of players each season you could say the manager has been responsible for all that success by changing the players, but this Arsenal side deserves a lot of credit too.

Brian Marwood:
George has identified what is going to be good for him. He hasn't been liked by everyone but I don't think he's bothered.

He wants to be remembered as someone who has been successful. And that's how people will view him. They will say he was successful! but not a great character – like Tommy Docherty or Ron Atkinson or Bill Shankly.

I don't think the fans love him. Now George would be happy if they did but I think he'd say, 'Am I here to be adored or am I here to be a success?'

The man runs a high-pressure football club and he's won two League Championships, two League Cups, an FA Cup and the European Cup-Winners' Cup. That is good going. Practically something every year.

He has kept Arsenal at the forefront and established a higher profile for the club than anyone except Herbert Chapman. As time passes he will become a greater and greater figure in Arsenal's history. People's view of you always becomes kinder with history. George is a success now. He'll be a terribly hard act to follow. I wouldn't like to think I was taking over from him.

The overwhelming impression from speaking to the players is of a deeply felt respect for what George Graham has achieved at Arsenal.

Discipline, character, resilience, organisation may seem like buzz-words from an aggressive piece of American corporate literature, but these are the consistent strands which, when pieced together, form the leitmotif for George Graham's Arsenal.

They seem quite simple things. Surely organisation and resilience are as easily attained at Halifax, Colchester or Barnet as they are at Arsenal and Manchester United?

Not so, according to Alan Smith, who believes these qualities need to be instilled by the manager over a long period of time. When asked if he could put his finger on one thing that set Arsenal apart under George Graham, Smith paused for some time before replying, 'You can see the manager in us more than you can in other teams.'

This is the ultimate irony for those who remember the 'Stroller' of old. A languid player with grace and finesse, but lacking many of the attributes needed for survival in the modern game.

This discrepancy between the attitude of Graham the player and Graham the manager, has been much commented on, leading Nick Hornby to claim that you cannot dislike Graham the manager because he is simply denying his true self for the good of Arsenal.

As for Brian Marwood's concept of man-management, anyone connected with the club would be horrified to think of the Arsenal manager stripping off in the back of the team bus and mixing with the crowd from below-stairs. This is Highbury, not Plough Lane.

Self-denial and repression are more in keeping with the air of austerity and rectitude that still permeates the marble halls. Amongst his charges Graham inspires respect, not a little fear and sneaking admiration, though, as yet, the reverence or affection accorded to Shankly and Busby is barely detectable. Perhaps when George Graham's reign is analysed in the soft focus of historical perspective, the gaffer will get the full credit he deserves.

St George and the Dragon

by Michael Collins

There are still those at Highbury who are grudging in their praise of George Graham. Unbelievable, isn't it? After six major trophies in eight seasons you would think undying gratitude was in order but, no, the chronically dissatisfied point to his emphasis on water-tight defence as if this is a failing, and his preference for solid effective grafters over those lissom magicians who reputedly 'entertain'. This species of critic does tend to be drawn from the gilded élite of Highbury fandom – the wiseacres who haunt the training ground spouting indispensible advice, and the fanzine contributors with their shedfuls of axes to grind. But such luminaries do not, I feel, accurately represent the views of the ordinary supporters, the men who have eschewed the bitter ironies of *Fever Pitch* and who revel instead in the self-satisfied 'George Graham' editorial in the official programme. Not for them the alternative publications with their buckets of venom, snide asides at Graham's deficiencies in tactical ploys, the transfer market and choice of tailor, the gloomy prognoses of unending underachievement. I mean, when you get down to it, George's all right, isn't he; won us the lot; done, so to speak, the business.

They have a point, although I do not go along with the extremist wing of the orthodoxy which maintains that Graham's managerial arrival in May 1986 was the Second Coming, the Son of Chapman descended from the celestial marble halls to redeem the faithful and consign Spurs to the pit of eternal torment. He has too many faults to be acclaimed as a Messiah, too much hubris, an all too mortal defect. But I can argue convincingly for a canonisation – St George, the slayer of the Arsenal Legend, that voracious red and white beast living in the heart of every Gunners fan, and which we released to consume lesser men over the years, the monstrous expectation that makes the Highbury crowd so difficult to pacify.

Look at Billy Wright CBE, superstar of his era, garnering more personal silverware than HM has stashed in the Tower of London; he got his double-nostrilled squirt of flame in 1966, otherwise a good year for English roses, having won exactly sod-all for the club. Billy's epitaph is the most damning in football – 'Well, he nurtured some fine talent in the youth team.' Sure, and a fat lot of use those pimply specimens are when it's the big boys of Liverpool on a Saturday afternoon. Here, then, was a career that should have ended gloriously on the pitch, not around a mahogany table with the knives politely stabbing.

Bertie Mee, a very perfect gentle knight, was next into the lists and he did put up one hell of a scrap – Fairs Cup 1970, Double winners 1971 – before succumbing to weariness at the end of the 75/76 season, when Arsenal went out of both Cup competitions by the third round and lost five of their last seven League games to finish seventeenth in the First Division. Seventeenth! The current generation of malcontents should try rolling those three syllables off their tongues whenever they feel Graham is getting them down, which is often.

The Highbury trumpets sounded for a new gallant to enter the fray and a few miles up the road, in the Castle of Groans, Terry Neill heard the summons. He made the short canter from White Hart Lane, took the plaudits for purchasing Malcolm MacDonald for a staggering £333,333 and sent out his new model army to lose 0-1 to a far from legendary Bristol City. Ho hum. Wasn't it all supposed to be different; hadn't the board promised us a new age of chivalry? Was Neill another wimp in rusty armour?

Not quite. His achievements are well documented but the standard histories tend to gloss over events from 1980 onwards, a key year which established the mood of quiet despair that prevailed at Highbury until Graham's appointment six years later. Losing the FA Cup to West Ham was woeful enough for any Arsenal fan; losing it to a headed Trevor Brooking goal was a cosmic league cruelty. To rub salt into this gaping wound, Graham Rix, just four days afterwards, took one of those 'My Mum could've done better' penalties and handed the Cup-Winners' Cup to Valencia, leaving the club with the one that runneth over with bile. 'Stop the year, we want to get off,' was the passionate plaint from the disappointed hordes. No chance. Liam Brady upped sticks in the close season and took himself to Juventus for a miserly £514,000. Neill, we then realised, was on that notorious Cresta run to oblivion against which there is no adequate brake, not even the successive signings of Tony Woodcock (' 'e were a lad, that one') and Charlie Nicholas (ditto). When fortune's always hiding it takes more than a fat chequebook to tempt it out into the open.

Two games – and games are the crucibles in which all fans forge the image of their managers – epitomise Neill's last days with Arsenal. The first was against Coventry on 15 October 1983, my personal most unforgettable Match to Forget. It was a day of biblical rain, of a deluge so prolonged and heavy that the referee hired a canoe to inspect the pitch. A shame he did not abandon proceedings because the watery garbage that followed did a profound disservice to local park football, let alone a professional stadium. What happened, or, more precisely, failed to happen in those abysmal 90 minutes, disabused 20,000 drenched souls of the illusion that Neill was to lead us to the Promised Land. The burning bush spluttered, hissed and went out. Arsenal lost 0-1 to a side so poor that, before kick-off, charitable collections were held for them outside the ground. Colin Hill, not a name resonating grandly in the Highbury annals, played at number 6, and the forward line included the unsurpassable Lee Chapman. Nicholas, supposedly our 'darling', did nothing discernible during the afternoon, apart from a few fancy-pants dummies on the half-way line, which sums up most of his time at the club. What became ominously evident in this disaster was that lovable, chuckling, avuncular Uncle Terry was not up to the job.

Final proof of his guilt was presented to a furious jury of 22,000 on the evening of 29 November 1983. Arsenal had beaten Spurs in the previous round of the League Cup three weeks earlier and had been rewarded for their endeavour by what amounted to a bye against Walsall. A fillip was required after the 0-3 League defeat by Leicester the preceding Saturday, so what could have been easier than a team so obscure that no home fan was even sure of where they came from? The old-timers on the North Bank touted their sepia recollections of an amazing upset perpetrated by the same club in prehistoric times, but no one listens to the aged. Life, say the Buddhists, revolves in circles. Walsall fought back from a one-goal deficit to win, on merit, 2-1, and for the disillusioned faithful enough was enough. The mob converged on the main entrance in Avenell Road to demand Neill's sacking. The dragon had him in its jaws and we wanted him swallowed alive. His charm, patience and easy-going humour were not the qualities to restore the club to the aristocracy, and likeability had become a liability. The job of Arsenal manager demanded attributes we as Arsenal fans pride ourselves upon – toughness, single-mindedness, even ruthlessness in achieving our aims. Incredibly, in the light of these requirements, the board opted to promote Don Howe to caretaker manager, confirming the position as permanent in April 1984.

For the next two and a half years, matches were won, matches lost and Arsenal never looked like winning a church raffle, never mind a trophy, with the players going through an increasingly perfunctory set of motions. Howe is essentially a coach, not made of the more valuable stuff that guides a club to glory, and this was abundantly clear to the more perceptive supporters from the outset. He is the enthusiastic physics teacher who coaches soccer after lessons, the one with the grass-stained tracksuit he wears in the laboratory while trying to enlighten disinterested hooligans in the nuances of Archimedes' Principle. Moreover, the enthusiasm is of a variety which comes across as slightly absurd, forever formulating plans to deflect attention away from the present inadequacies. Howe hatched more plans than a coopful of hens but lacked the charisma to motivate his players to spill blood for the cause. The fans were increasingly infected with the lethargy and lost their sparkle too, the North Bank reminiscent of a mausoleum on many occasions under his auspices.

Inconsistency was Howe's team's consistent fault, particularly evidenced by the form of Nicholas, who drifted in and out of games as the mood took him. We had probably given up the notion of Charlie as Saviour by then, and it seemed obvious that Howe could not motivate him. The problem extended throughout the team. How could a side, we asked, capable of walloping Liverpool 3-1, slither to icy FA Cup defeat at York City in 1985, much to the chagrin of the 2500 loyalists who made the long trip north? These are the days which fix the manager's stature in the fans' eyes; you weigh what you see against the other evidence he has given you and make the judgement. When Graham's team, seven years later, crashed to Wrexham in the same competition, the bitterness of defeat was tempered by the awareness of the successes he had brought. Howe had no such buffer and to stand out in sub-zero temperatures watching eleven men who embody all your hopes of glory performing like novices, does not inspire confidence in the man supposedly motivating them. It was actually a relief when Howe stormed out of the club just prior to a League match with Tottenham on learning that the board had tentatively approached Terry Venables about the job. Bye, bye, Don Howe, bye, bye . . .

The Venables rumours – and such manoeuvres are always just rumours to the ordinary fan – were worrying. Despite his itinerant career, the Essex Boy was indelibly associated with Spurs in the minds of the Arsenal faithful, and even considering him for the top post was tantamount to hiring Norman Bates to re-tile our Mums' bathrooms. He had achieved some managerial success, yet always seemed to leave his clubs in dubious circumstances. When the somewhat surprising announcement of George Graham's acceptance of the job was made on 14 May 1986, there was a feeling that we had escaped an even bigger mess than the one left behind by Howe. Not that there was any dancing in the streets of N5. New eras had the habit of fizzling out into the same old stuff at Highbury. Still, at least Graham was a step in the right direction. A member of the Double-winning side of 1971, he had spent three-and-a-half years learning the managerial ropes at Millwall, the ultimate School of Hard Knocks, turning around an outfit he had found languishing at the foot of the Third Division. Graham himself remarked that the job had given him ten years' experience in a third of that time. He was now, he professed, ready for the Big Challenge, which made him and about 50,000 others. The past six years had been atrocious; faith in the club's ability to win trophies had withered to a stump, and a £1 million debt was hanging over Highbury. Bring on George – he could hardly be any worse than his predecessors.

Graham's early pronouncements gave no indication of the scope of the revolution he was to create at Arsenal. There was a high moral tone to some of the quotes that gave the effect of oratory, the words of the re-former who had to make clear to *everyone* what he was about and what had to be done. We all conveniently forgot the FA Disciplinary Tribunal he had to attend just days after his appointment, for swearing at the referee during a Portsmouth-Millwall match, because even the most highly-principled must be forgiven their occasional lapses. In addition, there was a marked lack of activity in the transfer market, foreshadowing the later years when certain sections of the support wanted him to move on anyone who looked as if they might add zest to the mineral water. 'Eventually, it will be *my* squad at Highbury,' he told a reporter, 'but for the moment I'll wait to see how things develop.' We were happy enough with this statement. After all, an ingrained legacy of failure is not eradicated overnight, and no one expected the glittering prizes to fall into the trophy cabinet without a new culture first being introduced. We did not know it then, but that had already arrived.

The first League game under Graham's stewardship was a 1-0 win over Manchester United. A crowd of 41,000 came to watch and in truth it was a scrappy affair. Nicholas helped himself to a tap-in from Davis's shot, enough to beat a poor United side. At least Rix was galvanised by his new manager's presence, chasing after every loose ball and running back to tackle, a phenomenon never before witnessed at Highbury. We were satisfied, however, with an opening day victory, the first in three years, and Graham made all the right noises about seeing enough to work on. That work was needed was undeniable as the next two games at Coventry and Liverpool were both lost. An unhealthy sense of *déjà vu* assailed the loyalists. Surely a Scottish version of Neill and Howe had not snuck in through the back door to take our money and run? League form thereafter was much improved. Between the start of October and the end of January the only defeat was inflicted by Manchester United at Old Trafford. The North Bank began to swell with pride again – 'Arsenal are back' was the recurring refrain, this time chanted with genuine conviction. Graham, despite a worrying aloofness, was casting his spell.

The first real evidence of the magic came on 1 March 1987 at White Hart Lane. Arsenal had been beaten 0-1 in the first leg of the League Cup Semi-Final at Highbury, a result coinciding with a run of scoreless draws in the League. It would be an exaggeration to say there was a crisis of confidence, more a sense of anti-climax that something which started so well was threatening to evaporate at the crucial moment. Graham professed himself happy at the points being won, ignoring the vocal minority's call for more 'entertainment' along with the undoubted sweat. They were duly rewarded. In the days of yore a 0-1 deficit would have been seen as too large an obstacle to overcome. Arsenal were almost unbeatable if they took a lead, yet tended to deflate like an old Christmas balloon should the reverse occur. No such inferiority complex was displayed this time. The Spurs goal was put under siege, Quinn and Anderson nicked the decisive strikes, and the game was pulled around to 2-2 on aggregate. This was a world away from the miserable capitulations against Walsall, York City and their ilk. The decider, four days later, established Graham as the true pretender to Chapman's throne, and was the preface to the dazzling chapters he has subsequently written. Spurs again took the lead and despite the bravery of Arsenal's resistance, it looked as if it was all over. The old enemy were going to Wembley to meet Liverpool – we were stuck once more with the *ennui* of a meaningless end-of-season campaign. Against the run of play, Ian Allinson squeezed an equaliser, and the red and white army on the Park Lane terrace went berserk. From that moment onwards we just *knew* it was going to be all right. Cometh the moment, cometh David Rocastle to sweep in the winner at the death. The terrace ecstasy has rarely been equalled since. One-nil-down, two-one-up, that's how George got us to the final of the Cup. Never mind that it was only the League Cup, a poor relation to the Big One.

It was still a recognised trophy, a piece of silver to fill that cobwebbed cabinet in the marble halls. The story of the final is well-known – Arsenal winning a match in which Ian Rush had scored for Liverpool, a feat never before achieved – but it was the semi-final that made Graham's name. It was not always pretty, yet it was remorselessly effective. Graham just shrugged it off; as soon as the Cup had been lifted, the achievement was history, pleasant to recall, and totally irrelevant to the future. Here was the hardness Neill and Howe had lacked, the 'don't give a toss what you think' attitude that has become the Scotsman's way of showing his concern for us. Winning makes up for a lot, and there was a lot to make up for.

Basking in long-overdue glory, the Arsenal fans were further heartened by the arrival of Alan Smith from Leicester, Watford's Kevin Richardson and Wimbledon's Nigel Winterburn, none of them laying claim to be George Best, which was perhaps Nicholas's most grievous fault. Charlie had struck twice at Wembley to win the Cup but it was obvious his Highbury days were numbered, that he had fallen from favour with the manager. 'Charlie has to ask himself why he has totally failed to fulfill his potential in England,' commented Graham severely. And he had a point. The terrace idolisation, due as much to an engaging demeanour as ability, belied a decidedly average strike rate and concealed a definitely atrocious work rate. He was dropped after the 0-2 defeat by QPR on 22 August 1987 and never again kicked a ball in anger for Arsenal. The *afficionados* were disgusted. Charlie embodied the club and had a divine right to be out on the pitch, a plausible enough argument under Neill and Howe, who had precious little else to offer and who depended on the Scot's popularity with the fans to shore up their own positions. Graham was different. His uncompromising ambition to be the best Arsenal manager of all time did not permit players like Nicholas to stand in his way, whatever the opinion of the terraces. It was no more Mr Nice Guy – the gauntlet had been flung down to those who would challenge his vision. Flair, entertainment and attractive football only meant something if they contributed to quantifiable success. Despite protests from some quarters, Graham had calculated that Charlie had to go and unflinchingly rid himself of the turbulent Bonnie Prince, a decision of no small courage. The protestors howled with rage, to zero effect.

Not that he was missed overmuch. Smith proved a canny purchase in the goal-scoring department and banged in the chances in an unromantic yet consistent manner. The addition of Lee Dixon and Brian Marwood early in 1988 met with universal approbation; here, at last, was a team scenting glory and capable of attractive football. If Graham had a discernible weakness it was his misplaced loyalty to players who the fans could see were duffers. Perhaps the most ludicrous was Gus Caesar, whose name has an imperial resonance cruelly belied by the reality. The story of Caesar's contribution to the League Cup Final of 1988 is legend and confirmed Graham as a manager prone to errors of judgement. After a disastrous Wembley performance, Caesar was allowed to remain at the club in the face of unanimous disapproval from the supporters.

The burning question at Highbury in light of the Cup success was Graham's ability to bring the Championship to North London for the first time in eighteen years. Those disillusioned by Howe and Neill were flocking back to matches to witness both attractive play and the serious pursuit of glory. That Graham was serious was beyond doubt. He exuded the aura of success, a dapper Don impervious to the slings and arrows of outrageous rivals and dissenters within his own ranks. On his appointment he had said he would await developments and create a team to his own vision, which was, of course, totally shared by the Arsenal fans. Yet he so nearly abused the trust we placed in him by allowing the team to falter at the final hurdles of the 88/89 title race. For most of the season the players had responded magnificently to his inspired leadership. The collective failure of nerve against Derby County and Wimbledon hinted at shortcomings which we remembered all too well from previous years. Arousing great expectations among a mass following is fraught with danger; failure, should it strike, is doubly bitter for those expecting the ultimate prize. A lucky rebound to Mickey Thomas saw off the spectre, although it was much too close for comfort. The parties amongst the Arsenal contingent at Anfield, and the near anarchy on the streets of North London that Friday night, were as much about relief as joy, a celebration of Graham's escape from the ignominy that would have been heaped upon him, and us, should it all have gone wrong. The line between success and failure is a thin one and if Graham, in addition to all his other qualities, could charm Lady Luck into the Highway boudoir then he was truly the man we had been waiting for since Chapman.

Even at this moment of greatest triumph, however, Graham was not well-liked. Respect was due by the lorry-load, yet there was, and still is, a coldness in his demeanour which renders him unapproachable, even intimidating. Villa fans can love Big Ron, Sheffield United followers idolise 'Harry' Bassett and even the rare smile of Alex Ferguson comes from the heart. Graham, on the other hand, seems constantly preoccupied to the point of disdain and his ruthless pragmatism extends, in some eyes, to cold-heartedness. The Bond issue, following the strictures of the Taylor Report, was put to the Highbury public immediately after the 90/91 Championship success via a glossy brochure composed of the standard vacuous copywriting and jolly photographs. The most absurd of these shows Graham shaking hands with an 'average' supporter – in this case a professional model – who looks only too pleased to have been relieved of over £1000. Real average supporters were undismayed and not many ironic chords were struck; here, after all, was the man responsible for so much happiness washing his hands of many of the people who had embodied that happiness, written it large for players and manager alike. He had always maintained that there would be no deflecting him from the business of running the team, yet here was a veritable boomerang. Not once did he express genuine remorse for the loss of the North Bank which had acclaimed him as player and manager. 'You must never look back,' he told an intereviewer. 'You must always progress.' Nothing wrong in that approach, but a human touch at this point would have given him some sympathetic qualities. Still, another trophy had been won, and most of the fans did not fully appreciate at that time what they were losing. Very few people are capable of understanding that defeat can often be snatched from the jaws of victory.

An ambivalent attitude to discipline similarly troubles few of the loyalists. Public rebukes for Mickey Thomas and Anders Limpar over matters best left private were seized upon, inevitably, by the tabloid Press to the detriment of Arsenal's much-touted 'good' name. Berating employees in this fashion would be half-acceptable if it had any consistency, which it does not in Graham's case. Tony Adams' release from prison on drink-driving offences was greeted by the kind of red carpet treatment accorded to returning prodigal sons. Surely what Adams did was unforgivable within the strict moral victories Graham himself had espoused and a grievous contravention of the law of the land. The message to supporters seems to be that crime is acceptable as long as you play for Arsenal.

The mass punch-ups that have periodically erupted on the field also deserve examination. The fracas with Norwich in 1989 was hardly edifying fare, and the FA made its position clear, for once, by warning the club that a repeat performance would invite dire retribution. Yes, Your Honour, no Your Honour, thank you very much, Your Honour. Less than a year later at Old Trafford, another battle was staged in front of a full house and neither Graham nor Ferguson could find much contrition within themselves. The video of the 90/91 season shows a carefully staged performance of Graham urging on his troops to new exploits, but features not one word of apology to the fans. The resulting two-point deduction did no more than confirm the suspicion entertained by the majority that 'they' had it in for us. The more perceptive suspected that something within the manager had it in for us, although this chapter is not an exercise in cod-psychology. Graham, by all accounts, is one hell of an angry man; as long as that anger is channelled into lifting trophies we can forgive him most things, even the atrocious League form of the last two years.

Winning is the armour which protects Graham from the fate that visited his predecessors. Questionable forays into the transfer market – Jensen, McGoldrick, Schwarz et al. – are implicitly justified by the victorious context in which they are introduced to the club. Wright has been perhaps the most spectacular addition, having much of the sorcerer about him, although the others do not even qualify as apprentices. Graham does things his way and so what that the Double-cup triumph of 92/93 was a grind, that the European Cup-winners' Cup success was won by the slenderest of margins? We are all football fans – terrace casual and fanzine editor alike – and do not live in a world of conjecture. While Graham is doing what he does best, and what we love best, we are content, but the large irony, after all, is not yet apparent. By slaying one dragon, St George has created an even more fearsome beast for those coming after him to quell. Which bright-eyed pretender awaits his doom at our hands in the future? Who will fail miserably to fulfil our aspirations? We're not any old crowd, we are Arsenal. So, whoever he is had better be as hard as George Graham if he wants to live with that.

No One Likes Us

by Henry Winter

Arsenal versus Parma, European Cup-Winners' Cup Final, Copenhagen, May 94. They came, they scored, they conquered. What more could people want?

Arsenal's triumph over Parma, the holders of the Cup-Winner's Cup, will not go down as one of English football's greatest or most stylish European successes. But the lack of euphoria outside Islington simply confirmed the view in which the Gunners are held nationwide. Boring, unexciting. Strip away Merse and Wright and, so the theory goes, you are better off with a newly Duluxed wall and a magnifying glass. Highbury's bunker-mentality continued apace.

Few, even on the North Bank, would argue that Arsenal's against-the-odds victory over expensively assembled Italian opposition was a classic. One goal and a whole load of quality-defending proved sufficient. Yet think what the reaction would have been if Brolin, Zola, Asprilla and co. had struck early then defended like dervishes. Cue widespread applause for their Continental nous and professionalism.

The Gunners' achievement needs to be spelt out. Impressive away-performances, the key to European progress, read: win at Odense; 7-0 thrashing of Standard Liege; hold Torino in their imposing Alpine home; score draw with Paris Saint-Germain. Here were a series of great overseas successes, culminating in Alan Smith's settler in Copenhagen.

There's more. The knock-on effect of Smith's winner was considerable – it bought English clubs more UEFA points and gave Newcastle United a place in Continental competition.

Embarrassed by England's failure to qualify for the World Cup finals, George Graham's coup should have engendered a feeling of national pride. Here was tangible proof that we could compete against, and defeat, international opposition. After defeat to Arsenal, Parma players like Apolloni and Zola, of Italy, Sweden's Brolin and the Colombian Asprilla headed off to the World Cup. Italy and Sweden, of course, finished, respectively, second and third overall.

Arsenal, true to type, simply received grudging respect. Fans, not only Tottenham Hotspur's, argued that Graham's men had simply bored the opposition to death. The sentiments shown by a mid-season poll which revealed that more than 50 per cent of fans from all clubs felt Arsenal to be 'boring' were confirmed again.

This naive view, prevalent among so many rival fans, was captured best in a letter to *The Independent* newspaper following the Copenhagen final. 'To any objective reviewer,' wrote a reader from Beckenham, Kent, 'Arsenal's win in the European Cup-Winner's Cup must surely have been a profoundly depressing experience, truly a victory for the dullest virtues and a denial of the game's potential for grace, imagination, subtlety and beauty. In comparison with their opponents, Arsenal were clearly inferior in technical ability and only able to spoil the game, with the added weapon of persistent fouling.'

Bolshy of Beckenham had not finished. His pen still dripped indignation. The display 'devalues the game itself and will do nothing but harm football in England'. The correspondent insisted he did not have a club axe to grind, and he was not a fan of either Tottenham or Manchester United. From a purist point of view he simply disapproved of the Gunners' game-plan. 'Arsenal deserve neither credit nor respect for their victory,' he concluded.

Why? Parma's defeated players declared their respect. Arsenal had scored early and defended exceptionally; a common tactic in Italy.

The criticism directed at Arsenal, from Beckenham and elsewhere, goes deeper than any one performance, any one season. Its roots are buried in the 30s, when Herbert Chapman laid the foundations for the tradition of parsimony. Repeated success, and all that envy generated, ensured that 'lucky' Arsenal became 'boring'.

'Over the years clubs develop reputations,' argues Ken Jones, *The Independent*'s chief sports writer and a long-standing friend of George Graham's. 'Like Tottenham who have always been known for classy football, Arsenal are stuck with their reputation. In the 30s it was "lucky" Arsenal. In those days Arsenal had outstanding players, but when Chapman introduced a third defender, converting a centre-half into a stopper, he emphasised the value of defence. They were called lucky because they often won 1-0.'

Brian Glanville, a respected observer of events at Highbury, wrote Cliff Bastin's autobiography. 'In the 30s they were known as Lucky Arsenal for two reasons,' says Glanville, formerly of *The Sunday Times*, but now the voice of the *People*. 'Firstly they *so* often won on break-aways. Cliff Bastin used to say that if we had too much possession we would get worried.

Secondly, Eddie Hapgood and other defenders were very adept at clearing off the goal line. They were criticised because there was this feeling that they had such good players – like Bastin and Alex James – that they didn't need to play this type of football they called "renunciating".'

Ken Jones takes up the historical thread, which underpins the club's negative reputation. 'The double team was hardly renowned for class – although Charlie George was the type of player crowds thrill to. Frank McLintock used to recall how many times they played poorly and still won 1-0 or 2-1 scuffling for results. When they set that Double achievement, people said, "Yes, it was a marvellous achievement but not as stylishly done as Tottenham".'

The current crop of players depresses Glanville. 'They have been boring for some time. Every time I go to Highbury and sit in the East Stand I hear people complaining about the quality of football. There's no comparison with the teams of the 30s. They had players like Alex James, who could go past players easily and pass the ball intelligently. Arsenal now have no one like him, except possibly Paul Davis. John Jensen can just about pass between you and me – 5 yards.'

Ken Jones disagrees, arguing that much of the flak aimed at Graham and Arsenal is 'unfair'. 'Do you want an attractive team that falls short or a team that consistently wins?' Jones counters. 'I think the fans are just happy with a team that wins. There is a montage behind George's desk with Herbert Chapman, George Allison, Tom Whittaker, Bertie Mee and himself on it. Chapman won three League titles to George's two, but George has won more trophies, although of course there was no Europe or League Cup in Chapman's day.

'I feel sometimes that football supporters must get misled by newspapers and TV. They are fed so much stuff they don't understand. Last year when George was feeling low about the criticism I asked him, "How much stick do you get in board room meetings?" He said "none". I told him he was employed by Arsenal Football Club, indirectly by supporters, but the people you need to keep most happy are the directors. Anyway, I can't imagine the supporters are disappointed by the recent success.' Brasso sales in London N5 must have soared since Graham began his silverware-collecting tenure at Highbury.

As is the way with these matters, the blame for Arsenal's unflattering reputation lies in a number of areas. The media, particularly the printed variety, are partly responsible, both reflecting and encouraging the 'boring' tag. Graham and the club are partly at fault, their poor grasp of public relations a contrast to the openness of, for example, Kevin Keegan's Newcastle United, and increasingly Tottenham Hotspur. A club as big and successful as Arsenal should have fewer chips on their shoulders. For many journalists Tony Adams' behaviour after his testimonial is a case in point. The media felt used. They had plugged his lucrative pay-day, from listing the fixture to writing deserved eulogies about the Arsenal captain and encouraging punters to turn up to support his big day. Reporters sent to cover the match were understandably angered when Adams refused to come up to talk afterwards. Most of the hacks were writing profiles about Adams with the game as an obvious hook, so to have no 'nannies' (from nanny goat, quote) from him made them – and Adams – look daft. Many of the journalists left Highbury having felt used simply as promotional tools. PR like this does a club few favours.

The argument that the Press deserve such treatment is naive at best. Most football writers write about football for one reason – they passionately love the game. Hence much of Fleet Street's criticism of Arsenal; they want to watch good football.

Being first and foremost fans of the game, rather than admitting any loyalty to one club, journalists object to players' assumptions that they are simply digging for dirt. Athletes in other sports, and in other countries, have few problems. All each hack asks, and intelligent clubs like Newcastle provide, are some decent quotes to keep sports editors and readers happy. Those papers which survive on quotes are most anguished.

Newcastle, like other clubs who understand the importance of good PR, have a system whereby the players can speak to the Press. Such assistance invariably encourages hacks to view kindly a club or player. When Shaun Teale, Aston Villa's likeable centre-half, was dismissed in an FA Cup tie at Grimsby Town in the 93/94 season, he appeared afterwards to explain his actions. The verdicts in the Sunday papers were sympathetic.

At least Arsenal provides excellent working conditions: free bar, good view (apart from an important-looking pillar), plentiful half-time sandwiches and a good-sized lounge for writing. It is perhaps symbolic, though, that the route into the Press area avoids contact with any part of the club. At most clubs, journalists trek through the club, and feel part of the event.

The chief gripe at Arsenal is access to players. With effectively none, the more intrepid reporters go off to scuffle around the car park in search of a hurried word with a player climbing into a BMW. A hugely tacky experience, demeaning to serious professionals in both football and writing.

For those representatives of Her Majesty's Press lucky enough to cover the World Cup, the American idea of access to competitors was a delight. Mixed-zone passes allowed journalists to question briefly all the players after the match. It was a scrum, of course, to reach the Maldinis and Romarios but you could return to your work station with comments – although invariably anodyne – to add colour and substance to your articles. Stefan Schwarz, a member of the open Swedish party, must have found the move to the Highbury bunker strange.

The irony is that the problem concerns one of the most eloquent, intelligent managers of his generation, as well as rivalling Alex Ferguson as the most successful. George's handling of a pre-season debate at a Football Writer's Association lunch was particularly impressive; a seasoned advertising executive pitching for new business could not have presented himself better. Graham began with a joke, something about setting the ball Brolin, as he had at the previous day's Rothman's Football Yearbook launch, before delving into weightier matters. Great tactics. He had taken a line from the journalist's handbook; hook their interest early with something witty or thought-provoking and then, with audience captured, make your points (or in the word of one seasoned hack, 'get your joke in the intro and then run for home'). It was a stroll for Graham.

The ease of delivery and clarity of thought and expression are trademarks of the well-groomed Graham, traits witnessed countless times in post-match Press conferences and on television and radio. Yet unlike his relaxed FWA performance, he often appears distrustful of interviewers, searching for hidden agendas in often straightforward questions.

'I believe a club's image comes from its manager,' says Christopher Davies of *The Daily Telegraph*. 'With Big Ron at Aston Villa you have an upbeat, positive image. You never see George on TV.

'He's paranoid about the tabloids. At Millwall, George was wonderful but that changed the moment he got the Arsenal job. It must be an incredible strain for him putting on that mask every day, when underneath he's a genuinely nice guy. I just wish he would relax a bit.'

Ken Jones of *The Independent* springs to the erstwhile Stroller's defence. 'Journalists probably find it confusing that George Graham as a player represented something different to what his teams now embody,' Jones says. 'He was a classical footballer. You often get that with players who become managers, they reverse their images. Don Revie, a classical player, produced tough teams. Bill Nicholson, a dour half-back, produced a classical team.

'In our many conversations when he was a player, George never suggested to me he would become a football manager. When we had conversations he would say "put the ball away". The chances of him becoming a moderately successful manager were long. Yet here he is.'

The 'curse', as Jones terms it, of Arsenal's boring image has been extended by Arsenal's shortage of inspiring employees. Those who witnessed the Gunners' training say, only half-jokingly, that Graham is the one to watch.

'If he had players like Liam Brady or George Eastham it would take the curse off,' Jones adds. 'George has been very impatient with players who appeal to the audience. In my view, understandably so with Anders Limpar, who is so in and out, so unreliable. That's what Arsenal supporters have complained about. I've never been convinced either by Paul Merson. He's too inconsistent. His shortage of flair players is an area where George leaves himself open to criticism – but maybe he cannot see anybody who is right. George also does not want to upset the wage structure. Rightly so.'

In his studious address to the Football Writer's Association, ironically meeting at the Holborn bar of Terry Neill, a less distinguished predecessor in the Highbury manager's office, Graham stressed that Arsenal were big payers, and that only one other club spent more on rewarding players. They didn't just have the best paid players, preferring instead to spread the remuneration around.

Such a sensible wages policy – and, after all, the money is generated by the fans – ensures that the likes of Jurgen Klinsmann do not come to Highbury. Arsenal get the less flamboyant but cheaper Stefan Schwarz instead.

Klinsmannia is particularly galling for Arsenal fans. The expensive arrival of the German and Romania's Ille Dumitrescu enervated a moribund side. 'Are you watching Arsenal?' chanted the gleeful Paxton-Road-enders. Probably not. It would be too frustrating, showing up Arsenal's paucity in the creativity department.

'George is the opposite of the Man from Del Monte,' says Chris Davies of *The Daily Telegraph*. 'He cannot be choosy because all the best players, the Babbs, the Klinsmanns and Alberts, have been signed up elsewhere. Who's there of the right quality for him to buy? He can only go for the ones that John West rejects.'

Over in Klinsmann country, Richard Weekes, the deputy Sports Editor of *The Sunday Times* and life-long Spurs fan, feels that Arsenal's 'boring' reputation is 'partly a media thing, partly a fan's thing. Speaking as a Tottenham fan, we are quite happy to do our bit to keep it going.

'Something like Arsenal's boring label has a life of its own. The image somehow carried on for a long time when it was mostly aptly applied.' The obvious addendum is that Graham could play ten attackers, and still not escape the 'boring' slur.

'It's like West Ham,' Weekes continues. 'They're not an Academy now. Recently they were playing it straight up the middle, but because they had a golden era of putting nice passes together they would always be referred to as the Academy. Once Arsenal were tagged with their label it didn't matter what they did.

'Certainly, the way George Graham has developed the team hasn't helped. He has not filled the team chock-a-block with ball players. Anders Limpar became a fringe player. At times, the boring label is justified, sometimes not. You cannot escape the fact that as attractive a player as Paul Merson plays for them.'

Chris Davies, who covered the Cup-Winner's Cup success at Parma, believes Press and punter criticism that Arsenal are 'boring' is completely justified. 'The main difference between Arsenal and Wimbledon is that Arsenal have better players and their long-ball games are different. Arsenal hit their long-balls to players while Wimbledon hit their long-balls into holes for people to chase.'

For all his team's lack of creativity, George Graham is widely respected, at home and abroad, as one of the best coaches in Britain. The longest-serving manager in the Premiership, Graham's only rival in the silverware stakes is Alex Ferguson at Manchester United. 'The Arsenal side who won the Cup-Winner's Cup were a very limited side,' Davies adds. 'No other coach but George could have done it with such a side.'

'People forget that Steve Morrow, a converted full-back, played in midfield against Parma and was a very significant influence. The players who got there, or who have left, say they have not played for a better coach than George. He's been a good seller of players.

'Given what he has achieved, all the pots won at home and abroad, he's not popular. The fans have shown their feelings. It was wonderful on the way to the European trophy but there was a hell of a lot of mediocrity in between at League games. The fans don't want another season of mediocrity in the League. Even though they won the Cup-Winner's Cup in 93/94 they still finished 21 points behind Manchester United. A massive margin.'

Interestingly, in a mini straw-poll of Fleet Street's finest, a theory emerged that the club's reputation differed from the team's. Boring team, professional club. Richard Weekes sums up the prevalent school of thought: 'The club has a different image. It's a supremely efficient, well-run family club, solid, uncontroversial, quite careful. The team are solid, of course, but you would not call the club boring.

'Compare it with Tottenham. In the Venables era, rightly or wrongly, Spurs had a very Jack-the-Lad image. Arsenal are much more stable. The ownership of Arsenal has modified with David Dein's influence growing, but there is no feeling of overnight coups or board-room battles like you get elsewhere.'

Brian Glanville offers a lone voice of dissent. 'It's hard to differentiate between team and club,' he insists. 'Arsenal were hated between the wars outside London because they dominated and were portrayed as strutting metropolitan millionaires, which of course they weren't. They used to talk about a cauldron of hate at Middlesbrough when Arsenal came. They had enormous popularity abroad until Manchester United overtook them.'

The debate will continue. Arsenal would need to sign Ronaldo and Romario, persuade Pele to take over coaching, and play 1-1-8 formation to eradicate seven decades of an inexorably growing reputation.

Next

The Story of Arsenal's Youth System

by Tom Watt

'This blooding of youngsters is a ticklish business. However promising a man may look in the reserves, you cannot know whether he will survive the extra speed, cleverer positioning and the tense atmosphere of the senior side . . . The grooming of an Arsenal youngster takes a matter of years.'

Bernard Joy, writing in the Arsenal programme, April 1951

'It's great. You grow up with them. You see them play in the youth team at London Colney, then the reserves and then the first team. It's like they are part of my family.'

Alex Froso, Arsenal supporter

Picking 'best-ever' teams is one of the great and enduring pleasures of life for the football anorak. The opportunity to indulge in trivia-rich nostalgia, while exercising a chronology-defying sense of omnipotence, has made this kind of hypothesising a favourite waste of time for generations of fans. Even the great and the good find it hard to resist. A few years ago, George Graham (whose anoraks, admittedly, are hand-stitched by Aquascutum) committed his best-ever Arsenal side to video. Even a slow-running autocue couldn't conceal his obvious enjoyment of the whole business.

A while ago, the *Daily Mirror* asked me for a best-ever team covering the years since I first stood at Highbury in 1965. Given that I am a particularly sad case, I set myself a condition which would narrow (and, therefore obsessionalise) my choice. I decided my dream XI would be drawn entirely from the past 35 years of Arsenal's youth system.

Admittedly I struggled for a goalkeeper, settling on Bob Wilson because, though a latecomer, he never played professionally for anybody else. From then on, the rest of the team (as the saying goes) picked itself: Rice, Adams, O'Leary, Storey, Armstrong, Brady, George, Rix, Radford and Stapleton.

Toggles flying, nylon crackling, it didn't take much longer to come up with a second XI to give my first team a game: Kelsey, Court, Keown, Simpson, Nelson, Rocastle, Sammels, Davis, Merson, Campbell and Cole. Players of real quality like Thomas, Kelly, Neill and Stewart Robson were left looking for a game.

I don't know if the man from the *Mirror* really got the point. I didn't labour it. Arsenal fans, after all, wouldn't need reminding. Simply, the Arsenal youth system – for quantity and quality – is the best the country has to offer and has been for 30 years. In fact, much to the satisfaction of all concerned – not least the Highbury crowd – no other club comes close.

Like all the best Arsenal stories, this one begins with Herbert Chapman. The team the great man assembled in time to kick off the 30s (with a victory in the Cup Final over his old club, Huddersfield), was built around players lured to Highbury from elsewhere. The forward line alone had cost what was then an extraordinary amount of money, nearly £35,000, and throughout the coming decade the club continued to rely on the transfer market – exploited with guile as well as financial clout – to provide the players for its winning teams.

Arsenal ran reserve and junior teams, though, and Chapman was insistent that they should play to the same system as that of the first XI. In 1931 he went a step further and attempted to take over debt-ridden Clapton Orient of the Third Division South, intending to run the club as an Arsenal 'nursery'. The idea was that young players would benefit from playing in a more competitive environment, in much the same way that youngsters today, on the fringe of the first team, will be sent out on loan to clubs outside the Premiership to sharpen their game.

As with so many of Chapman's ideas – it being in the nature of the authorities then, as now, to balk at any hint of the imaginative – the Football League put paid to the plan. George Allison, however, who succeeded Chapman as manager, very quickly took practical steps towards the same end. Recognising the League's misgivings at the prospect of Arsenal controlling another club, albeit one in a lower division, Allison turned his attention to the Kent League and set up Margate as Arsenal's 'nursery' club in 1934.

The 'nursery' was looked upon at the time as very much a long-term policy. Tom Whittaker's *Arsenal Story* gives an idea of what was expected of the Margate experiment, and the risks it involved:

'All our promising youngsters were sent down to Margate for grooming, mostly at the age of seventeen, and we got little out of them for at least five years. You cannot expect a boy to be ready for top-class football under a period of five years ... It was very expensive but the Arsenal have never quibbled on the grounds of expense ... The average wage of the boys [worked] out between £5 and £6 a week, say £300-plus a year. We had twenty boys in training, which is about £6000 a year – £30,000 over five years. Include masseurs, coaches, groundsmen, trainers, travelling expenses, benefits, and you will see what a terrific expense it was to the club. And then you might get only three worthwhile First Division players in the five years!'

Eddie Carr, a young forward who scored seven goals in eleven games during the 37/38 Championship season, was certainly a 'worthwhile First Division player' – going on to prove it with Newcastle, Huddersfield and Newport County – and was the first obvious success of the Margate experiment. Among his team-mates on the Kent coast was Alf Fields, who was given his first-team debut the season after Carr made his mark back at Highbury.

Although the war and injury cut short his playing career, Fields' links with the club continue to the present day and his involvement with the development of young Arsenal players spans the entire post-war period. Every youth team player at Highbury since the late 40s will have come into contact with Alf at some point. Many, like Paul Davis for example, remember the significance of his contribution:

'I think Alf Fields did more for me than anybody when I was a youth team player. He would take you to one side after a game to reassure you or advise you. More than anyone, you felt he tried to understand what it was like for you as a young player.'

Spotted playing junior football in the East End, Fields signed as a pro at seventeen. He was sent down to Margate immediately, to be brought on under the watchful eye of ex-Arsenal centre-forward Jack Lambert. Talking to Alf about his time at the 'nursery', it's very clear how much he enjoyed his preparation for first team football, even his own extra training: desperate sprints along Margate front to be back at his digs before 10 pm, when manager Lambert would arrive on his bicycle to check the boys were in bed! At the same time, his recollection of the apprentice's life and contemporary coaching methods offer a perspective on the future in which Fields himself would play an important part:

'I went down to Margate in 1936, but it was going before then. It wasn't a youth team as such, it was a nursery side: we played in the old Southern League against all ages, you know. There were quite a few of us down there: myself, Eddie Carr, Andy Farr, George Marks, all came through. Jack Lambert was manager and there was an old Manchester City player, Robinson, who was in his thirties and played to help us along. When they thought you were ready, they'd bring you back to Highbury or they'd let you go. I think I was on about £3 10 s when I signed pro – and 25 bob of that went on my digs down there!

'Our training then would be something like five double laps of the pitch, a few exercises, and then just shooting-in or some head tennis. There'd be some work on particular positions: the wingers would practise crossing in from different angles; as a centre-half, they might give me a centre-forward to jump against while the goalie would thump balls up to the halfway line.

'I'd say it's much harder now. You need more skill because of the pace of the game. You know, I remember going to see Woodison run at the old White City: 4.7 or something in the mile! And football's speeded up just the same, hasn't it? Of course, there was more discipline then. Things were stricter – not just in football, but generally. A youth player then couldn't even walk into the first team dressing-room. It'd be: *Mr* Hapgood and *Mr* Male! I'm still that way, really. I don't think it was a bad thing.'

Fields' progress in the first team wasn't the only thing disrupted by the outbreak of war in 1939. The building of the new East and West stands at Highbury had plunged Arsenal into debt. The suspension of League football for the next six years left the club only a nominal income. The gate receipts from the huge crowds of the 30s would, had they continued, have made repayment possible sooner rather than later. As things turned out, the club carried the debt through the war years and faced the return to football in 1946 under serious financial pressure.

Economies had to be made and, although two of Arsenal's brightest post-war stars – Denis Compton and Reg Lewis – were products of the 'nursery' side, the link with Margate, it was decided, had become too expensive to sustain. By now Tom Whittaker had replaced Allison as manager. He performed miracles in the transfer market and behind Highbury's dressing-room doors to bring the club success on the pitch and at the turnstiles. However, the teams that won Championships in 1948 and 1953, and the Cup in 1950, were older teams built around veterans in their mid-30s like Ronnie Rooke and Joe Mercer. Whittaker was painfully aware of the need to build for the future. Rising transfer fees meant that Arsenal needed to start that building from within. Joe Mercer, in an obituary tribute to the manager who had brought him to Highbury so late in his career, recalled that by the mid-50s Whittaker 'had already started a new phase in Arsenal history. He realised the days of big buying were over. His plans only included youngsters.'

Alf Fields, finally forced to give up playing in 1951, was very much a practical part of those plans. Whittaker entrusted him with the handful of youngsters on Arsenal's groundstaff, boys who ten years previously would have been sent off to Margate to be 'groomed' for a career at Highbury:

'After the war, we put a team in the Eastern Counties League which would be the few groundstaff boys made up with amateurs – young players the club were interested in. Later, that team played in the South-East Counties League. When I had to stop playing, Tom Whittaker took me on the staff and asked me to look after the boys on the groundstaff. I think there were just four of them then!

'We had our scouts, as we do now, and signed a few local boys as apprentices. Anyway, I had no other trade and was glad of the job: I went up to Lilleshall and got a coaching badge. The thing was, they could only train two days a week – they had to do their other duties around the ground. George Elliott, who was Clerk of Works then, wouldn't let them train unless their other jobs were done – sweeping up on the terraces and all that!

'Although we did quite well – we won the South-East Counties League, as I recall – it took a while for us to get the benefit of the youngsters. You know, during the 50s we might get one player through at a time. Gerry Ward, I suppose, was the first. It wasn't until later that we got the nucleus of a side together through the youth team.'

The late 50s and early 60s were depressingly unsuccessful by Arsenal's own high standards. However, successive managers Jack Crayston and George Swindin didn't allow their struggle to find the right blend at first team level to interfere with the work being done with young players behind the scenes. Although neither manager is remembered as being particularly adventurous in giving home-bred youngsters a chance, the steady decline in gate receipts and the lack of funds available for the transfer market served to highlight the importance of young talent for Arsenal's future. The Busby Babes team were an example of what could be achieved and Arsenal weren't alone in seeking to emulate the success enjoyed by Manchester United's youngsters.

Already though, a certain care and selectivity set Arsenal's youth policy apart. David Court, one of the first generation of 'home-grown' players who would take Arsenal back to the top in the late 60s, remembers the club's attitude to prospective youngsters as instrumental in his own decision to come to Highbury:

'I joined Arsenal in 1959. I could have gone to possibly a dozen clubs – certainly, all the London clubs were interested, Chelsea and Tottenham in particular. Chelsea, at that time, were taking everybody who was anybody in schools football. They had so many players there, like Terry Venables and Barry Bridges. But the thing that impressed my father, and myself to a degree, about the Arsenal was that they were interested in you as an individual, as opposed to the "come and join us because everyone else is" attitude. Clubs like Chelsea would take on as many as they could in the hope that one would make it. Anyway, I joined the Arsenal at fifteen with a good bunch of boys. It was obvious the club had scouts who could judge a decent player without him being a big star in the world of schools football. Those boys, as I say, would tend to get snapped up by the Man. Uniteds and the Chelseas. The Arsenal people, I think, must have been very astute judges as regards who they thought would actually be able to progress through.'

That progress through the apprenticeship of youth team football was helped by the fact that, in this period before the abolition of the maximum wage, Arsenal – like other clubs – were able to maintain a playing staff of 40 or 50 full-time professionals. Although Margate was a thing of the past, Court – and other boys like Terry Neill, George Armstrong and Jon Sammels – enjoyed the benefit of playing alongside and against seasoned veterans in the Metropolitan and Combination leagues, which served as links between youth and first team football.

'You'd be thrown in with older players like Dennis Evans and Len Wills, who were very supportive. You couldn't help but improve and we had great fun with those older players. I don't know that that's still the case today. The club carried a big staff then, which might include people who were pros for five or ten years without playing a first team game. They'd have been good players with lower division clubs but we ended up playing with them in the reserve and third teams.'

Without there being any kind of rigid structure governing the preparation of young players at Arsenal, Court remembers different aspects of the game getting attention from the particular member of staff responsible for boys' progress at each competitive level. While the youth team under Alf Fields worked very much on touch and skill, Ernie Collett – who ran the Metropolitan League side – would work on building up the physical side of a young player's ability.

'We used to have five-a-side games and you'd be on either Alf's or Ernie's team: Fields' Fairies against Collett's Crunchers! But there was a good mixture and you needed that. If you graduated quickly you'd be in the Metropolitan League at sixteen, playing against men.'

The abolition of the maximum wage in 1961 – and the subsequent decrease in the size of the playing staff – might, under other circumstances, have nipped Arsenal's developing youth system in the bud. Although young players like Dave Bacuzzi and Terry Neill were beginning to suggest a way forward, the club still hoped big-name signings like Mel Charles, Tommy Docherty and George Eastham would bring the success which continued to prove elusive. Billy Wright's arrival at Highbury as manager in 1962 was to prove significant.

Faced with the task of bringing the club honours for the first time in a decade Wright, too, was quick to spend heavily, paying £70,000 to Torino for Joe Baker. The habit of mediocrity, though, had set in. Change was needed and Wright's hand was to be forced over the coming seasons, ironically as much by his own shortcomings as a manager as by anything else. Despite years of experience as a player at the highest level himself, Wright proved unable to handle Highbury's established stars:

'I began to realise that I had some senior players who didn't want to play for Arsenal. They wanted to do well for themselves but they weren't Arsenal through and through. I wanted the types who lived for the club, and by continuing the good work started by George Swindin with the youth policy I could see the potential of the youngsters coming through.'

Although his treatment of young players could be as ill-advised as his handling of senior pros – Pat Rice, for one, remembers extra running for the young apprentices as 'punishment', second-hand, for a poor showing by the first team the previous Saturday – Wright was prepared to give young players a chance at the earliest opportunity. David Court, like his contemporaries Jon Sammels, John Radford and Peter Simpson, wasn't too concerned if frustration with the older pros, rather than any real foresight on the manager's part, was what pushed him into League football so early.

'Billy Wright joined the Arsenal on the back of him being England Youth coach, which meant he'd had the chance to meet one or two of the boys – including myself – at some of the training sessions. His problem was that he couldn't really handle older players and so it suited him to get involved with the youngsters who'd be more attentive and wouldn't give him so much hassle. Like many managers, I suppose, he was better at dealing with players who didn't have too much to say for themselves! And, in fairness to him, I think he probably felt that youth was the right way to go. He inherited a team that wasn't doing well and probably felt he had nothing to lose. Except, of course, that Arsenal wanted success yesterday, not to-morrow, and youth was a long-term policy. Whether he could have made it work, though, I don't know. But he helped me a lot. He gave me a lot of confidence in myself by letting me know he believed in me. On the other hand, there were other lads he shouted at and was very destructive towards, while not being able to be hard with the older players who, perhaps, were the ones that needed it.'

Although Wright was unable to arrest the decline in the first team's fortunes, the progress of Arsenal's youth policy became apparent to a wider audience when, beaten finalists the year before, a youth side which included Pat Rice and Sammy Nelson won the FA Youth Cup in 1966. Nonetheless, a month later Wright was gone. His successor, Bertie Mee, inherited a first team squad stripped of many of its 'star' names, and full of youngsters whose fire and commitment were to be instrumental in Arsenal at last finding a blend to compete with the best.

Seven of Mee's first side at the opening of the 66/67 season were former youth team players. Four of them – Armstrong, Storey, Sammels and Radford – would go on to win the Fairs Cup and end Arsenal's long spell in the wilderness. Mee set a precedent which serves to define Arsenal sides to this day: of the team that took the field in Copenhagen against Parma last May, six had been youth team players – Adams, Selley, Morrow, Davis, Campbell and Merson. In terms of how Arsenal sides were put together, the 60s saw a revolution at Highbury. David Court gives the credit to Mee for turning promise into success.

'You can look back through the records and see how many young players were given their chance in the early 60s. A lot of the players in the Fairs Cup and Double sides had been weeded out from the many lads who'd had a chance in the first team over the years. Bertie inherited the cream. That said, you've still got to be able to get the best out of them. In Billy Wright, the club was taken over by someone prepared to give the youth policy its chance. Bertie Mee was a man who could push it on and actually start to win things with it. Of course that's continued since.'

Even in the 60s, a youth policy wasn't necessarily a cheap way of putting a side together. Bertie Mee estimated that each young player breaking into the first team would have cost the club £70,000, still a headline-making transfer fee at the time. Since then, of course, the disproportionate rise in the prices asked for established players has made the youth policy increasingly cost-effective. (Furthermore, the transfers of rising home-bred stars – from Tommy Baldwin through to Neil Heaney – have meant the system has proved, amongst its other virtues, to be almost self-supporting.) In any case, after the Double in 1971, which put Arsenal on an economic footing secure enough to justify the British record transfer of Alan Ball, cost became a secondary consideration. The youth policy continued, above all, because Arsenal's 'own' had brought the club success again at last.

In the last 30 years (apart from buying goalkeepers, who tend to be ready for first team football rather later than outfield players) the backbone – at least half – of every successful Arsenal side has been made up of players brought on from the youth team. Indeed, the slump in club fortunes during the early 80s coincided with a brief period when imports outnumbered home-developed players in the side. This basis for team-building is without doubt what has given recently successful Arsenal teams the resilience so satisfying to Highbury regulars and so exasperating, apparently, to everybody else.

The achievements of the late 60s and early 70s were remarkable enough testimony to the success of the youth system. The fact that the same system has continued to bring results under Terry Neill and, now, George Graham, is an even greater tribute to the staff involved. Other clubs in the past – West Ham, Man. United, Chelsea – have been able to enjoy a particular generation of great home-bred players. It is the capacity of Arsenal youth teams to push quality professionals through year after year – satisfying and often exceeding all expectation – which sets the Highbury system apart. Last season, while the first team was winning the European Cup-Winners' Cup with six former youth team players in the side, a new generation was busy at home, beating Millwall over two legs to win the 1994 FA Youth Cup.

George Graham himself, reserve team manager George Armstrong and youth team manager Pat Rice, were all around in 1971. Armstrong and Rice, of course, were youth team players at Highbury themselves while Graham would be the first to recognise how much their willing legs – and those of Eddie Kelly, Peter Storey and John Radford – helped make room for his own more relaxed contribution to the Double side. When he returned to Highbury in 1986, Graham brought with him the memory of how success had been achieved during his own playing career at the club. He'd also had the experience of looking after young players at Crystal Palace and managing another club, Millwall, who have traditionally set great store by an effective youth policy.

Graham's arrival meant the end, sooner or later, for imported big names like Mariner, Woodcock and Nicholas. Raw youngsters like Quinn, Hayes and Thomas were given their chance and the side that won the Littlewoods Cup the following March, predictably, included six youth team graduates. Arsenal's young side ran Liverpool into the ground that afternoon, quite unwilling to admit the possibility of defeat. Little wonder that, since 1987, Graham's Arsenal sides have all drawn so heavily on the virtues of hard graft and an indomitable team spirt. While the Highbury crowd may sometimes grumble about a shortage of 'flair' players, the likes of Nicholas, Limpar and Wright have been quick to recognise – as did Graham himself before them – that the team's relentless workrate earns them a platform on which to perform.

Over the past 35 years, no player has typified more completely an Arsenal 'attitude' than George Armstrong. Had the term 'a good engine' been current in the 60s and 70s Armstrong would have consigned it to the dustbin of spent cliche's well before his playing career came to a close. Somehow it's inevitable that the job which many would describe as the most thankless at Highbury should have fallen to him.

Without a Metropolitan League side (and with a smaller professional playing staff), the reserve team job now involves challenges that didn't have to be faced 25 years ago. Arsenal can no longer afford to retain senior pros like Dennis Evans and Len Wills to complement young players' apprenticeships out on the pitch. Any senior players Armstrong has at his disposal from week to week will be playing reserve team football under duress. Injury or loss of form mean they'll be there for purely selfish reasons, chasing a return to fitness or the first team and, therefore, less disposed to make a contribution to the development of the youngsters they are playing alongside. The progress, too, from youth team to first team has become increasingly foreshortened. The strongest younger players will often go out on loan at the first opportunity. All told, the contemporary environment of combination football at Highbury means more and more of the responsibility for boys' introduction to the man's game falls to the enthusiasm and willingness of Armstrong who, for his own pride if nothing else, likes to win the odd game too!

One thing Armstrong has going for him, as does George Graham when the boys are ready for the first team, is that any young player pushed up to the next competitive level – whatever his technical shortcomings – will already have a pretty clear idea of how he'll be expected to fit into the pattern of team play. By his own admission, youth team manager Pat Rice was not born but made himself a quality professional player. His progress from Arsenal schoolboy to club captain and Northern Ireland International was made possible by his own and others' willingness to recognise that what Rice lacked in natural ability could be made up for with a willingness to work at his game. The patience and hard graft he needed to unlock his own potential Rice now lavishes (forcefully and at full volume) on the youngest pros on Arsenal's playing staff.

While he may have a reputation as a hard taskmaster, Rice's understanding of the harshness of the apprentice's life is sincere. So is his commitment to each young player enjoying (is that the right word?) the best of a unique opportunity whilst a trainee at Highbury.

'The first year for a youth team player is very, very hard. The discipline, the long days. Getting up in the morning is a major shock: remember what you were like when you were sixteen! It may be the first time they're away from home. Plus the fact they have me on their backs as well. That first year's a nightmare for some of them. Especially now, when there are so many distractions for kids at that age.'

Rice first started working with young players at Watford under Graham Taylor and was brought back to Highbury as youth team manager by Don Howe. He's very enthusiastic about both these much-maligned characters, who helped him to settle on an approach of his own to the job. By the mid-80s, only a few years after he'd stopped playing, Rice was sure enough of himself to relish the responsibility given to him by a new Arsenal manager:

'When George Graham came, he knew the way his team was going to play – the shape the team would have. The only directive was: everybody plays the way the first team plays. How you worked it, that was down to you.'

Rice isn't under pressure to produce winning teams, although he doesn't hide his satisfaction when his youngsters achieve the kind of success enjoyed last season. While he may pick what he sees as his best team for Youth Cup games, Rice promises each boy equal opportunity to develop in the South-East Counties League competition during the season.

The youth team manager's remit is to ensure that every lad called into the reserve or first teams has sufficient awareness of Graham's overall pattern of team play to ensure he'll know what's going on around him. Rice himself remembers that, as a player, it took him some time to adapt to a different playing style at Watford. He finds that boys now who have trained at Lilleshall need time – three or four months in some cases – to learn the new habits that are part of a different team pattern at Highbury. It's time well spent: a youngster like Ian Selley or Ray Parlour, breaking into the first team at eighteen, has enough on his plate without having to wonder about how the senior side is organised.

All this may sound very structured and, indeed, goes some way to explaining how well-organised Arsenal teams are, whatever the circumstances. Last year's success in Europe, the side depleted by injuries and suspensions to senior players, is again an obvious example. Rice, however, stresses the importance of young players' time with him as an opportunity to develop their own style, at their own pace:

'With the youth side, they've got to be able to make mistakes. Otherwise they're never going to learn. If they're frightened to make mistakes in the youth side, what's going to happen when they move up to the reserves? They'll never make decisions for themselves. I've got to let them get on with it. All right, I'll shout at them, but they've got to have the chance.

They'll make a mistake that costs a goal one week but then they won't make that mistake again.'

Rice doesn't have much time for 'good old days' nostalgia. While he accepts that players of his generation may have been better passers earlier than youngsters today, he's full of admiration for the touch and ball skills that his trainees have developed to cope with the demands of a game in which the ball – if not the player – moves around faster than it did only ten or twenty years ago. Much of his coaching reflects changes in the way the modern game is played:

'We've all got to work hard. We've all got to do the physical stuff – the running, the heart and lung stuff – and sometimes that's tougher for the younger players who are having to make themselves stronger. But I believe that you can work hard *with the ball*. Twisting, turning, shielding the ball, keeping the ball up, playing small-sided games – all of that will take it out of you! It's been policy at the club, since before I came back, that the young players work with the ball.

'The training is different now, though, especially since George came. The areas you're playing in are smaller, the play's more condensed. Where the aim in a five-a-side used to be simply to stop the other team scoring and to score yourself, now we'll set different targets – nearest man to the ball closes down, say, and everybody else closes in on that side; or when the back players have the ball everybody else has to spread. There are more intense, specific things being worked on now than I remember as a player, when we used to just go out and play. What I'll try and work on in training now is particular things they'll try to put into practice on the Saturday.'

When asked to explain his continued success in pushing young players through to the Arsenal first team, Rice is quick to point out that what's most important is the quality of the raw material he has to work with: 'I am very fortunate because, with Terry Murphy and the scouting network, I get good players to work with. And with quality around them, youngsters can't help but improve. You know you're always going to get one or two who'll come through.'

Terry Murphy has been at Highbury for nineteen years and full-time Youth Development Officer for the last ten. He is one of the few men behind the scenes at the club without a history as a player – although his performances at centre-half in the end-of-season staff games are memorable in their own way. Murphy has a fan's unflagging enthusiasm for the game and the benefit, perhaps, of an 'outsider's' broad perspective to help him liaise with young hopefuls, their parents, their schools and, increasingly, the powers-that-be at Lancaster Gate.

It's perhaps ironic that the Arsenal team photo hanging behind Murphy in his office is of Tom Whittaker's successful, but veteran, side of the early 50s. While his working day is devoted to the club's future, Murphy retains a firm sense of tradition and sets great store by what he sees as an 'Arsenal' way of going about the job. This is perhaps most relevant in relation to the club's policy in choosing which young teenagers Murphy will try to involve in a career at Highbury:

'Unfortunately, you do get clubs who'll play the numbers game, taking every boy they can in the hope the odd one will come through. That way you're not really caring about the boy and you're not bothered if you have to disappoint him. I am asked what's made our policy successful and it's no single thing – obviously it's a team effort. But being selective is one of the reasons it works. We're selective from day one and once a boy comes here I think he does feel a bit special.'

Arsenal tend to involve only a few boys in the youngest age groups – so much can change so quickly – and from under-eleven onwards, up to youth team level, Murphy will be working with only ten to fifteen carefully chosen youngsters in each age group. The select few are invited along to training at the centres of excellence, not on the off chance, but in a real belief that they could have a long-term future at the club. The judgement of Murphy and the club's scouts (and Pat Rice and George Armstrong, who coach two age groups each at Centre of Excellence sessions) is given every chance to prove itself in practice. The degree to which they tend to get it right is clear: a look at each age group shows that at least three-quarters of each year's intake will move on to the next level of development, with the odd extra one or two being added as a result of an ongoing process of scouting and trials.

Although Murphy is hard-pressed to define exactly what it is about a youngster that will attract his or a scout's attention, he is able to outline some of the considerations made when decisions are being taken:

'When you're watching a game, something has to catch your eye. They can all play but someone, suddenly, will do something that'll make you watch them in particular rather than the game. You wait to see what else they're going to show you. For example, when I first saw Martin Keown he was a big thirteen-year-old and the one thing he could do was move that yard quicker than anyone else. His football was no better than the other boys in terms of his touch or knowledge of the game – but that one thing made him a bit special. And you hope you can work around something like that. You hang your hat on the one thing and hope you can add to it in time.

'Although at the younger ages I'll make most of the decisions, as things go on it's a team effort: scouts may see more of a boy than I do and will push him very strongly; some scouts like a particular kind of player and will pick a boy out who other people might not notice. Of course, there's a big difference between training and playing. At every stage you want to see the boy play. Whatever you work on with them in training, you have to see what happens in a game. Experience teaches you: Andy Myers I never saw play. In training he looked awkward and, after a month, we said we'd have to see him in games before taking things further. Before we could, Chelsea had watched him play and stepped in. Since then he's played for their first team and been capped at under-21. You just have to learn from that!

'Nowadays, too, you're looking for character as much as skill. You need to get to know the boys. Although I don't think it's right to get too close – it falls to me, after all, to tell them if we're not taking them on – I think we're all friendly here. Obviously, if a boy is extremely talented but has flaws in his character, you'll take him on and hope that you can change him. On the other hand, there are some who you really hope will make it because they're such good lads. Every year you look back at your kids and there'll be one or two who surprise you with how they've come on. Those are the boys whose common denominator is a strength of character.'

It's as well that Murphy is as committed as he is. Although he doesn't waste time complaining about it, his description of his job is hedged with ifs and buts that are not of his own making. The relatively settled, if archaic, world of schools and junior football has for decades offered Arsenal a background on which to draw when building a coherent youth policy at Highbury. Over the past few years, however, the world in which Murphy works has changed profoundly, and continues to do so. Youth development has become a political issue for the Press, the public and, above all, for the FA. Many of the changes Murphy must keep up with are well-meant, an attempt to strengthen the national game at grassroots level. Unfortunately, much of what comes through from above is all too obviously designed by and for a bureaucracy. More importantly, some of the planning has been so shortsighted that the entire structure is increasingly open to abuse, given the cut-throat nature of the football business which the FA's good intentions are there, in part, to serve.

Clubs offering illegal inducements to boys and their families, in order to attract the brightest young talent, isn't a new story. David Court remembers rumours of the practice from his own days in youth football in the 50s. It's a present-day problem, though, which if not actually on the increase is becoming increasingly prominent. It's increasingly relevant, too, in the context of a transfer market lacking any sense of proportion. Schoolboys are a futures market. Without doubt, some dealers will do whatever they can to acquire lads they see as gilt-edged prospects.

Terry Murphy, for obvious reasons, is unwilling to be drawn on specific incidents but recognises the ways in which changes to FA regulations have helped to make the offering of inducements an attractive option to those who want to get involved. In trying to ensure freedom of choice for the boys themselves, new legislation makes it possible for youngsters to be approached at each stage of youth development. The old 'schoolboy' forms no longer operate and youngsters need make no formal commitment, until they're sixteen, to the club they've been training with for perhaps seven or eight years. The compensation scheme brought in to counterbalance approaches by competing clubs carries little bite and is itself open to abuse. (After 50 first team games for the 'new' club, compensation of £120,000 is due to the 'old' club. A First Division player recently changed hands for £1.5 million after 49 league games.) Murphy himself has had youngsters return from Lilleshall Centre of Excellence sessions with their ears burning. The gossip's been about money and contracts – just as it is at senior England sessions – and boys come back to Highbury asking if Arsenal are prepared to offer what they've heard their peers are getting. Inevitably, agents are starting to get involved. After all, if money – at whatever stage – is on the table, boys and their parents will be ready to listen to 'professional' advice.

In the same way as there are good reasons, other than parsimony, why George Graham is unwilling to loosen Arsenal's wage structure (despite a long list of players – from John Barnes through to Chris Sutton – who may have gone to other clubs as a result), Terry Murphy is in no doubt why Arsenal should continue to refuse any involvement whatever in the acquisition of young players on the promise of inducements:

'Although it's illegal, it's talked about and I'm sure it does happen. Why else would a boy be with one club for so long and then suddenly go somewhere else? But, as I see it, if money's involved at an early stage, a boy is under pressure. From his peers and from coaches and staff. Of course, some boys will be strong enough to come through that. But they're a minority. For the rest, had they gone to clubs for the right reasons in the first place, there wouldn't be so many drop out of the game, or not achieve what they should, along the way. That's why we won't tolerate anything like that here. We want lads who come here for the football and because they want to play for the club.'

Commitment counts for a lot at Highbury, in the dressing-room and up in the stands. For a player like Tony Adams, it defines a ten-year relationship with the club. For an 'import' like Ian Wright, his arrival is a success thanks, in large part, to his obvious and infectious enthusiasm for the Arsenal cause. That commitment, as George Graham and Terry Murphy would agree, is something that can't be bought. It's the quality which, above all, has brought them both – and Arsenal – the remarkable success enjoyed over the past decade.

The future of the club's youth policy, and which steps Arsenal should take to sustain a now traditional pre-eminence in the field of youth development, are legitimate grounds for speculation, not least within the club itself. George Graham relies, as each of his predecessors over four decades has done, on a steady stream of willing, capable and, occasionally, brilliant youngsters coming through the ranks. They bring Highbury the success, in the short-term, that the club's status and a discriminating support demand. They promise, too, a long-term foundation on which to build a future, without compromising traditional values of honesty, integrity and stability. These traditional values, in turn, help Terry Murphy attract young players of real quality to Highbury. While a boy's parents may not get any immediate benefit from their son joining the Arsenal system, the lad himself can rest assured that under Murphy, Rice and Armstrong he'll get an apprenticeship that will stand him in good stead however things work out. And if he's good enough, Arsenal's a club where a young player can be sure he'll get his chance – at the very highest level.

That picture of the youth system's future is, obviously, an optimistic one, though not nesessarily unrealistic. The Highbury set-up's strength may lie, over and above the virtues of its component parts, in it being able to continue to operate on its own well-established terms whatever happens in the rest of the contemporary football environment. The same may be said, perhaps, of George Graham's approach to team-building. What's certain is that the two areas of policy are interdependent at Arsenal to an extent not seen at any other Premiership club. In the meantime, Highbury watches and waits for players like Selley, Parlour and Dickov to fulfil their very obvious promise. The diehards out at London Colney may well be chatting with Alf Fields about last year's Youth Cup winners. Which of them (Hughes, maybe? or Black?) will be first to push one of a previous generation of youth team players (Merson, say, or Campbell) for a place on future Arsenal teamsheets?

Sleeping with the Enemy

by Paul Hawksbee

'Is Gascoigne going to have a crack . . . ? He is you know . . . OH, I SAY!'
Barry Davies, Wembley, 14 April 1991, 12.05 pm

An extra body in the wall might have helped, but I doubt it. Maybe if Seaman had tried to reach it with his *left* hand then . . . who knows. Alas, you can't turn back the clock.

Thankfully, you can rewind the video.

I like to. At least a couple of times a year, switching to super slo-mo just as Gazza begins his run-up. Tick . . . Tick . . . Tick . . . Tick . . . BOOM!

Masochism? Not at all. You see, along with riding shotgun at the birth of my son (a bit like winning 3-0 at Bramall Lane – messy but rewarding), and witnessing an equally spectacular Wembley goal a decade earlier ('Ricky Villa, *still* Ricky Villa!'), Fatboy's 30-yard screamer remains one of the most sublime moments of my life.

As you've probably gathered by now, I'm a Tottenham fan. West Stand season ticket. Cockerel tattoo on bum. *Extensive* Chas 'n' Dave collection. Your worst nightmare.

'Well, piss off then!' you're probably thinking. 'And take your Amstrad word processor with you!'

I understand. I'm sure if I'd shelled out serious money on *Peter Shreeves: The Wonder Week*, and some smart-arse Gooner insisted on carting me back to one of the bleakest afternoons of my existence, I'd be a mite put out as well. But please, hang in there. I know at the moment it looks as if I'm just shamelessly getting my rocks off at your expense (which, of course, I am) but this really is leading somewhere. Honest.

There's a simple reason why that Semi-Final – and especially that free-kick – enjoy mythical status among Spurs fans. There's a simple reason why, for a good week after the match, I was drunk with joy – well, drunk, anyway.

It was an emphatic victory, probably one of the most complete performances by a Spurs side in modern times. Intelligent, industrious, incisive; had the opposition and the occasion been less celebrated it would still have ranked as impressive. But at Wembley, in an FA Cup Semi, against the Arse – the team of the moment, well, of *that* moment, anyway – you were talking a conquest of epic proportions.

Coming as it did during a spell where scoring Brownie points over the enemy was proving tougher than offloading Mitchell Thomas, it's easy to see why our joy was unconfined. On that wondrous spring afternoon, when the sun shone, the birds sang, and David Seaman *was* Mr Blobby, we could truly consider ourselves, 'The Pride of Norf London'.

One afternoon, in nearly nine years. I blame that George Graham. It was a sad day for us when he went back to Highbury. I still recall how moments after news of his defection from Millwall filtered through to the Lane, the skies blackened, the heavens opened and the rains came – 40 days and 40 nights. All right, they didn't, but they should have.

Virtually from the moment George settled back and surveyed his plush panelled office, we've played Ernie to your Eric. Close inspection of our respective trophy cabinets speaks volumes. Two Championships, one FA Cup, two League Cups, a European Cup-Winners' Cup, plays ... One FA Cup, in 1991. Even then, our joy was tempered by the fact that you would be parading a bigger, shinier and more prestigious trophy along Upper Street a few days later. The story has been much the same off the field. At the beginning of the 90s, we stared bankcruptcy in the face, and our only likely means of survival rested on the goodwill and hard cash of Robert Maxwell. A tasteless gag involving the Devil and the deep blue sea is tempting, but I'll let it pass.

This was just the first in a bizarre chain of events that eventually saw the club bailed out by Knight in Shining Roller, Alan Sugar; manager Terry Venables first hired, then fired as Chief Executive and finally, humiliating censure by the FA following an irregular payments scandal. (Oh, how you laughed when those points were deducted, how you laughed even harder when Status Quo offered to bail us out!)

Toss in the odd dodgy deal and the occasional bitter courtroom battle, and you have all the ingredients of a trashy, 'continued after the News at Ten' TV movie (Larry Hagman as Scholar, Stephen Berkoff as Sugar, Stephanie Powers as Venables, etc.) By far the most frustrating aspect of all this was that while chaos reigned at Spurs, over at Highbury it was like the bloody Waltons! Ken, Pete, Dave and George linking arms and skipping merrily through the Marbled Halls; never falling out, rarely screwing up. If the Bond Scheme hadn't been handled so insensitively, I reckon it would only have been a matter of time before Esther showed up with the Hearts of Gold.

Then there's your ground, of course. Last summer, the magazine I edit, *90 Minutes*, voted Highbury their favourite stadium, and deservedly so. It's an impressive sight, made even more impressive by that all-singing, all-dancing scoreboard. Calling it merely a 'scoreboard' fails to do it justice. What we're talking about here is a 200-foot telly that can conjure up anything from last week's goal action to enthralling features like *Whatever Happened to Pal Lydersen?* or the seminal *Citizen Pates*.

Unfortunately, the pre-match entertainment at The Lane isn't quite so state-of-the-art. Via some neon nightmare that the New York Cosmos probably junked in 1975, we're treated to distorted, bright-orange stills of the players' faces, which make them look like victims of some cruel medical experiment.

OK, so it's only a scoreboard, but it's symptomatic of the way you've eclipsed us on practically every count. Not content with simply kicking us while we're down, you've now started nicking our fans. I live in Enfield, about three miles north of White Hart Lane. As you'd expect, it's a traditional Tottenham stronghold. Well, it used to be, anyway.

Over the past few years, I've noticed the balance of power slowly shifting. Maybe I'm just being paranoid, but wander around the town centre any Saturday morning and you're likely to see as many kids in Arsenal – and, of course, the obligatory United – shirts as you are Spurs.

It's easy to blame the parents, but they can only exert so much influence over their gullible, misguided offspring. Kids, bless 'em, want to be associated with winners, and Tottenham haven't really fallen into that category for some time.

Having said that, if my boy – currently a mere two-year-old – were to announce he fancied an Arsenal season-ticket, there would be hell to pay. Make no mistake, voices would be raised. Hearts would be broken. Electrodes would be attached to the willy.

Allow me to share with you one of my many recurring nightmares. Cut to the year 2006 . . .

'I found this under your bed. You make me so . . . so *ashamed*.'

'Oh, God. Dad . . . what can I say?'

'Don't say anything. I want you out of this house by this evening!'

'But, Dad!'

'No, son, my mind's made up. Hard-core pornography I could have accepted, maybe even a small quantity of mind-bending drugs . . . but a signed photo of Ian Selley . . . !'

★   ★   ★

For the most telling indicator of Gooner domination since George began weaving his magic, look no further than the derby record. Based on our meetings in the League and major Cup competitions – I've not worried about the no-mark matches, like testimonials and the, er . . . 1988 Makita Tournament – you run out winners in a good 70 per cent, with a majority of the rest being draws.

Why do we get so worked up about these games when they rarely justify the hype, and the pattern of play is frighteningly predictable?

Usually, the ball pings aimlessly around midfield until someone decides to liven up proceedings with a career-threatening tackle. The two players involved square up. Handbags at five paces ensues until the peacemaker (usually Gary Mabbutt) gets between them. The yellow card's shown, the free-kick's taken quickly, Wright reacts before the Spurs defence, latches on to it and drills the ball low into the corner. Final score: 'H'one-nil to the Ar-sen-nul!' As a spectacle the derbies, played at breakneck speed, littered with sloppy passing and rarely settled by more than a solitary goal, fail to deliver in practically every department.

Then again, who gives a damn? For once, the performance is immaterial, the result is all.

Spurs fans generally accept defeat with a smile and a shrug as long as there's been a few goals, the boys have tried to keep the ball on the floor and the entertainment value has been high. I'd like to think this is a popular misconception, that we're really far more ruthless and ambitious than that. But as we keep returning to the scene of the crime week after week, despite the team's relative lack of success, I'm not so sure.

The derbies, however, are the exception to the rule. Frankly, on these occasions, I don't give a toss whether the lads hump the ball into no-man's land for 89 minutes. If we manage to nick it with a 3-yard toe-poke in injury time, consider me sated. The derby victory is the sweetest victory of all. Moments after the final whistle, you're counting the minutes to Monday morning, when you strut into work or school, head held high, and parade past the gaggle of forlorn enemy fans wearing a grin that's part Cheshire cat, part serial killer.

I don't think outsiders fully appreciate just how much we hate each other, you know. At supporter level, the rivalry between Tottenham and Arsenal is arguably far more intense than among any of the other big English clubs.

Man. United-Man. City isn't really comparable; after all, United's real grudge match is against Liverpool. Likewise, the Merseyside derby tends to be played out in a boisterous, but generally good-natured atmosphere, with little or no segregation. Then again, this is mainly due to the fact that most of the crowd are related to each other ('Hey, Degsy, don't batter me – I'm your second cousin!'). Our 'relationship' is much more akin to that of Rangers and Celtic, without the sectarian overtones obviously, but still potentially as explosive.

Maybe that's why there's always a hint of menace in the air at the derbies; always the feeling that it could go off at any moment, especially outside the ground. Fighting at football matches may no longer be fashionable, and high-profile policing has effectively put paid to those ugly pitched-battles at Seven Sisters and Finsbury Park tube. Even so, a couple of tanked-up gangs of thirtysomethings still usually manage to find a way. Having watched football through much of the 70s and feared for my life on a few occasions (picture a young innocent – snake belt, scabby knee – being chased across London Bridge by knife-wielding West Ham fans. Ah, the good old days) it's thankfully rare to feel threatened at a match these days, even with supporters of dubious reputation like – yes, let's name names – Leeds and Chelsea. Only after the derbies do I ever really feel the need to be a little bit streetwise on the way home. Untie the silk scarf from my wrist, hide the blue and white striped top hat . . . You get the picture.

Strangely enough, you tend to find that the bigger the occasion, the less malevolent the atmosphere. That's probably because the victors are just too darned happy to fight, while the vanquished are so emotionally destroyed they've barely got the energy to put one foot in front of the other, let alone wade in with fists flying. This was true of Wembley in 91, and, as I painfully recall, the 87 Milk Cup Semi-Final saga.

Two games that spawned a fanzine. Two victories that must have been almost as sweet as winning the Final itself.

They were ominous matches from my point of view. Although we'd won the derby at White Hart Lane earlier that season, I think it was the first time I realised Graham was capable of building a formidable side.

Sure, Charlie Nick was there, noncing about as usual, as were makeweights like Ian Allinson who, despite a modest talent and a woeful 'tash, still usually managed to stick one past us. But it was the kids who shone, especially in the replay. Adams, who I'd previously dismissed as little more than an OK stopper, was suddenly doing a passable impression of Bobby Moore. Thomas and Rocastle, once tricky but lightweight, now seemed to be everywhere. I half expected to find one of them standing next to me in the crowd.

And then there was Martin Hayes, the brightest prospect of them all. A future England regular. A star if ever I saw one. Martin, *what happened*?

Graham can consider himself fortunate to have taken control of the club at a time when there was such a wealth of fine young players. After all, it was their hunger, passion and exuberance that was so influential in delivering the title in 1989. Handling precocious talent must be one of the toughest aspects of football management. Bring them on too quickly and there's a danger they'll buckle under the strain and let you down on the big occasion. Bring them on too slow and, impatient for first-team football, they'll soon be looking for a move.

Although the names Gus Caesar and Andy Cole immediately spring to mind, Graham's record in this area still remains impressive. Back in 87, he took a calculated risk throwing a bunch of rookie teenagers into the world's most physically demanding League and it paid off – big time. I suppose his secret was knowing the ones who'd rise to the challenge and those who'd crash and burn. I doubt if Big Tone and Rocky would have come on quite so quickly at Spurs, if at all. Our track record of retaining the fruit of our loins is pretty woeful.

Since the Graham era began, Tottenham have released, among others, Norwich's Mark Bowen – having already packed Ian Culverhouse and Ian Crook off to Carrow Road the year before – and John Moncur and Mark Robson.

That's five pretty good players. I'd certainly trade Kevin Scott or Jason Dozzell for any one of them. Then again, I'd probably trade Scott and Dozzell for a set of jump leads.

Admittedly, there have been some successes. Vinny Samways, for all his faults, showed occasional flashes of brilliance, and I suppose you could argue at a stretch that Nick Barmby was a product of the youth system – although he was more or less the finished article before he joined us. Hardly the local lad made good.

Tottenham will always struggle to hang on to their most talented youngsters, because fundamentally we are a star-led club. When we're having problems on the pitch, the first call isn't to the reserve or youth coach to see who might be worthy of a run-out in the first team, it's to the bank manager to see how much we can afford to spend.

We've always been a club who've bought themselves out of trouble. Stars sell season-tickets, stars keep the supporters sweet, stars keep you up among the game's major teams, even when you haven't won the Championship for 33 years.

Summer 1994 was a classic example. With the fans still reeling from the points deduction, the £1.5 million fine, the FA Cup ban and the fact that we'd only just avoided relegation the previous season, Alan Sugar went out and bought us all a pressie.

Now, I would have been satisfied with one of the coveted Britpack, maybe Chris Sutton (but not at £5 million), or even Phil Babb. I'd have probably been equally content with a pacey, no-nonsense Swedish midfielder who fires in the odd good cross.

But that is not the Spurs way. You can keep your stars, sunshine – show us your supernovas. Jurgen Klinsmann, come on down. Now, I wasn't complaining. I even struggled to find an Arsenal fan who thought £2 million for one of the best half-dozen strikers in the world was a bad piece of business. But there was something about the whole episode – the clandestine meetings with Sugar on his boat in the South of France, followed by the eleventh-hour scramble for season-tickets, replica shirts and *lederhosen* – that was just *so* Tottenham.

George would never have bought Klinsmann.

'You're looking to earn *how much*?' he would have said. 'Fifteen grand a week? Oh, no, son, I can't help you. But I know a man who can . . .'

His reluctance to break the club's wage structure is well documented and no doubt a constant source of frustration to the supporters. During that desperate search for a quality midfielder, when the likes of Townsend and Keane weren't even bothering to show up for the interview, you must have been bracing yourself for the ultimate indignity: *Jimmy Case says no to Gunners*!

It's difficult to criticise Graham's methods when his teams have always delivered the goods. Even so, there are some who believe the club could have enjoyed even greater success had he ventured into the transfer market more often, and been a little less inflexible when it came to negotiating terms. I'm not so sure. In fact, you could argue that Arsenal have probably succeeded because of, rather than in spite of, his penny-pinching.

By guaranteeing that no one earns substantially more than anyone else, Graham spares himself the constant hassle of fending off disgruntled players. This is not a luxury too many Spurs managers have enjoyed over the years. As recently as the 93/94 season, Steve Sedgley, now thankfully with Ipswich, was demanding to know why he earned less than Teddy Sheringham. I'd imagine it's the same reason Frank Sinatra commands more for a gig than Roger de Courcey and Nookie.

It's also meant he's been able to sustain a remarkable team-spirit at Highbury. This 'all for one' attitude that the whole squad appears to share shouldn't be underestimated. As a Spurs fan, I regard it as one of the enemy's most enviable qualities. Cut an Arsenal player and they all bleed; cut one of my lot and the rest seem relieved they're not the one who's bleeding. Tottenham do not get involved in ten-man brawls. We prefer to get *our* points docked in less strenuous ways.

Maybe Graham's reason for choosing not to pursue the big names isn't purely financial. There's always a danger that having spent big money on a player you feel obliged to pick him every week to justify your decision, even when he's not cutting it. This was certainly true of Ardiles in the cases of Dozzell and Calderwood in the 93/94 season.

George has proved over the years that he's incapable of ignoring a player's shortcomings, even if it means flying in the face of popular opinion or putting some very expensive noses out of joint. When it comes to egos, he is a very poor masseuse.

There's a game that sticks in my mind – Lord knows why – that gives a pretty good illustration of this. A few weeks into the 92/93 season, Arsenal went to Sheffield United. It was goalless at half-time and, unhappy with their workrate, Graham took Limpar and Merson off, replacing them with Hillier and Parlour. The switch paid off. The midfield dug in (fancy that!), wore the Blades down and Wright scored the winner in the dying minutes. I remember the fans and the Press got on Graham's case over it, but the three points were all the justification he needed.

I sometimes wish Spurs were as versatile tactically. We only know one way to play and when it comes off, it is a thing of rare beauty. When it doesn't, which is often the case, we just don't have a Plan B to revert to.

You know, I'd actually quite enjoy watching us grind out a result once in a while. Take the lead after two minutes, get plenty of men behind the ball and shut up shop. You can count on the fingers of a mitten the times Tottenham have gone in front early-doors and eventually won 1-0. Our trouble is we're just not cynical enough. Only Arsenal fly to Turin midweek and grind out a mind-numbing goalless draw in the Cup-Winners' Cup, then travel to the South Coast three days later, give an awesome display of attacking football and hammer four past Southampton. If that was us, we'd have slaughtered Torino then been spanked by Saints.

I suppose it's a bit rich of me to accuse my team of being inconsistent when I'm guilty of much the same thing. Let's be honest here, I've just given a classic Spurs performance. After a positive start, everything was nicely in place for a full-frontal assault on the enemy. Here was a great chance to get in amongst them, go in late once or twice, leave the foot in when the ref wasn't looking. Instead, I've fannied about in midfield, lost all momentum and ended up showing the opposition far too much respect.

How many Tottenham supporters are given the opportunity to slaughter the Arsenal manager in print? Why didn't I grasp it with both hands and work off almost a decade of pent-up frustration? Maybe it's time to face the truth. Maybe, deep down ... (*dramatic pause*) ... I *like* George Graham. (*Blood-curdling scream followed by clap of thunder.*)

Even though he champions a style of football that would be met with a hail of rotten fruit were it ever adopted at White Hart Lane? Yep, 'fraid so.

That doesn't mean, however, that I'm blind to his shortcomings. Graham is the baddest of bad losers. He would probably argue that the best managers usually are, but is it really necessary to look for a scapegoat *every* time the result doesn't go your way (the grass was too long, the ref was too crap, the crowd were too Welsh, etc.)?

Unfortunately, TV viewers are rarely given the opportunity to hear George's version of events, as his refusal to face the cameras after a defeat is legendary. If Arsenal win, of course, he's out of the dressing-room and under the lights before Motty's even managed to climb out of his sheepskin.

Graham's relationship with the media generally is fairly prickly. As Joe Lovejoy of *The Independent* once wrote, George is quick to tell you that he doesn't read the newspapers, but still usually manages to take you to task over something you've written about him.

Should he eventually decide to try his hand at coaching in Italy or Spain, where the Press have far more power to build or destroy reputations, the sparks may fly.

Despite this reputation for being cagey and confrontational with the back-page boys, I've never personally found Graham to be anything but a willing and able interviewee. Thankfully, he likes – and hopefully trusts – *90 Minutes* and consequently tends to give us very relaxed, enlightening pieces. Getting anything other than the usual platitudes out of a football manager isn't easy, but George always has something interesting to say.

When you hear on the grapevine that the Arsenal manager is championing your magazine, it's tough not to be flattered. It's even tougher to maintain the irrational dislike of him that, as a Spurs fan, should be ever-present.

This kind of thinking worried me. Although professionally I try not to allow club loyalties to cloud my judgement or colour my copy, I've never understood those journalists who profess to be fans of football in general and no one team in particular.

What exactly is a fan of football? Someone who gets as big a kick from watching Blackburn-Leicester as, say, Norwich-Newcastle? If so, I feel sorry for them. They must spend their whole lives feeling like gatecrashers at a private party.

I'm not suggesting that you shouldn't enjoy watching teams other than your own, but surely true passion for the game can only stem from your undying love for one club. And this was the heart of my dilemma. Did forming a kind of mutual appreciation society with George Graham mean I was losing my affection for Spurs? I got to thinking that maybe I wasn't the only Tottenham supporter who felt this way. Surely there were others who, if they were honest, would admit to a grudging respect for the architect of their misery?

I decided to put my theory to the test with a mate of mine, a fellow season-ticket holder and generally a fairly switched-on, intelligent sort of bloke:

'What do you think of George Graham, Dave?'

'Hate him.'

'Why?'

''Cos he's the Arsenal manager.'

'Yeah, but look beyond the obvious for a moment. Consider what he's achieved, how he's given the club direction, stability, success – all the things we haven't got. Now what do you think of him?'

'Still hate him.'

'*Why*?'

''Cos he's *still* the Arsenal manager!'

So it was true after all. Suddenly everything fell into place; the sudden inexplicable desire to rush out and buy a JVC video, the alarming increase in body hair – I was becoming an Arsenal fan. Maybe it was something I'd been subconsciously repressing for years. You see, I could so easily have been one of you lot in the first place.

I was born – and lived for seven years – in Stoke Newington, about two miles from Highbury. This, in itself, was no reason to suspect I'd once shown Gooner tendencies, so I asked my mum if she could remember anything that might offer a clue to my terrible affliction.

What she told me was so horrible, I can barely relate it. It appears that for my fifth birthday, I requested 'a football kit', but didn't specify which one. Big mistake.

We took a stroll to the poky little sports shop that used to sit on the corner of Church Street and Green Lanes, opposite the Robinson Crusoe pub, where there hung two lonely football shirts, a white one and – yes, you've guessed it – a red and white one. Mum wasn't to know. She probably thought the Arsenal one, with its extra colour and that, represented better value for money. And so the deal was done. The jersey was joined by a pair of white shorts and black and white hooped socks. Many Happy Returns, son! If I knew then what I know now, I would have asked for a taffeta ball-gown instead. It would have been less humiliating in the long run.

In the course of our traumatic conversation, Ma also reminded me that I'd been to watch the Arsenal shortly after my first visit to Spurs. I can't remember the score or even the opposition, but I've got a vague recollection of George Graham – or at least of the way he walked.

I could never understand why he was nicknamed 'Stroller'. He didn't stroll, he strutted. He reminded me of Foghorn Leghorn, the redneck rooster from the Warner Brothers cartoons. The first time I heard Graham interviewed, I fully expected him to say, in a Mississippi drawl: 'I was pleased – I say I was *pleased* with my performance today, boy!'

Despite this angst-ridden stumble down memory lane, I still refused to accept that I'd pocketed all 30 pieces of silver. Then the fickle finger of fate pointed me towards Lakeside Shopping Centre and a chance meeting with an Arsenal star that proved beyond doubt that I was a lost cause.

While queuing in the Food Hall for my chicken chow mein (they're dead cosmo down in West Thurrock, you know), I caught sight of a shadowy figure dressed in black, clutching two trays choc-full of Essex's finest fare. It was Tony Adams.

As the only other celeb doing his shopping that day was a bloke from *London's Burning*, Big Tone obviously turned a few heads. While kids crowded round him pleading for autographs, even though he clearly didn't have a free hand, I carefully weighed up my options. I could:

a) Sneak up behind him and shout 'Offside!', in which case he'd automatically throw an arm in the air and coat his expensive leather blouson in bacon double cheeseburger.

b) Stroll up to him casually and send both trays flying into the air, catching the horror and surprise in his face as I coolly remarked, 'That's for the winner in the 93 semi-final.'

c) Smile at him.

Guess what I did?

Well, that was it then. There was clearly no way back. Nothing left to do but cash in my season-ticket, auction my 12-inch white label of *Rabbit* and buy a house in Gillespie Road.

Then, just as I'd all but given up hope, along came salvation, in the form of two unbearably smug Arsenal supporters.

It was the night of the European Cup Final and I'd been invited out for a pint by the co-compilers of this book, Messrs King and Willis. The idea was to watch the match in the pub, then discuss this very chapter over a boozy biriani.

The trouble was, rather than watch Milan slaughter Barcelona, they decided it would be far more fun to slaughter Spurs. There was barely a player, manager – even a tealady – past or present, who didn't come in for dog's abuse or at the very least a Nescafé handshake.

Now I like to think I'm a pretty tolerant kind of guy, and as some of their observations were valid – if a little condescendingly delivered – I took them on the chin. And then they started on Glenn Hoddle.

Insults I could handle, but I drew the line at sacrilege.

Suddenly, I was up at the count of eight, bobbing and weaving, giving as good as I got. The names Ure, Marinello, Caesar and, inevitably, Groves tripped effortlessly off my tongue. Within minutes, the conversation had degenerated into not so much 'My Dad's bigger than your Dad!', more 'My Dad may not be bigger than your Dad but at least he plays prettier football!'

Don't get me wrong, this was all pretty good-humoured stuff. Rival football fans getting on each other's case, top-quality entertainment. But for me it was more than that. For me, it was a cleansing experience.

It made me realise that when push comes to shove, I will always stand in Tottenham's corner. That however deep my respect and admiration for George Graham and what he's achieved, I still basically loathe and despise the Arsenal.

I hope you feel the same way about us?

Good. I wouldn't have it any other way.

The Mystery of George Graham

by Brian Glanville

George Graham might, at times, like to borrow the catch-phrase of a famous American comedian, Rodney Dangerfield: 'I don't get no respect.' Alternatively, he could seek solace in what that great golfer, Ben Hogan, replied, when accused of sinking a lucky putt: 'Are we playing how, or how many?'

Under Graham's aegis, Arsenal have won Championships, FA and League Cups, now the European Cup-Winners' Cup. But his teams are not loved; even, in many cases, by their own supporters.

I know what I'm talking about because, time after time, match after match, I'm besieged by season-ticket holders in the East Stand, who deplore the sterility of the side, its negative approach, its, well, let's be honest . . . its capacity to BORE.

In the 30s, the cry was one of 'Lucky Arsenal!' Now it's 'Boring, boring Arsenal'. Comparisons between those teams, like comparisons between Graham and Herbert Chapman, are not so much odious as irrelevant, though a few facts might be of some interest.

'Lucky Arsenal!' were so-named chiefly because in so many matches they had far less of the play, but won through a series of breakaways. A secondary consideration was that their alert full-backs, George Male and Eddie Hapgood, were forever clearing off the goal line with their keeper beaten.

Counterattack was the very essence of those Arsenal teams, from the time, in 1925, when Charlie Buchan suggested and Chapman implemented the Third Back Game. Cliff Bastin, when I helped him to write his autobiography, *Cliff Bastin Remembers*, told me that when they had a lot of the play, his Arsenal team used to get worried.

Now, you can criticise the Gunners, as some did then and later, for their essentially functional, unpoetic approach to the game. But to call them boring would have been a misnomer. Unlike the present team, they had superabundant talent in what is now, but wasn't then, called the midfield.

Above all, in their prime, they had Alex James, the little Scot whose passing set off attack after attack, whether with a through ball down the middle for Lambert or Drake, a pass inside the back for Bastin, or a raking crossfield pass on to which Joey Hulme could run.

Nor was James only some kind of quarter-back. He had glorious control, and a photograph exists of him speeding past a posse of grounded Manchester City defenders, left hopelessly marooned by his swerves and feints and touches. David Jack, at inside-right, could do the same. Wing-halves like Charlie Jones and Jack Crayston were fine users of the ball.

Graham's Arsenal doesn't go in for that. The tradition that went from James via Bryn Jones (his career was spoiled by the war), the electric little Jimmy Logie, Jimmy Bloomfield, George Eastham to Liam Brady, seems to have withered on the vine.

All the more surprising when you remember what kind of a player George Graham was. One I admired; but who'd never be admired today by Graham, the manager. His nickname was 'Stroller'. He began as a centre-forward, with Aston Villa and Chelsea, metamorphosed into an elegant, technically accomplished, midfield attacker, a member of that under-rated, much abused but surely formidable Arsenal side which did the Double in 1971. Could any team which included Graham himself, the remarkable Charlie George and Eddie Kelly be written off as merely pedestrian? Not by me.

But Graham, you might say, has done a Revie. Gone the way of the Don. Of a player whose finest hour surely came at Highbury. There, where he had often played for Leicester reserves – I used to watch him – Revie mesmerised the defence of a Portsmouth team then heading for the Championship. It was creative inside-forward play at its best, and Leicester won that Semi-Final with ease, only to lose Revie – in almost every sense – for the Final, victim of a blow on the nose.

When Revie became a manager, however, all such apparently soft options at first went out of the window. His original Leeds United sides were hard, harsh and combative, even if things mellowed later on.

So it has been with Graham. A penchant not helped by his evident unwillingness to forget and forgive. A player who defies him is all-too-likely to become a non-person: even though it is at the expense of the team. Paul Davis is a pertinent example. Whatever the rights and wrongs of the notorious incident with Glen Cockerill, Davis has without doubt been, in his Highbury career, one of the pitifully few Arsenal midfield players capable of inventive football.

He fell out with Graham and, a couple of seasons ago, was banished to the reserves, even though the first team screamed out for someone who could give it the element of surprise, could pass the ball with flair. Finally, belatedly and surprisingly, Davis was brought back from outer darkness and put into the team at Ipswich, where he did so well that he had to stay. Am I saying that George Graham can sacrifice objectivity to personal predilection? Well . . . yes, I am, indeed.

The tribunes of the popular Press don't like him very much. They say, rightly or wrongly, that while he was all over them when he managed Millwall, the doors figuratively clanged shut when he got the job at Highbury. It does, certainly, seem absurd that training sessions out at London Colney are barred to the Press. In Italy, they are even open to the fans.

But George's Press relations are, to put it mildly, strained. Criticism wounds him. He says from time to time that he doesn't read most papers, but he always seems to know what's been written about him. Not least by me.

He detested it when I made fun of his penchant for collecting centre-halves. Rivalled only by Blackburn's obsession with centre-forwards. A few pre-seasons ago, when I was still with *The Sunday Times*, I attended the Press Conference when Arsenal had just been beaten on penalties in the Final of the Makita Trophy.

Looking down on the Great Unwashed from his dais in the interview room, George said he'd been astonished by what he'd read that morning in *The Sunday Times*. That 'our back four was over-rated. Over-rated! We only gave away X goals all season! That was my pre-match tactical talk!'

I was the one who'd written that; despite Arsenal's supposedly hermetic defensive record when they'd won the Championship, the previous season. I reminded him that Manchester United had put six past that defence at Highbury in a Cup match. He brushed it aside. And hadn't Lee Dixon got under the ball, when Sampdoria scored their goal? He brushed that aside, too.

Afterwards, I approached the dais. 'So glad to see you're reading *The Sunday Times* again, George,' I said.

'I expected a bit more quality,' he said.

'When I see it, I'll write it,' I told him.

Which doesn't alter the fact that, for me, Arsenal were the team of last season. This is despite the evident fact that Manchester United did the Double, and played by far the best football. But when it came to Europe, when it came to the crunch, United failed wretchedly, humiliated by modest Galatasaray, while Arsenal turned the trick, beating Parma in the European Cup-Winners' Cup Final.

Chapman and Graham. Well, odious or not, I'll make another comparison – the way George treated Tony Adams, when he was jailed for his motor accident, and the way Chapman would have behaved. Graham and Arsenal paid Adams his full whack while he was in prison. Morality surely turned on its head? Chapman, as tough a disciplinarian as George, but a much less selective one, would surely have followed Liverpool's example when Jan Molby was jailed after a driving incident. They didn't pay him.

Chapman, of course, lived in a much easier era for managers. 'He told you how to dress,' his illustrious skipper and left-back, Eddie Hapgood, once said to me. 'He told you how to do your hair.'

But around the same time, in the 60s, Eddie's partner, George Male, who remained at Highbury for decades, said to me that a player might, at that time, respond, 'Well, I'm not staying here for this.'

Pampered stars. No maximum wage. Limitless earnings. Endless public pressures. Chapman, the grand paternalist, wouldn't have found life as easy now as he did between 1925 and 1934. Even though I scornfully reject the view of Peter Hill-Wood, who's said that Graham is the greatest manager Arsenal have ever had.

For one thing, he inherited a going-concern. Chapman took over at Arsenal when they were just one more mediocre London team. Chapman made Arsenal. Let's not forget it.

And then, there's Graham's transfer policy. Bizarre at times. Showing a weird reluctance to buy creative players. Or, if he does buy them, to give them their heads. As in the vexed case of Anders Limpar, who could have done so much more for a largely negative team had he only been given a long, clear run. All those silly squabbles over his going off to play for Sweden looked no more than a smokescreen.

Graham let Andy Cole go. Manifestly a mistake. Yet he bought Ian Wright, which seemed to me an error at the time (when there were so many good strikers on the books) but which has unquestionably been justified by the goals which Wright has scored. One up to Graham, here.

But one down when you think of the money he has spent on players like John Jensen, £1 million for a ball-winner *par excellence* whose one great goal, in that Final in Gothenburg, is receding into the mists of time. And has had no equivalent at Highbury.

While Graham constantly averred that the right players were not available, clubs like Liverpool – before their collapse – and Manchester United seemed well able to find them. He might assert that neither Michael Thomas nor David Rocastle has set football alight since they left Highbury. But who, since his departure, has done what Rocastle could do?

George's post-match Press Conferences are usually collectors' items. An event in themselves, bearing little or no relation to what's been seen on the field. A series of essays in obfuscation, even distortion. Why argue with a man who insists the world is flat?

And yet . . . and yet . . . I've still a lingering liking for the fellow. Perhaps because I liked him so much as a player. Perhaps because, long, long ago, I myself was once an Arsenal supporter. Thin-skinned he may be. Stubborn he may be. But in his desperate yearning to be loved, there's a kind of pathos.

George, George! Buy Arsenal someone who's like you!

Part Two
The Magic

Season's Review 1986/87
One-Nil Down, Two-One Up . . .

'We're not looking for short-term success. We want to build something that will last for decades – the way Liverpool have gone on winning honours. In the long term no club can just buy success. You have to build from the bottom. We're looking on this season as a year of development with our new manager George Graham – hopefully with a trophy at the end of it – but we don't expect honours overnight.'

With the benefit of hindsight, the thoughts of Arsenal chairman Peter Hill-Wood shortly after George Graham took over at the club in May 1986, may seem strikingly prophetic. At the time, few could have predicted their longer-term significance, but they certainly reflected how quickly the new manager had set about dictating the agenda at Arsenal: Hill-Wood's comments were nothing if not a voicing of Graham's own philosophy on where the club was going and how it was going to get there. If further evidence of who was now pulling the strings was needed, Hill-Wood would later reveal: 'When George Graham came to Arsenal I asked "What do you want from me?" He said, "I want you to come to football and have a good time on a Saturday." '

That the powers-that-be at Highbury desperately needed Graham to get it right was glaringly obvious, even if he wasn't their first choice. Don Howe had resigned as manager the previous March, unhappy that the board had been negotiating with Terry Venables behind his back, especially when he was convinced that happier times were just around the corner. Howe's last game in charge – a 3-0 home victory against Coventry – was actually the Gunners' fourth consecutive win and left the team in a very handy fifth place. With games in hand, there was still an outside chance of winning the title. However, a crowd of just 17,189 for that game reflected widespread scepticism about Arsenal's title aspirations. Recent frustrations in the Fifth Round of the two Cup competitions (Arsenal had crashed 3-0 to Luton in a second replay of the FA Cup and lost at home to Aston Villa in the League Cup after doing the hard bit and drawing in Birmingham) were more accurate indicators of Arsenal's real potential – a team with plenty of talented individuals, but not one that any sane person would put money on when the going got tough. Though Howe's coaching ability was renowned and he was popular amongst the players, he had also gained a reputation for being a bit of a soft touch. And neither time nor titles were on his side. His last seven years of influence – he returned to Highbury as coach in 1977 and eventually took over from his erstwhile boss, Terry Neill, at the end of 1983 – had not yielded a single trophy. Arsenal's last glimpse of the silverware, the 1979 FA Cup triumph over Manchester United, was an increasingly distant memory. In recent seasons, a half-decent run in one of the Cups (with the emphasis most definitely on the half, given the debacles against Walsall, York, Oxford, etc.) was the nearest Arsenal got to even a flirt with the honours. For a coach who was fast approaching veteran status it was an unimpressive calling-card. And with the European ban on English clubs firmly in place, there wasn't even the consolation of being able to sneak into the UEFA Cup by finishing fourth or fifth in the League – a hope that had kept many a disappointing season alive long after Arsenal were out of the running for more tangible honours. The burning question at Highbury was: how much longer could a club of Arsenal's prestige afford such peripheral standing when the major honours were being dished out?

Nevertheless, the fans did rate Don Howe as being 'genuinely Arsenal', and the terrace opinion was that such a loyal servant could have been allowed a more dignified departure. The fact that Venables was associated with the *enemy* across North London didn't help either. With Howe gone and Steve Burtenshaw temporarily in charge, Arsenal's wafer-thin title aspirations soon crumbled and consecutive defeats to Spurs and Watford (twice) led to a search for new scapegoats. The final games of the season at Highbury saw unprecedented and vociferous post-match demonstrations calling for the resignation of Hill-Wood and his board, the first such manifestations of popular discontent since the 65/66 season when the fans had effectively got rid of the then manager, Billy Wright. In Wright's fourth and final year at the club, Arsenal finished in fourteenth place, their lowest League position in 41 years, and what amounted to a fan boycott (this was the year of the infamous 4,554 crowd against Leeds, the lowest First Division attendance since the First World War) forced the board to oust the manager. On that occasion, the somewhat surprising choice to take over was Wright's assistant and long-time physiotherapist, Bertie Mee. It was an unexpected move, but it turned out to be an inspired one. The prevailing circumstances and parallels with the appointment of the relatively inexperienced George Graham, twenty years later, make for uncanny similarities, especially in the light of subsequent history.

In 85/86, Arsenal eventually finished in seventh place, a massive nineteen points behind the champions, Liverpool. The board, massively under increasing pressure, were acutely aware that the fans' patience was starting to run out. Nick Hornby summed up the prevailing terrace view of the pre-Graham state of play in *Fever Pitch*: 'That Arsenal team – full of cliques and overpaid, over-the-hill stars – would never be bad enough to go down, but never good enough to win anything, and the stasis made you want to scream with frustration.' Indeed, Arsenal had become so predictably iffy that many of their long-suffering fans, rather than waste time talking about the actual football and thus running the risk of harbouring illusions that were bound to be dashed, preferred to amuse themselves with the latest chit-chat and lurid tales from the thriving Highbury grapevine. An unhealthy number of players in that squad seemed more assiduous in their duties as members of London's exclusive nightclubs than in carrying out their responsibilities at the club that paid their not inconsiderable salaries. (The gossip-mongers should be eternally grateful to George Graham for achieving so much with a bunch of players who at times seem so determined to imitate their less successful on-field predecessors in the laddish behaviour stakes!)

As for the Saturday afternoon entertainment pre-Graham, the most enjoyable days tended to be those when Arsenal were so utterly bad and/or downright uninterested that you just had to laugh. The FA Cup demise at Third Division York in 1985 sticks in the mind as one such occasion: on a bitterly cold January afternoon on an ice-rink of a pitch, Arsenal's seasoned professionals gave a new dimension to the word 'listless'. God knows where most of their minds were (Stringfellows?) but they certainly weren't on the job in hand. Just when it seemed that Arsenal would secure an undeserved replay with a goalless draw, Steve Williams gave away a last-minute penalty with a challenge that was so clumsy and/or incompetent and/or unnecessary that it was positively suspicious. Maybe Stevie had got the nod – you know, who needs another game on Tuesday against this bunch of cloggers. Not that half the team fancied it in the first place – the looks that several of the players exchanged when they came out to inspect the bone-hard pitch before the match were more eloquent than a thousand post-mortems.

A 3-1 defeat at Luton in May 1985 meant absolutely nothing in the historical scheme of things, but for the few thousand Arsenal fans who made the short trip from London it was an unforgettable occasion. That afternoon, Howe's team produced a performance of such staggeringly pathetic proportions that it produced mass hysterics on the terraces amidst jibes about total football *à la* Johan Cruyff's Holland. You know, the Dutch had great players who interchanged positions constantly, were all comfortable on the ball and could all perform equally well anywhere on the park. Admittedly, this was about the time many of the lads started to have a 'puff' on a Saturday afternoon – for Arsenal devotees in particular, an activity that helped put an agreeably different perspective on their team's bizarre antics. Just like Arsenal: crap players who bump into each other constantly, are all bungling idiots on the ball and can all perform equally badly anywhere on the park! The game ended with Paul Mariner all at sea at centre-half and David O'Leary hobbling around on the wing, whilst the desperately out-of-sorts Graham Rix gave the ball away so often in 90 minutes he might as well have been playing for Luton. As the fans headed back to London on the train, a lively debate ensued about which player had earnt the lowest-ever marks out of ten in *The Sunday People*. The smart money was on ex-Newcastle skipper, Bobby Moncur, at two out of ten. As the day-trippers dispersed at St Pancras, one apposite question floated in the air; would the unfortunate reporter who the paper had despatched to Kenilworth Road that day dare to give minus ratings? Yes, it was that bad.

Charlie Nicholas's first season at the club in 83/84 provided another memorably surreal moment. As Christmas came and went, the man who was supposed to inspire the Gunners to fresh heights with his goals still hadn't scored at Highbury. On a bleak afternoon amidst something that masqueraded for a game of football, Charlie finally broke his duck. It was an otherwise meaningless goal in a dreadful match against even worse opposition – Birmingham City. (The games that best sum up the pitiful fare of the latter Neill/Howe years were all those miserable goalless draws at home to a dire Birmingham side that must surely rate as the worst ever to grace the old First Division.) All right, it was only a penalty, but who cares? As the ball hit the back of the net, the chants of 'Charlie! Charlie! Charlie! Charlie!' resounded around Highbury – yes, *all* around the ground. And no, this wasn't some kind of mass exercise in irony; the celebration was genuine. The Arsenal supporters were really that desperate for something to get enthusiastic about.

It's easy to get blasé about George Graham's achievements at Arsenal – that's why these vignettes of life at Highbury pre-George are so important. To say that the level of expectancy at Highbury has changed is the understatement of the footballing century. Suffice to say that the very same fans who as recently as 1984 cheered a meaningless penalty goal until they were hoarse, were probably moaning about the style of football Arsenal were churning out as George Graham posed with any one of the six major trophies the club won during the wonder years.

Howe's departure, perhaps long-overdue, marked the end of an era at Highbury. It's not a question of having a downer on a great Arsenal servant, it's simply a case of every Don has his day. When all is said and done, a man who in his two different spells at the club coached the team to the Double, four FA Cup Finals and the European Cup-Winners' Cup Final, could walk away from the club with his head held high.

Changing managers wouldn't guarantee success (guaranteed success is a bigger non-starter in football than just about anywhere else) but at the very least, the Arsenal hierarchy needed an ambitious new manager with a high profile: a man who could lead from the front when the going got tough and deflect unwelcome attention from the heavily pressured board. In the end, Terry Venables, unimpressed by the manner and timing of Arsenal's approach and annoyed by snide remarks about Don Howe from his would-be employers, decided he could live without the club's offer, thus clearing the way for George Graham to step into the breach. (In fact, it was the second time Venables had passed over the Arsenal job – he was first offered the post just before Terry Neill took over in 1976.) Despite subsequent attempts to re-write history, the club ended up with another 'Arsenal man' more by accident than design. Not that Graham was bothered; the illustrious old boy had the job he had always cherished and, characteristically, he would waste no time on the whys and wherefores.

The new man at Highbury didn't arrive with the pedigree of his great friend Venables or the longer-term track record of Graham Taylor, another man who had been touted as a likely successor to Howe once Venables had dropped out of the running. But in his three-and-a-bit years in charge at Millwall, the Scot had proven conclusively that he had the stomach for a battle. When he took over at the modest South London club in 1982, they were on the brink of relegation to Division Four and eventually only a skin-of-their-teeth win at Chesterfield in the last game of the season kept them up. After this early crash course in the footballing facts of life, Graham quickly set about transforming the club from top to bottom and, by the time he left to take over at Arsenal, Millwall were firmly established in the upper reaches of Division Two and the foundations for subsequent promotion to the top flight were firmly in place. Graham's team had also attracted considerable media attention thanks to their exploits against First Division teams in runs to the Quarter-Finals and Fifth Round of the FA

Cup. And all this was achieved despite the fact that the rookie manager regularly had to sell his star players to balance the books.

At Millwall, George Graham's reputation as a coach was immediately at loggerheads with the considerably more laid back image he had acquired as a player. In no time at all, he had made a name for himself as a formidable coach and a strict disciplinarian. He also swiftly attracted the disdain of the purists who accused him of being 'defensive and negative'. The negative jibes may or may not have been fair, but the Graham philosophy was clear: you set out to make a team work by getting it right at the back. He did once say, 'I'd rather win matches 3-2 than 1-0 because it's good for the game', but anyone who believes that should be answering questions on gullibility on *Mastermind*. Still, nobody at Millwall was complaining. Graham had forged a side that were extremely difficult to beat, especially at the Den, and transformed the club in no uncertain terms (in 1988 they were promoted to the First Division for the first time in their history). In less than glamorous circumstances, Graham had done more than enough to earn a shot at the big time.

On arriving at Highbury, the new boss was at pains to insist that everybody on the staff would get a fair crack of the whip, but when Tony Woodcock and Paul Mariner were summarily dispatched, the writing was on the wall for the old guard. As Graham later admitted, 'When I first arrived at the club, I had a look at the staff and decided there were a lot of prima donnas who'd probably seen their best days, so it was time to get the broom out and start sweeping a few out the door and give the youngsters a chance.' The fact that the cupboard was bare – Arsenal were some £1 million in the red – provided considerable justification for getting rid of the non-performing high-earners. On the other hand, letting the highly promising Martin Keown go because he reputedly asked for a £50 a week rise seemed to be a case of biting off your nose to spite your face. Graham insisted that no player would get a pay rise without proving himself first. However, the Keown affair was an early example of the financial inflexibility that would cost Arsenal numerous signings over the years. On the other hand, it wouldn't take long for Graham to demonstrate his knack for squeezing the best price out of fellow managers who came shopping at Highbury – in January of that first season, the injury-prone Stewart Robson was sold to West Ham for £750,000. As for giving the young players their head, Graham was probably aware that the fans would concede an extended honeymoon period to 'one of their own' after so many barren years, and he figured that this goodwill would allow him a certain leeway to experiment in his first season.

In private, Graham was sceptical about some of the bigger names that initially stayed – North Bank darling Charlie Nicholas especially – but in his treatment of the players he was initially as good as his word. In pre-season training it was made clear that everybody, including the youngsters, would start from scratch – after all, reasoned Graham, the experienced players had won nothing. From day one, he assailed the players with his plans for the club: he intended to make Arsenal great again and restore the reputation the club had enjoyed under Bertie Mee. Time and time again he would insist on restoring the values that held sway in his days as a player in that legendary Double-winning side. Sloppiness or lack of discipline would not be tolerated, nothing less than total commitment to Arsenal would do.

But his was most definitely a carrot and stick approach. When Graham said, 'Look, this is Arsenal, I want to win things and so do you, let's get it right together', he said it with such conviction that the players couldn't help but believe him. And if there is one thing that unites footballers, it is their ability to put up stoically with the most demanding of managers if they are convinced he can bring them success. Despite their very different personalities and managerial styles, Brian Clough (hardly his players' bosom pal) is George Graham's most obvious and eloquent predecessor in this sense.

The pressure on a new manager to wave the cheque book around in headline-grabbing fashion is considerable, especially at a club like Arsenal, but Graham insisted on biding his time before delving into the transfer market. 'Let me have a good look at what I've already got' was the oft-repeated message. True to his word, the season got underway with only the unknown Perry Groves added to the squad. The 1-0 win over Manchester United on day one – which Graham described as 'great result, bad game' – was only notable for an untypical goal from Charlie Nicholas; a tap-in from 5 yards, precisely the kind of goal the Scot had failed to notch up with anything like the required frequency since his move down south from Celtic. But just one more victory in the next seven League games, and not a single goal in the last four of the spell, soon provoked questions about Graham's failure to strengthen the squad.

When injuries swiftly deprived the team of Stewart Robson, Graham Rix and Charlie Nicholas, it looked like this inertia in the marketplace could prove to be a gross error. However, what initially looked like a recipe for all-too-familiar mediocrity, proved to be the turning point of Arsenal's season. Steve Williams – out of favour with Don Howe towards the end of the former manager's spell in charge and the sort of man who is the antithesis of Graham's model player – stepped into the depleted midfield alongside Paul Davis, and the pair immediately forged an impressive partnership which is still remembered fondly by Arsenal fans today. In the past, Davis had never quite assumed Liam Brady's mantle as Arsenal's playmaker, and when midfield changes were made he was almost inevitably the first to get the chop. Under Graham that situation changed overnight. Davis sensed that here at last was a manager who really rated him, and responded accordingly. While the graceful South Londoner would cajole in his own inimitably cool fashion, Williams (a local lad who had supported Arsenal as a boy but had arrived at the club via the roundabout route of Southampton) would constantly moan and groan, berating all and sundry (his own team-mates and referees included) in his efforts to throw the opposition off their game. Davis and Williams may have been a chalk and cheese combination, but they were both gifted and intelligent footballers with a quick eye and a subtle touch. When they were good there was arguably no better midfield partnership in the country. George Graham has subsequently built much better teams, but many would argue that he has never improved on that early double act at the heart of Arsenal's midfield.

Up front, Nicholas's injury meant that the youthful red-head Perry Groves (not even an automatic choice at Fourth Division Colchester) was thrown in at the deep end, much earlier than Graham had originally intended. Groves was never going to be a world-beater, but by overcoming his technical deficiencies with pace and enthusiasm, he proved to be a snip at £65,000. However, George Graham's good luck – something that all successful managers need – was best illustrated by the impact of Martin Hayes. The young winger from Walthamstow had flirted briefly with the first team under Don Howe, but Graham had obviously decided he was surplus to requirements when Arsenal agreed a £25,000 fee with Huddersfield in November. Hayes actually travelled to Leeds Road and agreed terms, only to have a last-minute change of heart about moving up north. When Groves was pushed inside to replace the injured Nicholas, Graham was forced to turn to Hayes to cover Rix in an unaccustomed role on the left side of midfield, and to almost everyone's surprise he immediately looked the part. Using his winger's instincts and pace to take on defenders from deeper positions, Hayes presented a constant goal-scoring threat, especially when cutting inside on to his favoured right foot. Circumstances conspired to heighten his impact still further: in the dressing-room before Hayes' first League game against Watford, Graham asked for volunteers to take penalties in the absence of the out-of-favour Ian Allinson, the previous season's spot-kicker. With no takers among the more experienced players,

Hayes – who, whatever his talents, hardly gives the impression of being assertive – surprisingly volunteered. Some 90 minutes later he was back in the dressing-room, having taken and scored his first-ever penalty, and about to embark on a once-in-a-lifetime goal-scoring streak.

In almost accidental fashion, a somewhat improvised Arsenal set about giving George Graham a dream start at the club. A 1-0 victory against Everton on 4 October was the beginning of a 22-match unbeaten run that saw the team go top in mid-November and stay there for three long months.

If the permutations offered by Hayes, Groves and Williams had not originally featured in Graham's planning, the club's defensive solidity – the real base for that unbeaten run – most certainly did. From his very first day at the club, Graham spent an enormous amount of time in training and working on defensive organisation, convinced that getting the shape of the side right could only be achieved by building a solid foundation from the back. The work on the training ground soon paid off and the defensive strength that would characterise all his teams at Highbury was established immediately. When Arsenal entered the New Year at the top of the table, four points ahead of Everton, you didn't need to be a genius to work out where the roots of the success lie. 'Clean sheets' was the pre-match rallying cry in the Arsenal dressing-room as John Lukic remained unbeaten in 13 of the first 22 games.

It would be churlish to deny Graham credit. He may have inherited quality defenders but he proved a master at getting the best out of them. At left-back, Arsenal's captain Kenny Sansom may have seen it all with England, but he had never won anything at club level. He immediately realised that Graham was a man that could change that. In his book about the 86/87 season at Highbury, *Going Great Guns*, Sansom claimed that George Graham reminded him of Terry Venables – Graham's own coaching mentor at Queens Park Rangers and Crystal Palace, and the player's manager at the latter. The full-back cited Graham's all-round professionalism, his minute attention to detail, and the ability to bring out the best in his players, as qualities he shared with Venables. He also revealed that Graham was not averse to seeking advice from senior players in his early days at the club (this would certainly change as time passed) and that he actively encouraged players to air their views in the dressing-room.

At right-back, Viv Anderson was recovering from the immense disappointment of a second successive World Cup stretch without making a single appearance. Under Graham, he quickly put that setback behind him to play the best football of his career. Of the defenders, Daddy-Longlegs

125

Anderson was the player given most licence to get forward. Whether surging down the right with that idiosyncratic and leggy stride to combine with his young charge, David Rocastle, or creating havoc at free-kicks with his ability in the air, Anderson spent as much time in the opposition box as many a forward! Off the park, he was an equally positive influence, with his infectious character a key factor in creating the burgeoning team-spirit that Graham was so keen to establish. All the youngsters loved him and, for Rocastle and Michael Thomas in particular, it must have been a great boost to have such a popular and respected senior black player in the side to encourage them at an embryonic stage of their careers. Anderson's tremendous season was rewarded by a well-deserved recall to the England side at 30, an indelible reminder in the history books that the coupling of Anderson and Sansom at full-back was one of the best-ever in English football.

At centre-half, the long-serving David O'Leary was just the kind of dedicated, totally professional and dependable performer that any manager loves, let alone a man like Graham who sets so much store by these very characteristics. It was now thirteen years since the Irishman had made his League debut, and his burning desire remained intact – to win a Championship medal with Arsenal. In Graham he recognised a kindred spirit; the new boss was an 'Arsenal man' and would not settle for second-best. He was the ideal catalyst to bring out the best in a player who, though highly rated within the game, had taken a back seat in the public recognition stakes due to Arsenal's recent lack of success (playing for a modest Republic of Ireland side in the years before Saint Jack took over the reins didn't help his profile either). As a youngster in the Arsenal team that had reached three successive Cup Finals at the turn of the 80s, O'Leary had been touted as potentially the best defender in Europe, and the way he marked the Argentinian ace Mario Kempes out of the Cup-Winners' Cup Final in 1980 cemented his reputation on an international stage. But he had grown quietly frustrated by Arsenal's lack of ambition and in the latter stages of Don Howe's reign the Irishman's career had taken a visible step backwards.

With the cumbersome Tommy Caton failing to convince Graham, and with hot prospect Martin Keown being shown the door, O'Leary found himself lining up alongside young Tony Adams at centre-back as the season kicked off. Adams had made his debut as a seventeen-year-old back in 1983, but despite a couple of brief periods in the first team, the rangy teenager from Essex had fallen behind Keown in the pecking order under Howe. Nonetheless, he had always been highly rated at Highbury: even as a schoolboy, his character and leadership qualities had singled him out as a big name for the future. In one of the best decisions he would ever make, Graham didn't hesitate in giving Adams his wings. In his first full season in the team, the youngster with the old head on his shoulders created a formidable partnership with O'Leary, and people were soon talking about him as a certain international and future Arsenal captain.

Tony Adams was eventually chosen as the PFA Young Player of the Year, though it must have been a close-run thing with another young Gunner in his first full season, nineteen-year-old David Rocastle. 'Rocky' had already made a considerable impression under Don Howe before injury cut his first season short. His uninhibited style down the right flank – that rare combination of a winger's ability to take on people with an all-action style more akin to that of a midfield player – made him a great favourite with the crowd at Highbury, and the supporters would eventually vote him their 1986 Player of the Year. Great things were expected of the modest and likeable youngster from South London. Without any question, Arsenal's best attacking performances in Graham's first season came when Rocastle and Anderson were blasting down the right flank.

The Press were quick to latch on to the changes that Graham had made at Highbury and were soon talking about Arsenal as genuine Championship challengers. After the 3-0 victory against Luton at the end of December, David Lacey wrote in his resolutely hype-free column in the *Guardian*: 'Saturday's victory stretched Arsenal's unbeaten run to a dozen matches, ten of which have been won. Four of their last five wins, moreover, have been by three goals or more. This is the stuff of Championships, make no mistake.' The fact that it was Arsenal's centenary year inevitably focused additional media attention on the club, but amidst all the Press attention and speculation about a title bid that the long unbeaten run attracted, George Graham always insisted that, while delighted with his side's progress, they were too inexperienced and too lacking in depth to maintain their challenge in a League marathon over nine months.

The unbeaten run finally came to an end on 24 January in a right old rumble at Old Trafford, on a day when the experience and sheer intimidatory presence of Bryan Robson and Norman Whiteside in midfield proved rather too much for Arsenal. The roughneck Whiteside, in particular, did his best to kick Arsenal out of the game – afterwards the normally uncontroversial David O'Leary accused him of being a 'crazy nutter' – and one very late challenge on Rocastle had the desired effect, provoking the youngster into retaliation and a consequent sending-off. A couple of weeks later the eventual champions, Everton, went top as Arsenal prepared for their Sunday Littlewoods Cup game against Spurs. A subsequent combination of injuries, loss of form, and the pressure of competing on two fronts with a still shallow squad, saw Arsenal slipping out of the title race, just as Graham had always predicted.

But glory was at hand. It was the titanic struggle against Spurs in the Littlewoods Cup Semi-Final saga that not only defined Arsenal's first season under Graham, but set the standard of what was to come; his sides would never, but never, lie down and die, however adverse the circumstances. A Cup Semi-Final against the old enemy was never going to be an occasion for the faint-hearted. On this occasion, measuring up to probably the best Tottenham side since the glory days of the 60s (a side, remember, that was a serious candidate for major honours on all three fronts) provided the sternest of tests. David Pleat, the other half of the new managerial duo in North London, had astutely moulded a five-man midfield around Glenn Hoddle, giving his midfield genius the completely free rein he had always coveted. And ploughing a lonely furrow in Spurs' attack, Clive Allen (the man whose blink-and-you'd-miss-it Arsenal career forged the way for Kenny Sansom's arrival at the club) was in once-in-a-lifetime form. The have-goals-will-travel striker eventually finished the season with 49 goals and as Footballer of the Year. As it turned out, he so very nearly proved to be Arsenal's executioner as well.

For the first leg at Highbury, suspensions deprived Graham of his right flank wedge of Anderson and Rocastle and an untypically lacklustre performance saw a solitary goal from Allen hand Arsenal their first home defeat of the season. If that reverse appeared to have tipped the scales in Tottenham's favour, a 1-0 half-time lead in the second-leg, courtesy of you-know-who, saw the ides of March shaping up to deal Arsenal a fatal blow. However, as the Arsenal players sought solace in the dressing-room at half-time, they were astounded to hear the public address system announcing ticket arrangements for the Final and spouting out 'Spurs are on their way to Wembley' from Tottenham's Cup Final song. Tactless and arrogant it may have been, but in reality, if the half-wits on the staff at White Hart Lane had deliberately gone out of their way to motivate the Arsenal players, they couldn't possibly have done more. Affronted by this slight, Arsenal ran out for the second half like men possessed. Skipper Kenny Sansom would later cite Tottenham's half-time jumping of the gun as the turning point: 'It's difficult to describe because it is a feeling that rarely happens to you. You get a goosepimply feeling and you know that you are not going to lose the game ... it was obvious as we trotted out that Arsenal were not going out of the competition.' Charlie Nicholas was equally convinced: 'When we came out for the second half trailing 2-0 on aggregate, I looked at the faces of the Tottenham players and then at the Arsenal lads, and I just knew we were going to do it.' In the second period there was indeed only one side in it, and goals from Niall Quinn and Viv Anderson left Spurs reeling to set up a dramatic third game. George Graham lost the toss to decide the venue – not something that would have bothered Arsenal unduly, given their ongoing run of results at White Hart Lane – and the following Wednesday it was back to London N17 for what had to be a dramatic final instalment. If 90 minutes and extra-time couldn't separate the teams, penalties would.

With the psychological advantage firmly on Arsenal's side and Glenn Hoddle missing through injury, the smart money suggested it would be third-time lucky for the Gunners. But Graham's men still insisted on doing it the hard way. The game was an end-to-end, raw-blooded battle against a sea of noise, in the very best tradition of English Cup ties. With just eight minutes to go the Gunners were trailing to yet another Clive Allen goal. His only other contribution to the proceedings was a horrific kung-fu-style tackle on Paul Davis that the referee somehow deemed only worthy of a booking, an incident that would deprive the Gunners of the man George Graham had described as their most consistent performer for several subsequent games.

Ian Allinson, at best a bit-player under Graham, was on for Charlie Nicholas, who had been carried off with a twisted ankle. The talented Scot had been a peripheral figure in such a raw affair but his understudy immediately took centre-stage. With the Tottenham fans already picturing the walk down Wembley Way, Allinson chased a long punt from Paul Davis into an unpromising corner of the penalty area. As the ball bobbled around uninvitingly, he managed to shake off the attentions of Richard Gough before hitting a speculative shot that somehow squeezed through the defender's legs and past a surprised Ray Clemence at the near post. In that instance, Spurs palpably (and perhaps understandably) *went*, and against the wall of noise emerging from the travelling North Bank at the Park Lane end, it was simply a question of when the final twist of the knife would be delivered.

As the game entered injury-time, Arsenal swarmed forward. Allinson again drove the ball in from wide on the left, and a ricochet off Danny Thomas left David Rocastle with the ball invitingly at his feet and with only Clemence to beat. His left-foot shot was anything but true, but it sneaked under the hapless keeper and Arsenal were suddenly and dramatically ahead . . . for the very first time in the saga. Moments later it was all over. Graham's team had given the Arsenal fans their most ecstatic moment in years and the ensuing high jinks on the pitch at White Hart Lane brought back memories of that momentous night in 1971 when Arsenal secured the first half of the historic Double. As a song was born on the terraces – 'One-nil down, two-one up, we knocked Tottenham out the Cup' – the walls of Arsenal's dressing-room echoed to the chants of 'Spurs are on their way to Wembley'. Tottenham had been made to pay for their startling presumptuousness, and how! The legend of George Graham's durable Arsenal had been forged. Their reward for beating Spurs? A final against the side Graham had always insisted were his benchmark, Liverpool.

It would be exaggerating to say that the young Gunners arrived at Wembley as sacrificial lambs: injuries to Mark Lawrenson, Steve Nichol and Jim Beglin had deprived the Merseysiders of three-quarters of their defence and Kenny Dalglish's unusually vulnerable-looking team were slipping behind in the title race after two consecutive defeats. But the talent and experience of Ian Rush, Alan Hansen, Bruce Grobbelaar, Jan Molby et al. certainly made them favourites. Arsenal's recent form had been even worse than Liverpool's; in the aftermath of the Spurs game they had dropped off the pace in the League in vertiginous fashion and a home defeat by their Wembley opponents a month earlier had effectively ended any Championship pretensions – that defeat was part of a dismal run-in to the big day of five defeats and a draw. The alarming slump saw Arsenal notch just one goal, and that was a meaningless consolation in a 3-1 home defeat against Watford in the FA Cup. The latter defeat may have been unfortunate: after a melée in the Watford area, the Arsenal players saw a linesman waving his flag for a foul by Steve Sims on Niall Quinn and stopped momentarily, waiting for the penalty that never came. Meanwhile, Watford raced upfield for Luther Blissett to score the killer third goal. The resulting mayhem may have been borne of injustice, but the whole incident was an accurate reflection of Arsenal's accident-prone form. They still weren't conceding many goals, but at the other end the forwards were proving stubbornly shot-shy. Neither Quinn nor Groves was ever going to be a prolific scorer, and Nicholas had been missing again after sustaining that knock in the Spurs Semi-Final. As for Hayes, he had hit a dry spell that was to prove far more representative of his long-term potential than the early season flurry of goals.

With not only the weight and tradition of Liverpool's recent past to deal with, but also their own poor form going into the Final, it wasn't a surprise that Arsenal went into the game as underdogs. What is more, for most of the Liverpool players Wembley was like a second home. By contrast, only

David O'Leary, Viv Anderson and Steve Williams had trodden the sacred turf at club level. Kenny Sansom had been a frequent visitor with England but, as he himself recognised, and as a nervous start demonstrated, it wasn't the same thing.

On a gloriously sunny Sunday in April, in front of a 96,000 crowd, the heat was most definitely on for Graham's young charges, and at first they seemed likely to buckle under the pressure. The manager had insisted that the first twenty minutes were vital, but his warnings didn't prevent his players succumbing to the butterflies as Liverpool dominated the early exchanges; only Steve Williams occasionally threatened to ruffle the feathers of Jan Molby and Steve McMahon in midfield. Worst of all, Arsenal's normally safe-as-houses defence was looking exceedingly vulnerable as Liverpool continually sought out the pace of Ian Rush with searching long balls. The Welshman had already escaped the clutches of O'Leary on several occasions – most notably when he set up a golden chance for Craig Johnston, who was only foiled by a memorable save by John Lukic down low to his right – before the inevitable goal arrived in the 23rd minute. Molby's raking ball from deep in his own half found Arsenal's defence AWOL and McMahon racing free down the right. When he knocked the ball square, Rush found himself 'home alone' in the box and with enough time to write his own headlines before knocking the ball past the hopelessly exposed Lukic.

The signs were ominous, especially given Ian Rush's record: the Juventous-bound Welshman had scored for Liverpool in 144 matches and, amazingly, had never left the pitch on the losing side. When John Lukic picked the ball out of the net in game number 145, few would have bet against Rush flying off to Italy with his record intact.

But perversely, rather than signalling the start of a Liverpool goal-rush, the setback at last shook Arsenal out of their initial stupor. Liverpool, meanwhile, perhaps too confident of their own forces, seemed to shift down a gear. Paul Davis began to emerge from his own personal lethargy and within minutes had nearly put the Gunners level with a deceptively powerful 25-yard shot that caught Grobbelaar napping before coming back off the post. A couple of minutes later, the keeper was not so lucky; after Davis's free kick had rebounded off the encroaching Liverpool wall, Kenny Sansom lofted the ball back into the box (with his right foot!) where Viv Anderson, making a typical nuisance of himself, fed the ball invitingly to Charlie Nicholas. The Scot's first effort came back off the post, but in the ensuing scramble, the still loitering Anderson reacted like lightning to knock the ball back from the dead-ball line. This time Charlie made no mistake, flicking the ball past a crowd of defenders on the line to put his side level. Arsenal had taken just six minutes to equalise and were suddenly looking much the better side. As the antagonists went off at half-time, George Graham must have been proud of the way his young team had turned the game around.

For the first fifteen minutes of the second half, Liverpool fleetingly regained their grip and composure, but gradually, as Williams and, above all, the majestic Davis, started to tighten the screw in midfield, Arsenal took command. Now Charlie Nicholas was buzzing too; rising to the big occasion, the Scot was suddenly looking ball-hungry and goal-starved as he constantly tried to jink round defenders and create an opening. At the same time, Viv Anderson was beginning to take advantage of Wembley's ample proportions to get forward down the right, where Ronnie Whelan was looking decidedly uncomfortable as a makeshift left-back.

With eighteen minutes to go, Kenny Dalglish and Perry Groves entered the fray as both camps looked to tip the final balance in their favour. As it turned out, the legendary player-manager couldn't get in the game at all, but Graham's ploy of sending on the little-known winger for the ailing Quinn proved a master-stroke. Groves' impact was immediate; darting back and forth across Liverpool's rearguard and leaving tiring defenders giddy in his wake, his pace and enthusiasm soon tilted the balance, just as Graham had planned. And in one gloriously decisive moment he really did his boss proud; latching on to a long ball from Kenny Sansom, he jinked delightfully past Gary Gillespie along the left touchline, before cutting inside and knocking the ball square to Charlie Nicholas, who had checked and lost his marker on the edge of the box. Nicholas scuffed his shot, but a deflection off Ronnie Whelan was enough to leave Grobbelaar groping at thin air and the ball rolled agonisingly over the line. With eight minutes to go, Arsenal were ahead and yet another variation on the season's staple chant was born: 'One-nil down, Two-one up, Ian Rush's record's scuppered' (or words to that effect) rang around Wembley, and after what seemed an eternity it was all over. For George Graham and Arsenal it was third-time lucky in the League Cup after Final defeats in 1968 and 1969 but, more importantly, eight long years after Pat Rice had last climbed up the Wembley steps as a winning captain, Arsenal were back on the trophy trail.

The supporters were overjoyed to see Arsenal return to winning ways, especially against such formidable opposition, and the fact that Charlie Nicholas had played a decisive role was an added bonus. But George Graham was still unconvinced by his fellow-countryman's wayward talents and one match-winning performance at Wembley was not about to change his mind. 'Charlie – The Prince for one Glorious Day' was the poetic headline in the next day's *Guardian*. Unfortunately for Charlie's fan club, this was as prophetic as it was poetic. Alf Ramsey had once famously commented that he was quite willing to leave out the best player in the world if he wouldn't or couldn't fit into the team plan. Graham was clearly of the same school and you didn't need to be an Einstein to realise that Nicholas, although arguably Arsenal's most gifted player, was struggling to adjust to Graham's new order at Highbury.

As the season drew to a close, Graham admitted that picking up a trophy had been a vast bonus in a year when his main aim had been to assess his players and build a platform for the future. But he had quickly instilled good habits in his Highbury disciples, habits that ensured a high level of competitiveness. Picking up the League Cup after overcoming opponents of the calibre of Nottingham Forest, Spurs and Liverpool was no mean feat. More importantly, given the foundations of faith that Graham had forged, it was no coincidence. The players who took the field for Graham that first season may not have been the finished article, and in some cases never would be, but the new boss had quickly established a spirit and pattern of play throughout the club that made it easier for new players to step into the first team and do their job. Graham's philosophy would help young players to thrive at Highbury – that seven of the Wembley winners had emerged through the ranks (Liverpool couldn't boast even one) was a sure sign of things to come. That five of those players were aged twenty or under, speaks volumes for Graham's philosophy that 'if you're good enough, you're old enough'.

The form of youngsters like Adams, Rocastle, Hayes, Groves, Quinn and Thomas (the first three all won Young Player of the Month awards during the season while Quinn forced his way into the Ireland squad) was a massive bonus. They would not all go on to enjoy the same success at Highbury, but their contribution to Graham's good start was unquestionable. Don Howe has since implied that Graham was lucky to inherit such a talented group of youngsters. But by demonstrating such faith in his youngsters, even in the most compromising situations, and by resisting the pressure to panic-buy at the beginning of the season when things started badly, the new man at Highbury showed considerably more courage in a few short months than many of his fellow managers do in a whole career. It was not even a case of making a virtue out of necessity; Graham genuinely believes that this is the right way to do things. Tony Adams displayed an almost startling maturity in his first full season, and by February was making his full England debut at only twenty – the first player born after the 1966 World Cup triumph to win a full cap for England. After afternoon glory at Wembley in the League Cup he would dash off to receive the FA Young Player of the Year award in the evening. Not far behind was the talented and combative Rocastle; not since the days of Geordie Armstrong had Arsenal had such an eager and effective performer out wide. But Graham's 'if you're good enough, you're old enough' attitude was best illustrated when he entrusted a vital holding role in midfield to Michael Thomas in the League Cup Semi-Final against Spurs – this at a time when the youngster had only a couple of games, and those at full-back.

Not that Graham only demonstrated a knack for cultivating his younger talents in his first year at Highbury; seasoned professionals like John Lukic, Viv Anderson, Paul Davis and Steve Williams also played arguably the best football of their careers in the 86/87 season. For Peter Hill-Wood and company, the contrast with the situation of just a year before couldn't have been greater. Graham's achievements in his first season at the helm had exceeded even the wildest expectations, and the rumblings of discontent among the fans were by now just a distant echo. As the season understandably fizzled out in the aftermath of the Liverpool game, the man who had saved the board's skin was already beginning to plan for an even more glorious future. Before the summer holidays arrived, Alan Smith and Nigel Winterburn had both signed on the dotted line, as George Graham's quest to build a pedigree side continued.

BY GEORGE ...

'As the new manager, I'm in the process of bringing *my* ideas into the club and assembling the squad of players I want ... However, I'm not going out to buy players just to fill up the squad. I haven't bought anyone so far because the quality players I want are not available ... I plan to do my homework on players who'll be good for Arsenal, not sign them on their reputations. I've said before that our squad is not strong enough but I shan't be railroaded into signing a player until I think I've found the right man.'

A veritable Declaration of Intent as Graham embarks on his first season.

'If I could have looked into a crystal ball five months ago and discovered we'd be at the top come Christmas, I'd have been very surprised ... We've recovered our resilience again, the same resilience I remember when I was a player here ... I know the "lucky Arsenal" label has been resurrected after certain games when a break has gone our way. My answer is that you might get a break, but you still have to take advantage of it.'

George peers down on the rest from the Highbury Christmas tree.

'I am absolutely delighted things have happened so quickly. It wasn't planned this way. I think in the first year at a big club like Arsenal you try and set out your ideas and training methods and bring in new players. Up to now I have only brought in one (Perry Groves) and got rid of about six so we are a little bit short-staffed. But all credit to the young players who have come into the side. The combination of them and our experienced players has given us a lovely blend which has put us where we are today ... Getting to Wembley has come sooner than I expected, but looking beyond today, our target must be to emulate Liverpool's achievements and style ... Wembley is Liverpool's second home but our away record is very good.'

On the eve of the Littlewoods Cup Final.

'I think we've played better this season, and there were times when we looked a bit jaded ... but to give Liverpool a goal start through Ian Rush, then to come back and win the trophy, was a great performance. Liverpool are still the club I want to emulate, because they've been the most consistently successful side in the history of English football. We're working towards it.'

Liverpool may have been beaten ... but they're still the team to beat.

FOOTBALL LEAGUE DIVISION ONE 86/87

Final League position: 4th
Average home gate: 29,056

Manchester United	(h) 1-0	Nicholas	
Coventry City	(a) 1-2	Anderson	
Liverpool	(a) 1-2	Adams	
Sheffield Wednesday	(h) 2-0	Adams, Quinn	
Tottenham Hotspur	(h) 0-0		
Luton Town	(a) 0-0		
Oxford United	(h) 0-0		
Nottingham Forest	(a) 0-1		
Everton	(a) 1-0	Williams	
Watford	(h) 3-1	Groves, Hayes (penalty), Quinn	
Newcastle United	(a) 2-1	Anderson, Williams	
Chelsea	(h) 3-1	Rocastle, Hayes 2 (1 penalty)	
Charlton Athletic	(a) 2-0	Adams, Hayes	
West Ham United	(h) 0-0		
Southampton	(a) 4-0	Hayes (penalty), Quinn, Groves, Anderson	
Manchester City	(h) 3-0	Quinn, Anderson, Adams	
Aston Villa	(a) 4-0	Hayes, Rocastle, Groves, og	
Queens Park Rangers	(h) 3-1	Hayes 2, Quinn	
Norwich City	(a) 1-1	Hayes (penalty)	
Luton Town	(h) 3-0	Quinn, Adams, Hayes	
Leicester City	(a) 1-1	Hayes (penalty)	
Southampton	(h) 1-0	Quinn	
Wimbledon	(h) 3-1	Nicholas 2, Hayes (penalty)	
Tottenham Hotspur	(a) 2-1	Adams, Davis	
Coventry City	(h) 0-0		
Manchester United	(a) 0-2		
Sheffield Wednesday	(a) 1-1	Quinn	
Oxford United	(a) 0-0		
Chelsea	(a) 0-1		
Liverpool	(h) 0-1		
Nottingham Forest	(h) 0-0		
Watford	(a) 0-2		
Everton	(h) 0-1		
West Ham United	(a) 1-3	Hayes (penalty)	
Charlton Athletic	(h) 2-1	Davis, Hayes	
Newcastle United	(h) 0-1		
Wimbledon	(a) 2-1	Davis, Merson	
Leicester City	(h) 4-1	Davis, Hayes 2 (1 penalty), Nicholas	
Manchester City	(a) 0-3		
Aston Villa	(h) 2-1	Hayes 2 (1 penalty)	
Queens Park Rangers	(a) 4-1	Rix 2, Merson, Hayes	
Norwich City	(h) 1-2	Merson	

FA Cup 86/87

Third Round:
Reading (a) 3-1 Nicholas 2, Hayes (penalty)

Fourth Round:
Plymouth Argyle (h) 6-1 Nicholas, Davis, Quinn, Rocastle, Anderson 2

Fifth Round:
Barnsley (h) 2-0 Hayes (penalty), Nicholas

Sixth Round:
Watford (h) 1-3 Allinson

League Cup 86/87

Second Round:
Huddersfield Town (h) 2-0 Davis, Quinn

Huddersfield Town (a) 1-1 Hayes

Third Round:
Manchester City (h) 3-1 Rocastle, Hayes (penalty), Davis

Fourth Round:
Charlton Athletic (h) 2-0 Quinn, og

Fifth Round:
Nottingham Forest (h) 2-0 Nicholas, Hayes

Semi-Final 1st leg:
Tottenham Hotspur (h) 0-1

Semi-Final 2nd leg:
Tottenham Hotspur (a) 2-1 (after extra time) Anderson, Quinn

Semi-Final Replay:
Tottenham Hotspur (a) 2-1 Allinson, Rocastle

Final (Wembley):
Liverpool 2-1 Nicholas 2

Appearances

	League	FA Cup	League Cup	Total
Tony Adams	42	4	9	55
Viv Anderson	40	4	8	52
David O'Leary	39	4	9	52
Paul Davis	39	3	9	51
John Lukic	36	4	9	49
David Rocastle	36	4	8	48
Kenny Sansom	35	4	9	48
Niall Quinn	35	4	9	48
Steve Williams	33 + 1	3	7	43 + 1
Martin Hayes	31 + 4	4	7 + 1	42 + 5
Charlie Nicholas	25 + 3	2 + 2	6	33 + 5

	League	FA Cup	League Cup	Total
Perry Groves	19+6	2+1	4+2	25+9
Graham Rix	13+4	0	1+2	14+6
Michael Thomas	12	0+2	2+2	14+4
Gus Caesar	6+9	0+1	1	7+10
Rhys Wilmot	6	0	0	6
Ian Allinson	5+9	2	1+4	8+13
Paul Merson	5+2	0	0	5+2
Stewart Robson	5	0	0	5

Goal-scorers

	League	FA Cup	League Cup	Total
Martin Hayes	19	2	3	24
Niall Quinn	8	1	3	12
Charlie Nicholas	4	4	3	11
Viv Anderson	4	2	1	7
Paul Davis	4	1	2	7
Tony Adams	6	0	0	6
David Rocastle	2	1	2	5
Perry Groves	3	0	0	3
Paul Merson	3	0	0	3
Graham Rix	2	0	0	2
Steve Williams	2	0	0	2
Ian Allinson	0	1	1	2

Season's Review 1987/88

Buried by Caesar

I n many ways, George Graham's second season at Highbury was uncannily similar to the first, as for three months Arsenal again flattered to deceive in the Championship race before their aspirations evaporated. If at first glance the season was not an exact replica of its predecessor, it was only because the Littlewoods Cup Final saw 'North Sea' Gus Caesar all at sea and the ghost of Brian McClair returning to haunt Nigel Winterburn. In fact, there were major differences this time around. First, Graham seemed genuinely disappointed that his side were unable to sustain a challenge – during Arsenal's spell at the top there were none of the self-deprecating comments of the previous year and the 'we are not good enough' line was abandoned for a tone that was still realistic, but was definitely more ambitious. Second, the sheer brilliance of the eventual champions, Liverpool, would eventually convince Graham that his squad really did need strengthening if his team were to sustain a serious title challenge, an appreciation he made public as the season progressed.

Despite the pressure born of unfavourable comparisons with Kenny Dalglish's new model Liverpool (bolstered by the inspirational presence of big-money signings, John Barnes and Peter Beardsley, and with 29-goal John Aldridge more than making up for the absence of Ian Rush), the 87/88 champions were a team which ranks as one of the most spectacular the English game has ever seen. Graham stuck to his guns over transfer dealings, insisting that he would never pay inflated prices, even for players he really wanted. Unfortunately, John Barnes hadn't fallen into this latter category: as the season kicked off, many Arsenal fans were bewildered by Graham's failure to compete for Watford's wing magician when he had become available during the summer. Given that Arsenal were supposedly the player's first choice, this was an inexplicable decision. Liverpool eventually snapped the winger up for £900,000 and by the end of a stunning first year at Anfield, Barnes was not only savouring a first Championship triumph, but also basking in the glory of being virtually the most unanimous winner ever of the Footballer of the Year award. That Liverpool paid a mere £3,350,000 for the title-winning triumvirate of Barnes, Beardsley and Aldridge was a clear demonstration that you could still get value for money out of big names without gambling excessively. Word had it that Graham didn't fancy Barnes because he was sceptical about the player's work-rate and consistency, and apparently he didn't think he would fit into Arsenal's system. Caution can sometimes be excused when millions are paid for mediocrities, but Graham's failure to compete for Barnes infuriated the fans. The Scot's apparent aversion to big names, and/or unwillingness to match the salary offers of other big clubs, was a policy that cost Arsenal several signings in his first couple of years at the club. Undaunted, Graham would continue to go his own way in the pursuit of a Championship-winning side.

Arsenal's start was disappointing but, given the quality of the opposition (defeats against Liverpool and Queens Park Rangers were interspersed by a creditable draw at Old Trafford) hardly enough to throw the best-laid plans. So when Graham dropped Charlie Nicholas for the fourth game, at home to a vulnerable-looking Portsmouth side, the writing was on the wall for Bonnie Prince Charlie. If Graham wasn't prepared to give Nicholas the chance to forge a partnership with Alan Smith in a game that always promised goals, then quite clearly he had already seen enough. The fact that he chose Perry Groves to accompany Smith down the middle in place of Nicholas was further evidence of Graham's lack of faith in the gifted but inconsistent Scot. After all, Groves hardly offered any guarantees himself: he had been a winger for three years at Colchester before arriving at Highbury, and had so far scored only three goals in Arsenal colours.

Charlie had arrived from Celtic for £650,000 in the summer of 1983 after an incredible 48 goals in the 82/83 Scottish season had sparked off an almighty transfer battle between Arsenal, Liverpool and Manchester United. Somewhat surprisingly he chose to join Terry Neill's side, though the sweet-talking Irishman's blarney probably had less to do with the decision than the extra-curricular activities (commercial and otherwise) offered by the capital. Despite winning over the Highbury faithful with his undoubted charisma and an extravagant ability to do the unexpected, Charlie was never able to get near his strike-rate in the hoops of Celtic, notching up just 54 goals in 184 games in England. The fact that he produced a much better return in Cup games – 20 in only 29 starts – lent support to the argument that he might be the man for the big occasions but that he was never likely to buckle down sufficiently in the weekly bump-and-grind of the English League. His return in Graham's first season at Highbury was fairly typical: in the League he managed only four goals, but in the two Cup competitions he chalked up seven in only eight starts, including of course, the winning brace at Wembley.

Despite all the ifs and buts, the Arsenal fans loved Charlie, even if they accepted that Graham was right in demanding more, and the Charlie fan club turned up at Highbury that Saturday disgruntled by Graham's changes (Martin Hayes, top scorer the previous season, was also out after only three games). A 6-0 win marked by a Smith hat-trick (the centre-forward's first goals for Arsenal) was hardly going to change the manager's mind though, and helped put paid to any incipient rebellion among the masses. The fact that the opposition were pitifully weak was irrelevant. The Portsmouth game signalled the beginning of Arsenal's record-breaking run of wins and Graham became understandably reluctant to break up a winning team. Not that Arsenal would threaten to break any goal-scoring records: Alan Smith would only score another eight League goals all season and Charlie's grave-digger, Perry Groves, managed a mere six. With the forwards firing blanks, Arsenal would become over-reliant on their midfielders for goals. Even during the successful winning spell early on, the forwards were hardly prolific (Smith, for example, hit an eleven-match barren spell in November and December) but Graham stuck to his guns: with Hayes, Quinn and the emerging Paul Merson getting the nod as extras, Nicholas couldn't even make the bench. The die was cast. Graham simply wasn't prepared to carry a player he considered a luxury. The North Bank's favourite son would never play another game for Arsenal and in January 1988 he moved on to Aberdeen for £500,000; his destination and the bargain basement fee a reflection of how Charlie's stock had fallen in his four-and-a-bit years in London.

The Arsenal club record of fourteen consecutive wins was established in a run that lasted until a surprise home defeat by Southampton on 21 November, a sequence that took Graham's team from tenth position to the very top of the table. But the reverse against the Saints saw them immediately surrender their privileged position to the lurking giants from Liverpool and though mathematically Arsenal stayed within striking distance beyond the New Year, they never really looked like serious contenders in the face of such heavyweight opposition.

The catalyst for the impressive autumn run was again the defensive mean-machine and John Lukic kept no less than ten clean sheets in that fourteen-game spell. During the close season Graham had lost the influential Viv Anderson to Manchester United – at 30, and finding himself out of contract, the full-back was understandably tempted by a lucrative four-year deal at Old Trafford. At first, the manager reacted by looking for a replacement in the transfer market. However, twenty-year-old Michael Thomas stepped comfortably into a back four that carried on with business as usual, and the Arsenal faithful eventually breathed a sigh of relief when Graham's interest in Terry Fenwick waned. In his first two games, Thomas was faced with the daunting task of marking John Barnes and Jesper Olsen, a dual challenge he took to in his soon-to-become-familiar imperturbable manner. An early spell of goals, including a cracking winner in another 2-1 win at Spurs (the fourth consecutive derby victory at White Hart Lane since George Graham's arrival at the club) helped to seal his place in the side and made 'Steamer' an immediate favourite with the crowd.

Alongside Thomas, the international triumvirate of O'Leary, Adams and Sansom were performing as consistently as ever, while behind them, John Lukic (spurred on by the threat of competition from the Norwegian, Erik Thorstvedt, and Press speculation about the signing of Tony Coton) just got better and better. For a man who stood 6 feet 4 inches even before stepping into his boots, he was still at times surprisingly vulnerable in the air and he was fond of provoking the occasional flutter of the collective Highbury heartbeat with his indecisiveness when called to come off his line. But Lukic's agility for such a big man was rare, and he was justly recognised as one of the best 'shot-stoppers' in the League. As the wonder years got underway, John Lukic's reflexes were a regular match-winner for Arsenal.

As David O'Leary recognised at the time, Arsenal's defensive parsimony in fact started a long way from their own penalty box: 'Once more we're getting great protection because the midfield players close down so fast on their opposite numbers, making it very difficult for opponents to set attacks flowing.' Under Graham, the midfield had acquired the habit of hunting in packs, and it was common to see Davis and Williams leading a chasing band of Arsenal players all harassing a sole opponent. Until his injury at Christmas, Davis was again probably Arsenal's best player, at long last becoming a crowd favourite as he controlled the midfield with his waif-like poise. The player himself was quick to recognise the influence of his manager's positive promptings: 'It means a lot when you hear nice things about you from someone you respect – and that's helped convince the fans too.' Perhaps most eloquently, the ostensibly more aggressive Williams struggled to dominate without Davis alongside him. As for David Rocastle, after an uneasy first few games that found him out of sorts and looking perplexed by the tighter marking that his name now attracted (a learning period that saw him regularly hauled off by Graham), he soon came good again. Admitting that he needed to harness his attacking abilities by doing his best work further forward, 'Rocky' began to get into the opposition's box more often and would quickly boast regular goal-scoring to add to his already impressive repertoire, ending the season with a very useful tally of twelve goals.

Another midfielder who hit an early vein of goals was Kevin Richardson. The Geordie arrived at Highbury from Watford just a couple of weeks into the season, and with Graham Rix again sidelined with Achilles tendon problems and Martin Hayes out of favour, he stepped almost straight into the side in an unfamiliar position on the left side of midfield. Richardson himself had been out of the first team picture at Vicarage Road and George Graham's move for him raised more than a few eyebrows, but at £150,000 he soon proved to be a bargain. Five goals in his first eight games may have given a very false impression of his long-term goal-scoring potential, but the will to win acquired as a Championship winner with Everton was to prove more durable. What Richardson lacked in the flair stakes he more than made up for in good old-fashioned bottle. As Arsenal floundered into the New Year and as more talented team-mates were occasionally caught mincing around in tough away games (authentic battles at Portsmouth and Wimbledon immediately spring to mind), Richardson was always at hand, constantly showing himself for the ball and motivating the waverers.

The fourteen-game unbeaten run was followed by a period when Arsenal went seriously off the boil. The Southampton defeat at the end of November signalled the start of an eleven-match run in the League that yielded just one victory and saw Arsenal gradually slide down the table, never to regain momentum. Injuries to Davis and O'Leary (the midfielder needed a hernia op just before Christmas while the Irishman was plagued by a sore tendon) robbed the side of its two key organising elements; going into the New Year, Michael Thomas began to tire: and though Graham kept insisting that the side had to attack as a unit and share the goals around the whole team, the continuing drought from the men up-front was bound to take its toll eventually. The fact that Graham acknowledged this weakness was confirmed when he made an unsuccessful bid for Chelsea's Kerry Dixon in March.

Despite impressing with his all-round game, the resolutely unspectacular, and momentarily goal-shy, Alan Smith, was still struggling to win over the less discerning fans and he clearly needed a more effective partner than Groves to feed off his subtle lay-offs. When Smith first arrived at Highbury he almost certainly suffered by association with a more celebrated Leicester old boy, Gary Lineker. He certainly wasn't eye-catchingly quick or dynamic in the mould of his ex-striking partner and as he initially struggled for goals (any centre-forward's *raison d'être*, especially if he's an expensive one) the sceptics were handed an easy target. As for 'El Pel', by now he was very much the butt of the crowd's frustrations. The Arsenal fanzine *One-Nil Down, Two-One Up* suggested he wear a number on the front of his shirt as well as the back, so reminiscent was he of a wide receiver in American football. With Nicholas gone, Hayes and Quinn making little impact on the rare occasions they surfaced from the reserves, and the promising Paul Merson still a season away from really establishing himself, the second half of George Graham's second campaign at the helm was characterised by a distinct lack of flair and firepower up front.

At one stage the malaise threatened to spread, with defenders starting to make silly errors that cost the team goals and points, most notably in the Christmas period: in mistake-riddled games against Everton, Nottingham Forest, Wimbledon, and Portsmouth, Arsenal definitely took the season of goodwill rather too seriously. The fact that O'Leary often played when not fully fit obviously didn't help, though Graham's reluctance to rest his experienced Irishman was understandable given the identity of his understudy, Gus Caesar – an accident just waiting to happen. The introduction of the tough-tackling Nigel Winterburn at right-back eventually improved matters at the back; his wholehearted attitude proved as infectious as Graham had predicted. However, it was no secret that his longer-term future lay on the other flank, and Kenny Sansom, for one, was bitterly disappointed by his arrival. Unhappy at being rested on several occasions and disappointed at a prolonged impasse in talks over a new contract, Sansom was beginning to suffer a distinctly unwanted feeling. His strained relationship with George Graham eventually hit the headlines when the player voiced his festering discontent in a newspaper article on the eve of the Tottenham game at the beginning of March. That public outburst cost Sansom the captaincy and marked the beginning of the end of the full-back's Arsenal career. Tony Adams, who had already covered during Sansom's occasional absence, became captain for life (or as near as dammit).

If Arsenal had foundered on the rock of their own irregular form in the League, there was still the prospect of a trip back to Wembley in the League Cup if Graham could inspire his charges for the one-off occasions. After a much-needed rest, Michael Thomas came back into the side against Everton in the Semi-Final, this time in midfield for the injured Steve Williams, a move that was to prove permanent and that left Williams counting his days at the club. Graham had always believed that Thomas possessed far too much all-round talent and attacking ability to stay at full-back, although in the 1-0 win in the arduous first leg, the youngster had to rein in his attacking inclinations. If Thomas was magnificent in a more defensive role at Goodison – closing down the battle-hardened pairing of Peter Reid and Ian Snodin in uninhibited and insistent fashion – back at Highbury for the second leg, he was let off the leash to devastating effect, scoring one of the three goals on a night when Arsenal turned on the style in memorable fashion against the nonplussed Merseysiders. That game, without doubt among the most exciting at Highbury in Graham's long and successful reign, was witnessed by 51,148 people just four days after Highbury, bursting at the seams with 54,161 fans, saw Arsenal beat Manchester United 2-1 in the FA Cup 5th Round. These were only two of the 50,000-plus crowds in the 87/88 season, the likes of which the famous old stadium would never witness again. The United and Everton Cup games had seen Arsenal raise their game beyond their mediocre League form. Unfortunately, when Nottingham Forest arrived at Highbury for the FA Cup Sixth Round, a poor performance reflected what had gone on around it and the visitors were deserved winners. Circumstances conspired against Arsenal too; the palpably unfit David O'Leary had to go off early in the first half and an early Forest goal left Arsenal chasing the game without their most experienced defender to hold the fort at the back, hardly the ideal recipe for overcoming a masterful counter-attacking unit like Clough's team.

Still, as the season entered its final stages, Arsenal were back at Wembley. On paper, Luton Town didn't present such formidable opposition as Liverpool, but in the likes of Steve Foster, Mal Donaghy, Mick Harford and Brian Stein they did have good, experienced players and, as Graham insisted, they would be all fired up after their unfortunate defeat in the FA Cup Semi-Final against Wimbledon and an embarrassing 4-1 debacle in their previous visit to Wembley, against Second Division Reading in the Simod Cup Final.

The Arsenal side that took the field against the Hatters was considerably different from the one that had faced Liverpool a year earlier – Anderson, O'Leary, Williams, Nicholas, Quinn and Hayes were all missing from that line-up and, of course, the team were led out by their new 21-year-old captain. On another gloriously sunny April day, the first of many Arsenal sides that Tony Adams would lead out at Wembley was not only mean, but lean; it must have been decades since Wembley had played host to such a skinny team. Adams himself, Lukic, Davis, the still slimline Rocastle, Smith and Groves strode out looking more like a walking advertisement for a diet than a team of muscle-bound modern-day footballers!

Unfortunately, Arsenal's resistance to Luton's more positive approach was to prove as fragile as their appearance. The early signs were ominous as Adams and Gus Caesar struggled to get to grips with the gangling presence of Mick Harford and, just in case anyone didn't get the picture, the thirteenth minute proved to be unlucky for Arsenal. David Preece's free-kick found three defenders jumping fruitlessly with Harford, and when his knock-down fell to Foster, the centre-half's subtle touch found Caesar out of position and ball-watching. As the youngster vainly stuck his arm in the air appealing for a non-existent off-side, in slipped Brian Stein to latch on to his skipper's inch-perfect invitation and guide the ball smoothly past Lukic. Unlike Ian Rush's early goal the previous year, Stein's opening salvo failed to jolt Graham's men into action and Luton continued to dominate with their typically neat and enterprising football. Whatever George Graham said at half-time seemed to have fallen on deaf ears, too, as the only cohesion demonstrated by the Arsenal players in the early exchanges of the second half was in their uniformly bungling efforts to get on top of their game. If it hadn't been for some profligate Luton finishing and, in particular, one gravity-defying save from John Lukic to keep out Brian Stein's goalbound diving header, Arsenal might have been dead and buried well before an out-of-the-blue ten-minute spell – as crazy as it was unexpected – threatened to shift the balance in their favour.

Martin Hayes, so ineffectual in the previous year's Final, was now on for Perry Groves who, given the chance to repeat his match-winning deeds against Liverpool from the kick-off, had managed an equally feeble performance. In the 71st minute, Arsenal won a free-kick some 25 yards out, and Paul Davis – in what was a familiar, if not altogether popular ploy at Highbury – simply lofted the ball forward balloon-like into the crowded box. For once the 'route one' method worked and after a brief scramble the ball fell invitingly to Hayes with an unmissable chance to put Arsenal level. After struggling for so long, Graham's men suddenly scented blood. Just three minutes later – the sum total of Arsenal's dominance in the game so far – they were ahead. Michael Thomas won a tackle on the edge of the box and slipped the ball across to Alan Smith who had ghosted free to his right. The centre-forward's sweetly struck right-foot shot did the rest. Despite their woeful performance, Arsenal were ahead.

If the psychological blow of surrendering the lead after having dominated for so long wasn't bad enough in itself, prevailing circumstances suggested that a visibly deflated Luton would struggle to come back. Ricky Hill and David Preece – Ray Harford's two key men in midfield – were both back in the side after long spells of injury and were totally lacking match practice, and while Arsenal had enjoyed a nine-day break since their

Right: 'Stroller' in action for Arsenal during the double winning season 1970–71

Below: Life before Arsenal, with Terry Venables in Chelsea strip, 1965–66

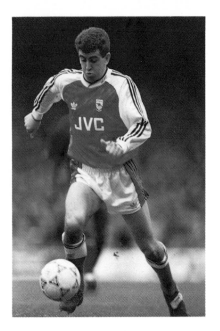
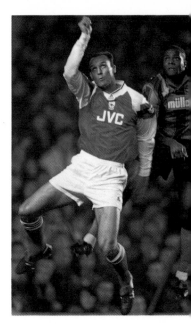

The rock on which George's empire is founded.
The ever-present back four (*clockwise, from top left*):
Nigel Winterburn (bought by George from Wimbledon 1987),
Steve Bould (bought by George from Stoke City 1988),
Tony Adams (at Arsenal since becoming an apprentice in 1984),
Lee Dixon (bought by George from Stoke City 1987)

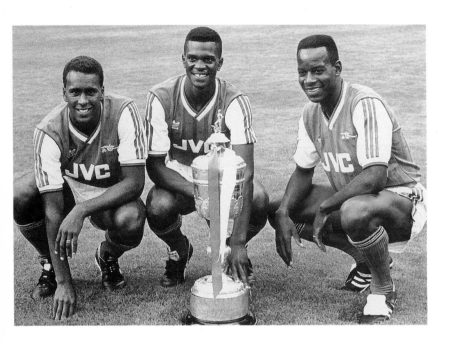

Above: The three degrees of midfield supremacy – with the First Division
trophy, 1989 (*left to right*):
David Rocastle (sold to Leeds in 1992, Man. City 1993, Chelsea 1994);
Paul Davis; Michael Thomas (sold to Liverpool 1991)

Below: The famous last-minute goal which stole the Championship
from Liverpool, scored by Thomas (*centre*). Nicol (*left*) can't believe it;
Winterburn (*right*) celebrates

George's misfits:
young, gifted and sold

Above, left: with Charlie Nicholas
(sold to Aberdeen 1987,
Celtic 1990)

Above: Andy Cole in rare photo,
wearing Arsenal first team strip (sold
to Bristol City 1992, Newcastle
United 1993, Premier League top
goal-scorer 1993–94)

Left: Superswede Anders Limpar
(sold to Everton 1994) with George

Making history again: the double Cup-winning season

Top: On the bus around Highbury with the Coca-Cola Cup (*left to right*) Ian Wright, George, Lee Dixon, David Seaman, 16 May 1993

Centre: The now familiar sight of Tony Adams scoring the only goal and winning the FA Cup Semi-Final against the old enemy Tottenham, 4 April 1993

Right: A delighted George congratulates Ian Wright who holds the FA Cup and his first winner's medal after beating Sheffield Wednesday 2–1 in the replay. Coca-Cola Cup goal scorer Steve Morrow looks on – he had to miss the FA Cup after breaking his arm celebrating Arsenal's first Cup triumph

Europe, the final frontier

Above: The agony. . .
George attempts to rouse the
team before extra time at home
against Benfica in the 2nd round,
2nd leg of the European Cup,
6 November 1991. They lose 1–3

Left: The expectancy. . .
George looking remarkably
relaxed in training before the
Cup Winners' Cup Final against
Parma in Copenhagen

Opposite, top: The ecstasy. . .
Paul Merson and winning
goal-scorer Alan Smith celebrate
taking the lead against Parma in the
Cup Winners' Cup, 4 May 1994

George smiles contentedly at his champion striker after the victory against Parma. Smith was bought by George from Leicester City in 1987 to replace Charlie Nicholas. When Ian Wright was bought in 1991, Smith was the player who most often made room for him

George with some of the family silver

last game (punctuated by a relaxing midweek break in Spain), Luton had played the previous Tuesday. If that wasn't bad enough, Mick Harford, the man who had given Arsenal's defence such a torrid time in the first half, had limped off with an ankle injury. Luton, however, were suddenly to discover an unexpected hero at the other end. Andy Dibble was only in the side because of an injury to Les Sealey, but for that intense ten-minute spell as Arsenal went for the jugular and as his team-mates wilted, the Welsh goalkeeper performed heroics in his efforts to prevent a miscarriage of justice. He had already tipped one goalbound header from Smith on to the bar (and then breathed a massive sigh of relief as Hayes' point-blank effort from the rebound somehow conspired to come back off the post) when David Rocastle was hauled down by Mal Donaghy. Arsenal had a penalty and the chance to put the result beyond doubt. The burning question was who would take it? Michael Thomas had started the season as penalty-taker but was presumably out of the running after a couple of misses. That left Martin Hayes as the obvious candidate: admittedly, he had been out of favour for most of the season, but his dead-eye exploits from the spot the previous year had brought him no less than twelve goals. And he was now on the park with the additional confidence-booster of a goal under his belt. Inexplicably, however, up stepped Nigel Winterburn to take his first-ever penalty, and as fate, and Brian McClair's ghost, would have it, his one and only spot-kick for Arsenal (hit true enough, but telegraphed) ended up in the arms of an unsung substitute keeper who would ultimately pick up the Man of the Match award.

With just eight minutes to go you still wouldn't have put your money on Luton coming back, but the seeds of Arsenal's demise were about to blossom from within their own ranks. George Graham had decided not to risk a half-fit David O'Leary, which left Gus Caesar to take his place. From the very first minute the affable but hapless youngster was a veritable bag of nerves, and he spent most of the game almost visibly willing the ball to stay away from him. But still nobody could have envisaged the bungling nature of his most glaring error. Just two minutes after Winterburn's penalty miss, Gus stumbled and miskicked (or should that be miskicked and stumbled?) in one practically simultaneous action on the edge of his own box, and in the ensuing pandemonium Danny Wilson equalised. Not that the sorry understudy was the only guilty party. If Winterburn hadn't clumsily tried to use his left foot instead of his right to block Kingsley Black's cross, the danger could still have been avoided. The fact that Gus hails from Tottenham might explain his aversion to effective defending, but that doesn't excuse the rest: Tony Adams never looked comfortable alongside Caesar, but he hardly asserted himself either; Kenny Sansom had an exceedingly poor game and Winterburn's two mistakes, though not as risible as Caesar's one crucial error, were arguably more damaging.

In fairness, Brian Stein's 'you're not coming back from this' late winner straight out of the Highbury textbook, did justice to the better side on the day. In an other-side-of-the-coin replay of the previous year's denouement, another carrot-topped substitute set up the last-gasp winner. Unfortunately for Arsenal it was a case of, for Perry read Ashley, as Grimes whipped in a superb cross from the right to give Stein the chance to edge in front of Adams and seal the comeback. After that, a stunned Arsenal barely had time to kick off again before it was all over and the country cousins from Bedfordshire began to celebrate their first-ever Wembley triumph (shades of Ipswich 1978). As the dejected and defused Gunners trooped off, how Nigel Winterburn must have rued the day he had theatrically taunted Brian McClair in front of a television audience of millions: the Scot's high-and-wide penalty miss in the dying minutes of the Fifth Round FA Cup tie at Highbury may have been decisive on the day (if McClair had scored, United would have drawn level after having been two down at half-time) but at least it wasn't in a Cup Final at Wembley!

Winterburn, though, would enjoy plenty of glory days at Arsenal and the erring full-back was soon forgiven. Footballers as ferociously determined as the Nuneaton-born hard man are a rare breed indeed and after some early teething problems at Highbury, mainly caused by having to play out of position on the right, Winterburn was soon demonstrating the unwavering consistency that had made him Wimbledon Player of the Year an astonishing four times in a row before arriving at Highbury. He would go on to become the only Arsenal player who was ever-present in both Championship-winning seasons. Less fortuituously, poor Gus Caesar would always have to live with the ignominy of his one fleeting appearance centre-stage.

As it turned out, the Wembley setback was only a minor hiccup in George Graham's long-term plans and, as the season drew to a close, the manager could allow himself a quiet pat on the back for Arsenal's progress in his first two campaigns. Just before Christmas he had secured a massive festive bonus for the club when Tony Adams, David Rocastle, Michael Thomas, Paul Merson and Perry Groves all signed new long-term contracts; at the same time Paul Davis also agreed on an extension to his existing deal. Graham was well aware of the dire consequences of letting home-grown stars escape. The still fresh in the memory departures of Liam Brady and Frank Stapleton had been a hammer-blow that Arsenal had taken years – the year until Graham arrived at the club, that is – to recover from.

At the same time, Graham recognised that after eighteen months at the club, and having taken a long hard look at what he already had, it was now time to bring in three or four fresh faces to add to the likes of Smith, Winterburn and Richardson, his first major buys. By the end of the season, Lee Dixon and Brian Marwood had both made their first appearances in the side. The 23-year-old Dixon had arrived unheralded from Stoke for £350,000 in January, while Marwood – a 28-year-old bundle of energy who Graham compared to his team-mate from the Double side, George Armstrong – had finally arrived from Sheffield Wednesday in March after an eighteen-month chase. Steve Bould would follow Dixon from the Potteries in the close season and along with the emerging Paul Merson would complete the first Championship jigsaw. As the season closed, Arsenal's victory in the FA Youth Cup Final threw up further names that would play a big part in Arsenal's future, though the likes of Kevin Campbell, David Hillier and Stephen Morrow would have to wait a while yet to make their mark.

Arsenal eventually finished sixth in the League, a massive 24 points behind the champions Liverpool. It was a performance that, on paper at least, didn't present much of an improvement from the Neill/Howe years. But a quiet revolution had taken place at Highbury: the mainstays of Don Howe's side were either gone (Woodcock, Nicholas, Robson, Anderson, Mariner, Caton, Allinson) or were on their way. Kenny Sansom, who was approaching 30, had seen the writing on the wall the day Winterburn arrived; the 30-year-old Graham Rix had been granted a free transfer after two injury-plagued years; and the 29-year-old Steve Williams had fallen down the pecking order with the emergence of Thomas as a midfield talent. By the time the 88/89 season kicked off, the team would well and truly be 'George Graham's Arsenal'.

149

BY GEORGE . . .

'I hope there'll be a difference this season . . . that if we get to the top, we'll last the whole distance instead of fading out as we did toward the end of last season. I've put a lot of trust in our young players, who've matured rapidly because of their experiences last year. Young players inevitably suffer ups and downs as they're learning the game. But if you believe they're the future of the club you keep faith with them. The mixture of our young players, allied with a solid base of experience – plus the occasional judicious buy – will put us on the right lines for many years to come.

'When I buy, the player must be right for Arsenal, not just in terms of ability, but in his attitude. We've built a great team spirit here and I intend to sign players who'll fit into that pattern – not disrupt it.'

Year two kicks off with George still hedging his bets
in the transfer stakes.

'With almost a third of the season gone, I'm delighted at the way we've bounced back after a disappointing start. We are tucked in nicely near the top. What we have to do is keep up our successful sequence, and wait for a slip from the teams above. That's what happened in 1971 when we last won the Championship.'

Looking back and forward with Arsenal lying third behind Liverpool
(October 1987).

'It was a shame our record-breaking run of victories had to come to an end – but winning the Championship is far more important to us than setting any records. All successful teams have a few poor games over the course of the season. If you could plan a Championship campaign to go how you wanted, you'd choose to have a strong start, your patchy games in mid-season and then peak again for a strong finish.'

After consecutive November defeats by Southampton and Watford.

'I'd like our forwards to be scoring more often. But I'm not going to get too alarmed about the situation. I've always emphasised that we should be scoring from every position – and that all-round power has made us one of the First Division's highest scorers this season. That's a healthier set-up than teams who rely on one player for the bulk of their goals.'

Coming up to Christmas, Rocastle, Richardson, Thomas and Davis
share the goals around as the forwards prove alarmingly shot-shy.

'Michael Thomas did a super job, first in midfield, then in the centre of defence, full-back, midfield, centre-back . . . He's like Captain Marvel. I'm just wondering what he'd be like if we played him up-front!'

After the Thomas-inspired FA Cup victory over Manchester United.

'Now I'm building the squad I want – with intense competition for places – it's inevitable that some weeks, good players will be sitting on the bench or playing in the reserves. That's part of being involved with a successful club. When players sign a contract, they sign for the club – not for the first team every week! Of course I expect players to be disappointed if they're left out. Then it's up to them to show me they should be in the side. It's the only way. I should know – I was dropped at least once every year during my playing career!

After adding Brian Marwood to his growing squad.

'We're still inconsistent. When we're on a good run, our momentum keeps us flying. But when we lose, it takes us a while to put our game together again. That's a problem we're bound to face, with so many youngsters in the team, many of whom are still maturing at the top level. I've heard all the talk about us starting Wembley favourites – and dismissed it. In recent Wembley finals the underdogs have an excellent record. I know Luton have suffered major disappointments in the FA Cup and the Simod Cup but our recent results have been nothing to boast about either. I expect Luton to be resolute and I'm anticipating a close game.'

A very prophetic George on the eve of the League Cup Final.

'Naturally, we were all very disappointed at the Littlewoods Cup Final result. It took us an hour to get started. But in the 20 minutes when we hit form, we made more than enough chances to have clinched the trophy for the second year running. If we'd managed a third goal when we led 2-1, that would have killed the game. Andy Dibble made a super save from Nigel Winterburn's well-placed penalty kick and he was clearly the man of the match, also making great saves to foil Alan Smith and Martin Hayes – and twice the woodwork came to his aid. Once again we only played in spasms. We're still not putting our best form together for 90 minutes. We need to sustain our productive spells for much longer, if we're to be consistently successful.

'When I was a younger player at Aston Villa, Joe Mercer always used to say that we should treat victory and defeat with the same dignity, and try and learn from them both. I'm sure we'll have gained a lot from Sunday's experience. I'm equally sure that we'll be back again at Wembley soon. It would have been a terrific finale to the season to have retained the Littlewoods Cup. But, taking the long-term view, I'm still very happy with the way the club is progressing. We're already the main force in London football. We're building a strong squad. Our ultimate aim is to win the Championship. The way we're developing – with two or three new faces – we can compete for the title next season.'

George looking forward after Wembley disappointment.

Charlie Nicholas: The Legend

by Jeff King (first published in *One-Nil Down, Two-One Up*,
January 1988)

Bonnie Prince Charlie, darling of the North Bank, enigma. The day Charlie Nicholas made his debut at Highbury, on a glorious sun-baked afternoon against Luton, an instant bond was forged. It wasn't just the sense of expectancy (that's normal with a big name debutant), there was something less tangible in the air. There was a feeling of goodwill which people normally reserve for one of their own, as if the 39,000 fans all had a son making his debut.

Four wonderful, teasing, fretful and ultimately frustrating years later, the goodwill largely remains, though the marriage, which for so long resembled an extended honeymoon, is finally over. The question remains, why does such widespread affection persist? Let's face it, Charlie has flattered to deceive, and ultimately failed to deliver, far more often than not. Even his most fervent fans would be hard-pushed to make a case for him as a consistently good footballer, let alone a great one. His flaws are legend: uncompetitive, unathletic and erratic, often a mere spectator when the going gets tough and one of the slowest players ever to grace top-class football. If he has a change of pace, it's from sluggish to snail-like. His capacity to tackle is non-existent, his ability in the air not better, and for a striker, he's never scored prolifically in the First Division. So what has he got?

I think we've got two things here. Firstly, there's his personality, his charisma, and secondly, there's his ability to do that something a bit special – something that most footballers could never visualise, and even if they could, would never attempt. And of course the two things are inextricably linked.

A well-known East End philosopher and Millwall fan was fond of saying to me of a mutual friend: 'That geezer is so warm you could fry an egg on him.' And warmth is what Charlie has in abundance. It's not easy to define but it's easy to recognise. Take the Littlewoods Cup Final and Barry Davies's spontaneous reaction to Arsenal's equalising goal: 'It's Charlie!'

Can you imagine how incongruous 'It's Ian!' or 'It's Kenny!' would sound? Bryan Robson is England captain, but he isn't a household name or an instantly recognisable face outside football circles. Yet everybody knows Charlie.

Whatever warmth is, George Best epitomised it; that something that makes everyone want to be your friend, a quality that engenders something approaching protective sentiments. To paraphrase the writer Jack Kerouac: 'Most of all I love those mad people, mad to give, mad to live.' George was like that of course, he may have been wayward, but for all his faults you rarely meet anyone with a bad word for him. And he recognises a kindred spirit, too. He's gone on record as a big, big fan of Charlie's.

I used to feel sorry for George Best – in the same way perhaps, that people feel sorry for Charlie – such a tragic waste. Then one day I realised it wasn't George I was sorry for but myself. Denied, prematurely, of the pleasure of wallowing in the glow of his unique footballing talent. George was, quite simply, *the* Best. I should feel sorry for him: fêted, idolised, rich, handsome, as much an icon of the swinging 60s as the Beatles. Living a boozy existence, surrounded by gorgeous women and even today living a luxurious life, despite the fact he doesn't seem to have done any obvious work for ten years. What a terrible life! OK, he's had his problems, but I should be so bloody lucky.

For much the same reasons as George Best, Charlie Nicholas is good copy. 'Champagne Charlie' has filled many a back page in the tabloids for want of a better story; a godsend in a modern game that is hardly bristling with colourful characters. In reality, Charlie is a pretty normal young Scot from Glasgow living in London, with a few bob in his pocket, a taste for the pop, and an eye for the ladies. In fact, just a normal single bloke. But in an age of identikit footballers with the detached in Hertfordshire, teen-age sweetheart as wife, and 2.5 kids, he sticks out like a sore thumb.

The fact that he occasionally acts like a bear with a sore head only accentuates the difference: 'Oi! Heard about Charlie slapping that bird in the chip shop in Ibiza?' Giggle giggle, nudge nudge. Like the naughty kid at school who the teacher has to reprimand but can't bring himself to dislike. Mischievous is the word that springs to mind.

Charlie could hardly be described as a players' player in the strictest sense of the term, but as Kenny Sansom makes clear in his recent record of the 86/87 season, his presence will be sadly missed. His bubbly personality and sense of humour made him as popular with the players and staff at Highbury as with the supporters, and particularly the kids, in public. When the media and fans were singing his praises he never suffered from an inflated ego, and when things were going badly there was no wounded sense of revenge, he was always the same Charlie.

Important as his personality is, though, it would mean nothing if it wasn't for the way Charlie plays football. When he's on song, something extraordinary is expected of him every time he gets the ball. A football fan's choice of favourite player tends to reflect the way they like to see the game played rather than who they think is the best player. At an inferior level, most of us have played football ourselves along the lines of a Brian Talbot or a Peter Reid. This is not to belittle two fine footballers, but nobody pays five quid to see bustle and harry for 90 minutes or, if they do, it's because their heart is with Halifax or Stockport, and their tribal instincts overcome such aesthetic carpings. Even Gary Lineker – to cite England's favourite son – very rarely does anything that looks spectacular. His ability is to make the difficult seem easy.

What makes Charlie – or a Best, an Osgood or a Worthington – different from the rest is the capacity to do that something out of the ordinary. That little touch which you'd never see on Hackney Marshes, of which very few professionals can say 'I could have done that', let alone the punter on the terraces. I remember one particular game against Hereford on a freezing night at Highbury in 1985. Against *who*? Yes, Hereford. But don't mock, the opposition is sometimes irrelevant. What is television's most replayed eulogy to George Best? Six goals against Northampton, that's what. And no one mocks that. Against Hereford it all came together. Seven goals, of which Charlie scored one and was the architect of four more. All the little tricks were on show that night. The jinks, the shuffles, the drop of the shoulder that leaves defenders lunging at thin air. The back-heels, the dummies and, above all, that lovely delicacy of touch; the weight on the passes married with peripheral vision. It was often said of Charlie that his problem was he was always thinking two or three steps ahead of his Arsenal team-mates, an argument that holds more than a grain of truth. Kenny Dalglish had a wonderful decade at Liverpool as the Kop's undisputed idol but, for me, he was never better than in the glorious Indian summer of his career, when he had Ian Rush, lightning of foot and instinct, to take advantage of his magisterial touch and vision. Charlie never had that kind of quality beside him, for which we can only be sorry. It's perhaps ironic that, when it really mattered, the sometimes shot-shy Scot outmastered the king of grubby goals at his own game, to bring the Littlewoods Cup to Highbury.

Everyone has their own particular memories of Charlie. The goals against Tottenham in his first season spring to mind, especially that dribble at Highbury – like the leading man who stinks in rehearsal only to shine on opening night, Charlie's timing was impeccable. And what about the memorable free-kicks against Grimsby on frozen Humberside, a scorcher against Leicester at Highbury, or that cheeky 40-yard lob into the North Bank goal against Chelsea – hit from within spitting distance of the dug-out, probably something no other player in Britain would have even dreamed of attempting. And has anyone seen a goal like his debut juggle and lob for Scotland? Most of all, though, I remember the reaction of the North Bank that night against Hereford. Towards the end, even the cynics and the wizened old so-and-sos were reduced to looking at each other and merely shaking their heads in a mixture of disbelief and approbation. Warm, despite the cold, happy in the knowledge they were witnessing something very special; luxuriating in the reflection of Charlie's wizardry.

Of course, Charlie's rapport with the Arsenal fans is legend and, despite his failings, it was only a few desolate souls, the hard and embittered, who ever really turned against him. There are moments aplenty that encapsulate the unique bond. A goal at Villa in the League Cup – some Arsenal fans are isolated in the Holt End, surrounded by hostile Brummies, but of course Charlie spots them. After scoring with a typically audacious solo effort, he rushes towards them, goes down on one knee with a flourish, and salutes them like a conquering hero waiting to be knighted ... Saint Charles indeed.

In that same season – before Don Howe's demise – there was a game against Spurs at White Hart Lane. Charlie has given the Gunners a 1-0 half-time lead with a shot that arrowed like a bullet across Ray Clemence and into the Park Lane net, right in front of the Arsenal faithful. But it's an interchange from half-time that sticks in the mind. After offering a shot of whisky to all and sundry, a total stranger in front of me spent almost the entire break shaking his head and mumbling, 'You dream about this, don't you? Dream about it'. You didn't need a post-graduate degree in Freudian analysis to realise what he was talking about – not seeing the ball hit the Park Lane net (sweet), or even beating Spurs on their patch (sweeter). No, he was talking specifically about Charlie, and only Charlie, doing the business in the one way that really matters (sweetest).

Almost as memorable, if only for its absurdity, was Charlie's goal against Birmingham in January 1984, his first at Highbury. We had waited and waited, the critics had had a field day, whilst opposing fans gloated. In a terrible game, on a horrible afternoon, against even worse opposition, Charlie's goal produced a response of rapture and relief. As if 25,000 people surfaced from underwater and let out their breath at the same time.

Rarely has a goal been greeted so joyously: 'Charlie! Charlie! Charlie! Charlie!' For a full five minutes the chanting continued and not just the North Bank choir, but all round Highbury. Never has a meaningless penalty been celebrated with such abandon!

It's highly unlikely Charlie will re-create this rapport with another crowd. He'll be fêted, but it won't be the same. Being a Scot who once wore the green of Celtic had a lot to do with it, given Highbury's catchment area, populated by many a son of Dublin and Glasgow. Beyond that, the crowds that flock to Finsbury Park and Arsenal every other Saturday for nine months of the year have their own distinct flavour. More than any other London ground, Highbury attracts the kind of fan that could identify and empathise with Charlie's particular brand of irreverence and style. Characterised by that peculiar blend of the cosmopolitan and the North London wide boy, Arsenal's lads had a mirror-image in their main-man – somebody they could identify with as a person as well as a player. I doubt very much whether a crowd as fickle as Tottenham's would have stuck by Charlie. David Speedie was a bigger idol at Stamford Bridge than Pat Nevin, which speaks volumes, and the more cynical repartee of the West Ham fans would surely have seen them turn on Charlie in the end. And the fact that Arsenal teams haven't exactly been overflowing with gifted individuals in recent years meant that Charlie would always enjoy more extended goodwill amongst Arsenal devotees.

Football used to be described as the panacea of the working classes. The theory was that if the plebs aired their pent-up emotions at Highbury, St James Park or wherever on a Saturday afternoon, they were less likely to turn their energies to more subversive outbursts. Whatever stands as the panacea of the masses in the late twentieth century (shopping malls? video? computer games?), it certainly isn't football. Nonetheless, it still remains our national sport and the world's game, despite the knockers. A wise man once said that apart from real landmarks in a lifetime – births, weddings, etc. – football provides many people with their best times and fondest memories. Maybe not often enough, but Charlie Nicholas provided more memories than most, and will continue to provide them, even though he's finally moved on.

George Graham is doing a wonderful job at Highbury and I have no doubts he will restore the rather tarnished prestige of Arsenal Football Club in the not too distant future. Certainly, it is very difficult to question his way of doing things. Nonetheless, deep down, there are a lot of Arsenal fans who are sorry Charlie can't be a part of it. To be among 30,000 or 40,000 human beings sharing a positive emotion is a great feeling and one of the main attractions of going to watch football live rather than sitting at home and watching games on TV. At its very best it inspires a warm glow. There is no doubt about it, Highbury will be a colder place without Charlie Nicholas.

FOOTBALL LEAGUE DIVISION ONE 87/88

Final League position: 6th
Average attendance: 29,902

Liverpool	(h)	1-2 Davis
Manchester United	(a)	0-0
Queens Park Rangers	(a)	0-2
Portsmouth	(h)	6-0 Smith 3, Rocastle, Davis, Adams
Luton Town	(a)	1-1 Davis
Nottingham Forest	(a)	1-0 Smith
Wimbledon	(h)	3-0 Thomas (penalty), Smith, Rocastle
West Ham United	(h)	1-0 Sansom
Charlton Athletic	(a)	3-0 Groves, Thomas, Adams
Oxford United	(h)	2-0 Davis, Williams
Tottenham Hotspur	(a)	2-1 Rocastle, Thomas
Derby County	(h)	2-1 Richardson, Thomas (penalty)
Newcastle United	(a)	1-0 Smith
Chelsea	(h)	3-1 Richardson 2, og
Norwich City	(a)	4-2 Rocastle 2, Thomas, Groves
Southampton	(h)	0-1
Watford	(a)	0-2
Sheffield Wednesday	(h)	3-1 Richardson, Groves, Merson
Coventry City	(a)	0-0
Everton	(h)	1-1 Rocastle
Nottingham Forest	(h)	0-2
Wimbledon	(a)	1-3 Quinn
Portsmouth	(a)	1-1 Smith
Queens Park Rangers	(h)	0-0
Liverpool	(a)	0-2
Manchester United	(h)	1-2 Quinn
Luton Town	(h)	2-1 Thomas, Rocastle
Charlton Athletic	(h)	4-0 Merson 2, Smith, Thomas
Tottenham Hotspur	(h)	2-1 Smith, Groves
Newcastle United	(h)	1-1 Groves
Derby County	(a)	0-0
Oxford United	(a)	0-0
Chelsea	(a)	1-1 og
Norwich City	(h)	2-0 Smith, Groves
Southampton	(a)	2-4 og, Davis
West Ham United	(a)	1-0 Thomas
Watford	(h)	0-1
Sheffield Wednesday	(a)	3-3 Merson 2, Smith
Coventry City	(h)	1-1 Marwood (penalty)
Everton	(a)	2-1 Thomas, Hayes

FA Cup 87/88

Third Round:
Millwall (h) 2-0 Hayes, Rocastle

Fourth Round:
Brighton (a) 2-1 Richardson, Groves

Fifth Round:
Manchester United (h) 2-1 Smith, og

Sixth Round:
Nottingham Forest (h) 1-2 Rocastle

League Cup 87/88

Second Round:
Doncaster Rovers (a) 3-0 Groves, Smith, Williams

Doncaster Rovers (h) 1-0 Rocastle

Third Round:
AFC Bournemouth (h) 3-0 Thomas (penalty), Smith, Richardson

Fourth Round:
Stoke City (h) 3-0 O'Leary, Richardson, Rocastle

Fifth Round:
Sheffield Wednesday (a) 1-0 Winterburn

Semi-Final 1st leg:
Everton (a) 1-0 Groves

Semi-Final 2nd leg:
Everton (h) 3-1 Thomas, Rocastle, Smith

Final (Wembley):
Luton 2-3 Hayes, Smith

Appearances

	League	FA Cup	League Cup	Total
John Lukic	40	4	8	52
David Rocastle	40	4	8	52
Tony Adams	39	4	8	51
Alan Smith	36+3	3	8	47+3
Kenny Sansom	34	4	8	46
Michael Thomas	36+1	2	7	45+1
Perry Groves	28+6	3+1	7+1	38+8
Steve Williams	29	2	5	36
Paul Davis	28+1	0+1	5+1	33+3
Kevin Richardson	24+5	4	6+1	34+6
David O'Leary	23	4	6	33
Martin Hayes	17+10	3+1	3+2	23+13
Gus Caesar	17+5	0	2+1	19+6
Nigel Winterburn	16+1	4	4	24+1
Paul Merson	7+8	1	0+1	8+9
Graham Rix	7+3	1+1	2	10+4

	League	FA Cup	League Cup	Total
Niall Quinn	6+5	1+1	1+2	8+8
Lee Dixon	6	0	0	6
Brian Marwood	4	0	0	4
Charlie Nicholas	3	0	0	3
Kevin Campbell	0+1	0	0	0+1

Goal-scorers

	League	FA Cup	League Cup	Total
Alan Smith	11	1	4	16
David Rocastle	7	2	3	12
Michael Thomas	9	0	2	11
Perry Groves	6	1	2	9
Kevin Richardson	4	1	2	7
Paul Davis	5	0	0	5
Paul Merson	5	0	0	5
Martin Hayes	1	1	1	3
Tony Adams	2	0	0	2
Niall Quinn	2	0	0	2
Steve Williams	1	0	1	2
Brian Marwood	1	0	0	1
Kenny Sansom	1	0	0	1
David O'Leary	0	0	1	1
Nigel Winterburn	0	0	1	1

Season's Review 1988/89

'It's up for grabs now . . .'

With the possible exception of *Billy's Boots*, football fiction is seldom more extraordinary than fact. Yet the climax to the 88/89 season would have been greeted with cries of 'unbelievable' even if it had appeared in the pages of *Boys' Own* itself. Arsenal's first Championship triumph for 18 long years may have actually been about a long haul over 38 matches, but it will always remain synonymous with that single moment in the dying seconds at Anfield, when Michael Thomas's goal sent half of North London into raptures and left football lovers everywhere – except perhaps on the Kop and in the other half of North London – with a moment they will always enthuse about.

The Gunners' season had started in similarly spectacular fashion; the 5-1 thrashing of Wimbledon at Plough Lane on the opening day was an early sign of things to come, for at the death, Arsenal's away record, and more specifically away goals, would prove decisive. Brian Marwood, who had arrived quietly from Sheffield Wednesday at the back end of the previous season, started the new term in revelatory form on the wing, his enthusiastic and insistent prompting helping Alan Smith to strike an early vein of goals that would continue steadily all season.

In the early games, the rearguard in general, and Tony Adams and David O'Leary in particular, were in uncharacteristically generous mood, though in Adams' defence, he may have been suffering from a European Championship hangover. Bobby Robson's team had gone to West Germany on the back of a great qualifying campaign and were well-fancied to put an end to England's barren record in the competition. But three defeats in as many games sent England scampering back home with their tails between their legs. Back in England, they were met by the predictable hunt for scapegoats. And surprise, surprise! Tony Adams was one of the fall-guys – in the wake of the Holland game in particular, he had been pilloried by the Press after an inspired Marco Van Basten had scored a hat-trick. The fact that the Dutchman was at the time the best forward in the world by some

162

distance, and was capable of giving any defender the runaround on his day, was a fact that conveniently eluded the geniuses of the tabloid Press.

Whatever the reasons, Adams and O'Leary started off the season looking like a couple on *Blind Date*. The misunderstanding and confusion that provoked the 3-2 defeat at home to Aston Villa – on a day when Arsenal played brilliantly going forward, only to bestow assorted free gifts at the back – was about par for the course. Fortunately, the mini-crisis proved fleeting, and the introduction of a fresh face at the back in the shape of the ice-cool Steve Bould saw the miserly ways of old restored. The Adams/Bould partnership clicked immediately, and with the Lee Dixon/Nigel Winterburn tandem settling in at full-back (Kenny Sansom had started the season on the transfer list and by Christmas was on his way to Newcastle for a cut-price £300,000, while Michael Thomas was now a fully-fledged midfielder). Arsenal's soon-to-become-legendary back four was swiftly looking as solid as a rock. Behind the back four, Lukic was growing more confident by the game. The giant goalkeeper had arrived at Highbury in 1983 with a reputation as one of the most promising keepers in the country. Initially, though, he had a difficult time of it as the evergreen Pat Jennings refused to budge. And when the legendary Irishman did finally bow out, the contender to the throne almost inevitably suffered in the immense shadow of his predecessor. But at last Lukic was starting to show the kind of consistent form that would make him a firm favourite at Highbury, combining a new assertiveness with his always peerless shot-stopping ability. Over the next couple of years it would be a mystery why John Lukic never got a look-in in the England stakes, especially when the resolutely ordinary Chris Woods was a fixture in the squad.

With firm foundations re-established, by Boxing Day Arsenal were top and looking like serious contenders. Was it too good to be true? In February and March the team began to stutter, and the first mutterings about a false dawn for the third successive year could be heard. Michael Thomas, so influential early on, went off the boil and the long-term absence of Paul Davis left a creative void in midfield. The lack of cover up front became apparent when both the experienced Brian Marwood, whose early zeal had proved so contagious, and the young Paul Merson, began to look jaded. Luckily, Alan Smith was still scoring, while Tony Adams, David Rocastle and Nigel Winterburn – the three players who best expressed the *esprit de corps* that Graham had successfully instilled in his players – were all running into magnificently determined form as the final hurdles beckoned. Still, without quite cracking up as the critics suggested (Arsenal never lost consecutive games) points were being frittered away, especially at Highbury. Predictably, Norwich's spirited challenge faltered, but Liverpool were closing ominously, putting together a run either side of the Hillsborough tragedy that was formidable even by their own standards.

Then with just eight games to go, George Graham shuffled his pieces in unexpected and headline-grabbing fashion. The sweeper system was criticised at the time for being defensive, but in fact it was designed to give freer rein to the attacking inclinations of Dixon and Winterburn while simultaneously unloading the defensive burden from Rocastle. The gamble appeared to pay off, with a 5-0 hammering of Norwich the high point of a five-game unbeaten burst which took the Gunners to within spitting distance of the title.

But Graham's men stuttered again, and in the space of a few crucial days the nerve finally seemed to crack. Perhaps inexperience was taking its toll? Lest anybody forget, the likes of Adams, Merson, Rocastle, Thomas, Hayes and Groves were still unusually young and inexperienced to provide the nucleus of a Championship challenging side, let alone a Championship-*winning* one. Not since Arsenal themselves had done the Double had a side so reliant on youngsters been in serious contention – Ray Kennedy, Charlie George and Eddie Kelly were all still teenagers when the 70/71 campaign kicked off and Pat Rice was just 21. Contriving to surrender five points at Highbury to Derby and Wimbledon in the final two home games, a Championship that had been there for the taking seemed to be lost. George Graham had always maintained, in public at least, that the title race would stretch right to the end of the season. Glaswegian's bluff or not, to the end it went: Liverpool's 5-1 drubbing of West Ham in their penultimate game left Arsenal needing to go to Fortress Anfield for the last 90 minutes of the season and win by two clear goals to snatch the title . . . on goal difference. Anything less, and the Championship would stay on Merseyside.

By defeating Everton in the previous Saturday's FA Cup Final, Liverpool went into the decisive game not only on the back of a 24-game unbeaten run in the League, but chasing the Double as well. Given that kind of form, and the veritable lion's den nature of Arsenal's task, few outside Highbury gave George Graham's men a prayer. On the afternoon of the game the bookmakers were offering 16-1 against Arsenal winning 2-0. 'You haven't got a prayer, Arsenal' proclaimed the *Daily Mirror*. Nor was history on the Londoners' side; Arsenal had lost their last seven First Division games at Anfield, and they hadn't managed two goals in a game there in fifteen years. But daunting as these precedents may have been, they were just statistics, and historical ones at that. In Arsenal's favour was a more recent and potentially much more relevant factor; Liverpool had played eight games in just 23 days in the run-in. If the game went the distance, it was always likely that Arsenal's young legs would last the pace better. Psychologically too, the pressure was on Kenny Dalglish's men. The weight of expectancy on Merseyside in the wake of the Hillsborough tragedy was enormous. The Liverpool players were well aware that for everyone connected with the club and, above all, for the supporters, this particular Championship had a far deeper significance than normal. George Graham, on the other hand, had succeeded admirably in taking the pressure off his young charges during the build-up. The last training session at London Colney before heading north was extraordinarily relaxed. According to David Rocastle, the general tone was laughter and jokes all round: 'We were mucking about even more in training than usual,' was how he described the atmosphere in the Arsenal camp. As Graham would later admit, he could hardly pretend it was just another game, but he did make sure that his players approached the game with a relish. Arsenal took the field at Anfield in a determined and positive frame of mind, conscious of their chance to make history. Liverpool may have been the better team and they almost certainly had more gifted players, but if the going got tough, Arsenal's indefatigable spirit was always lurking just below the surface.

No sooner had the game kicked off than the TV and radio pundits again laid into Graham's misunderstood and much maligned sweeper system, accusing Arsenal of stringing 'five across the back' and playing defensively. In fact, it was Liverpool who were guilty of being over-cautious, playing like they were more than happy to lose by the odd goal as long as they took the title. Arsenal were never overawed by the occasion and with the 'young Gunners' displaying a maturity beyond their years, a captive audience (it was the first time a television audience had seen a Championship played out live) soon sensed that the outcome was anything but the foregone conclusion everyone outside Highbury had assumed. If Steve Bould's early header had not been cleared off the line by Steve Nichol maybe the game would have taken a different track; would Liverpool really have dared to defend a one-goal lead for 82 minutes? As it was, Graham was happy to go in at half-time with a clean sheet; his first maxim had been 'don't concede a goal that will make our task practically impossible'. Once Alan Smith's glancing header had put the Gunners ahead in the 52nd minute, the feeling grew that Arsenal might actually achieve the impossible dream. (With the benefit of hindsight, has anybody been able to establish exactly what the Liverpool players were protesting about?) However, when Michael Thomas missed a gift of a chance with just fifteen minutes to go, even the most optimistic in the Arsenal camp must have been about ready to throw in the towel.

165

Liverpool were certainly ready to administer the last rites. As the game entered its dying seconds and with play held up to allow the Arsenal physio, Gary Lewin, to massage some life into Kevin Richardson's cramp-ridden legs, Steve 'one minute' McMahon could be seen geeing up his team-mates for one final effort. Meanwhile, John Barnes and John Aldridge allowed themselves a celebratory smack of hands, NBA style. When the game restarted, it was Barnes who made what proved to be a fatal mistake; presented with the chance to run the ball into the far and wide reaches of Arsenal territory and out of danger, he rashly opted to try to dribble his way into the box. Richardson of all people, dredging one last effort out of his weary legs, intercepted and nudged the ball back to John Lukic. With 92 minutes looming on the clock, the keeper swiftly threw the ball to Lee Dixon at right-back. The rest is freeze-framed on the memory: Dixon knocked it forward to Alan Smith, making himself available as a willing target for one last, crucial time in the season. The man whose goals had done so much to bring Arsenal this close, and whose opening goal on the night has often been overlooked amidst the attention focused on the dramatic finish, deftly controlled the ball before knocking it on to Michael Thomas who was off on a characteristic gallop towards Liverpool's box. Once there, fortune favoured the brave as the ball ricocheted off Steve Nichol and Thomas found himself, almost unbelievably, with only Grobbelaar to beat. As time stood still, Brian Moore announced in papal fashion, 'It's up for grabs now', the watching millions screamed 'Shoooooooot!', and, of course, after what seemed an eternity, Mickey did ... At 21, the coolest dude in town casually dropped a shoulder as if making a move on a crowded dance-floor (rather than holding centre-stage before the eyes of a transfixed nation) before almost flippantly knocking it past a flummoxed Grobbelaar and setting off on a handstand into history. Collective disbelief was written on the faces of the 41,718 Anfield spectators as a stunned Liverpool kicked off, but any notion that Thomas might justifiably be somewhere up in the clouds after his *pièce de résistance* were soon dispelled as the youngster charged back into defence to make sure nobody stole his headlines. George Graham must have been willing him to boot the ball into the crowd as the game agonisingly drew to a close, but Thomas was now on a different plane as he pounced on a loose ball and dribbled past Peter Beardsley into his own box before nonchalantly easing the ball back to Lukic. And to think that he had hardly trained all week with a knee ligament problem and, if Paul Davis had been fit, he wouldn't even have played.

For the first time since 1971, and only the second time in 37 years,

Arsenal were champions. It had taken the last 91-and-a-half minutes of the longest and most dramatic season ever for Arsenal to seal their triumph, but who was counting? As Thomas's baseball cap would remind everybody wo days later when Arsenal paraded the trophy before a quarter of a million people in Islington, 'MICKEY DID IT', and in doing so he had helped George Graham become only the fifth man in English football history to win a title medal as player and manager. Thomas's goal, scored as the game and the season moved into injury time, left Arsenal and Liverpool with identical won, drawn and lost records, and locked together on goal difference. The delicate balance only shifted in the Gunners' favour because they had scored eight goals more. By a supreme irony, 'Boring, boring Arsenal' had grabbed the title thanks to their superior firepower.

The victory at Anfield was memorable and then some. Neither the lucky few who were there or the millions watching it on TV (more incidentally, than had watched the all-Merseyside Cup Final the previous week) would ever forget it. Memorable performance? Undoubtedly. For Arsenal to go to Anfield in such circumstances and win was achievement enough. That they totally outplayed *the* club side of modern times was even more praiseworthy. Nobody, but nobody, could deny that Arsenal were worthy winners on the night. After the game, George Graham was quick to place the victory, and his part in securing it, in its historical context: 'I want to join the Highbury Hall of Fame alongside great managers like Herbert Chapman, George Allison, Tom Whittaker and Bertie Mee. We have laid a foundation of belief at Highbury. If you lose hope, or lose belief, you may as well get out of football. Tonight was a fairy tale, the unpredictable that makes us all love football.'

Amidst the post-match revelry on the pitch at Anfield, it's unlikely that the arch-realist Graham bothered to pinch himself to make sure it was all really happening. But what about the rest of the season? Was it really that memorable? In the sense that Arsenal ended an eighteen-year famine to bring the Championship back to the Marble Halls, yes. George Graham would quite properly say that it was all about the end result and that any other assessment was just so much hot air. To which the Arsenal fans, starved of success for so long, would chorus 'and so say all of us!' But scratch beneath the surface gloss of the results and it is arguable that much of Arsenal's football in the 88/89 season was at best functional and at worst downright mediocre. Most frustrating of all for Arsenal fans, was the side's tendency to play well in brief spells instead of imposing themselves over 90 minutes. The most typical menu of the day offered short bursts of inspiration interspersed, or overwhelmed, by long periods of mediocrity and/or lack of ambition. At Highbury in particular, there were few performances truly worthy of champions: the only really convincing win was the 5-0 deflowering of Norwich's title aspirations. Otherwise, victories tended to be etched out, at times agonisingly so. The Norwich game apart, only against relegated Middlesbrough did the Gunners manage to score more than two goals. At the time, Graham argued that even the weakest First Division sides were capable of making a tight game of it at Highbury. On their own patch, teams were expected to open up and make a game of it, but they would come to Highbury with the sole intention of shutting up shop and defending – this was bound to spoil the game as a spectacle, Graham claimed. Clearly you don't win Championships without digging in on the bad days; but even though Graham's protestations contained a grain of truth, they couldn't possibly justify the poor fare that was served up for most of the season at Highbury.

On the plus side, without playing great football, the ratio of quality goals was extremely high. Take your pick from this selection of striking prowess: David Rocastle's acute lob at Villa or his breathtaking individual effort against Middlesbrough; Michael Thomas's long dash and cool finish when confronted by Peter Shilton at Derby, his cracking shot against Coventry and, of course, *that* goal at Anfield; and what about Nigel Winterburn's astonishing right foot (yes, *right* foot) strike against Wimbledon? Then there was Alan Smith's volley against Norwich, Paul Merson's cool finish to a sweeping move at Everton, or Paul Davis's spectacular diving header after running practically the length of the park against Charlton.

Davis, once the butt of persistent criticism from the Arsenal fans for his inability to impose his graceful touch on the game more than fleetingly, had developed into one of the best midfield players in the country under Graham. It has often been said that his languid and laidback style make him the current Gunner who most resembles Graham the player. Like the erstwhile 'Stroller', Davis lacks pace, but he too possesses the invaluable knack of finding time and space in the most crowded midfield. He may lack the finishing power of the boss, but he is a better passer of the ball. His lengthy absence in the aftermath of the Glenn Cockerill incident was probably the main reason that Liverpool got so close at the death. A nine-match ban was excessively harsh for a player with an impeccable disciplinary record (God knows what the Southampton player could have done to provoke such an out-of-character response) but that flash of autumn madness and a subsequent thigh injury cost both Davis, poised at the time to break into the England side, and Arsenal, dear. His appalling bad luck came to a head in February. Back in the Arsenal side after suspension, he was called up to the England squad for the game against Greece, only to suffer a thigh injury in training literally minutes after hearing the good news. As fate would have it, Davis of England was never to be. With the team's only genuine playmaker limited to just twelve games, the Arsenal midfield sometimes resembled the headless chickens that Graham Taylor would later give such a bad name. With no experienced cover – Graham Rix had left for Caen on a free-transfer in the summer and Steve Williams had moved to Luton for £300,000 – a lot of responsibility fell on still very young shoulders.

The feeling at Highbury was that Michael Thomas was potentially a great player. And despite an inauspicious international debut against Saudi Arabia in November, his awe-inspiring athleticism and ability to get on the end of things after irresistible surges from deep, made him an obvious candidate to succeed Bryan Robson in the England team. Brian Marwood came on as substitute for the last nine minutes of that game, too – the sum total of his international career, as it turned out. In Riyadh, Thomas felt uncomfortable and out-of-sorts in a deeper role, saying afterwards, 'I see myself as a Bryan Robson-type going for goals, not a Ray Wilkins type.' But despite the potential, Thomas was still at the learning stage of his career, and when things were going wrong he tended to drift around on the periphery of the action. For a long spell in the second half of the season his confidence disappeared totally – the uncanny knack he developed for avoiding the ball for impossibly long periods was a tell-tale sign of a player at odds with himself. At one stage it got so bad that Arsenal fans would actually take bets during games on how long his unique form of non-contact football could last! When the season was over, George Graham admitted that he would have liked to have given the youngster a break: 'Michael Thomas went through a dodgy spell after his England debut last November. If Paul Davis had been fit, we'd have rested him, but he had to keep on playing.'

But with Davis unavailable, and no other reliable cover in midfield, Thomas had to soldier on, and thanks to the Anfield finale it was eventually a case of 'all's well that ends well'. The Arsenal fans set off on their holidays hoping that the Anfield goal and 'Steamer's' new-found hero status would help him approach the forthcoming season with renewed confidence. Alongside Thomas, the wholehearted Kevin Richardson – the only man in the squad with a Championship pedigree – had already proved a welcome addition to the team in his first season, but he lacked the vision or flair to shoulder the creative burden in midfield. With Rocastle still doing his best work down the flanks, the creative hole at the heart of midfield was very nearly expensive for Arsenal in the run-in, especially in those sterile home performances. Game after game cried out for a touch of imagination though, to be fair, the unusually poor state of the Highbury playing surface didn't help. In the second half of the season, the conditions certainly didn't lend themselves to flowing football – at one stage, the pitch was so cut up and bumpy that even a playmaker raised on the beaches of Copacabana would have struggled to do his party tricks, let alone the journeymen of more typically British mould.

As it was, strength in other departments and the formidable team-spirit proved enough to carry the handicap of a not always convincing midfield. Once again, there was a tremendous contribution from the home-grown players. The evergreen David O'Leary – winning a Championship medal an astonishing fourteen years after his League debut – and the new wave of Rocastle, Adams, Thomas and Merson were all leading players in the drama; and though Paul Davis, Niall Quinn, Gus Caesar and Martin Hayes never threatened to make the Oscar nominations for Best Supporting Actor, each played their own small part. Hayes, the top scorer in Graham's first season at the club, only managed one goal this time around, but it sure was an important one, earning a vital three points at Middlesbrough with just three games to go.

Nobody represented the Arsenal spirit better than the ever-present David Rocastle, and the First Division's youngest captain, Tony Adams. Rocastle started the season in untypically subdued mood and early on George Graham was forced to admit that, 'by his own standards "Rocky" has been a bit quiet this season'. Luckily, he just got better and better as the season progressed; few players have ever worn the red and white of Arsenal with such pride, and in those last few games, as others visibly wilted under the pressure, 'Rocky's' burning ambition and will to win was vital. For his part, Tony Adams, already the man opposing fans and the tabloid Press loved to hate, came through all the flak superbly. It may be a cliché, but he really was an old head on young shoulders and he was already being talked about as a future captain of his country. Then there was the PFA Young Player of The Year, twenty-year-old Paul Merson. Gifted and charismatic in just about equal portions, the young Londoner was not only the heir-apparent to Charlie Nicholas in the skill stakes, but was also fond of the kind of off-field activities that were guaranteed to raise a snigger amongst his peer group on the terraces, thus making him an even firmer candidate to succeed Charlie in the hearts and minds of the North Bank.

You would certainly need a long memory to recall the last Championship-winning side with so many home-grown players – six played a part in the Anfield finale – and it is to George Graham's eternal credit that he was prepared to give youth a fling, however demanding the occasion. The reliance on Highbury-produced talent was very much by design: the Scot is a firm believer that players brought up at the club will form a more solid bond than a team based on outsiders. Arsenal were also the cheapest champions of recent times by some distance – only Alan Smith at £850,000 would have registered on the Richter Scale of big money transfers.

On the tactical front, the sweeper system was to prove a successful but short-lived experiment although, to be fair, an injury to Steve Bould prevented Graham from introducing it earlier. With David O'Leary slotting comfortably behind Adams and Bould, and Dixon and Winterburn getting forward at every opportunity, the system was more akin to an adventurous 3-5-2 configuration than the ultra-defensive ploy that its critics would have had us believe. But George Graham is nothing if not a student of the game and he would have realised that a tactic that takes its name from one specialist player, the sweeper, becomes a caricature without the genuine article rather than a converted centre-half at its heart. And, quite simply, English football doesn't breed specialists *à la* Beckenbauer, Koeman or Belodedici. Arsenal's trio of Adams, Bould and O'Leary were excellent defenders, but they remained precisely that – out-and-out defenders, with neither the ability nor inclination to assume a more pivotal role in the overall scheme of things.

Tactical niceties aside, in three short years George Graham had turned the club around spectacularly. Lest anyone forget, in the barren mid-80s Arsenal were as spineless and as far away from winning titles as any recent Tottenham side you care to mention, and now look at the gulf between the two great rivals. The shifting balance of power in North London in the wake of Graham's arrival at Highbury is comparable to the increasing chasm between the Glasgow giants, as Spurs increasingly find themselves as adrift of their erstwhile rivals – on and off the pitch – as Celtic do.

The basic foundations for long-term success were now firmly established. Arsenal were an efficient, resilient, and well-balanced unit, moulded together with a healthy dose of home-grown players – all characteristics redolent of the Double side that Graham so often cited as a decisive influence. Above all, George Graham's Arsenal had acquired the very healthy habit of winning, even if their football ran the gamut of the good, the bad and the ugly.

BY GEORGE . . .

'George Graham: London Pride'
Interview with Jeff King (first appeared in *Football Today* July 1989)

Football, like all sport, is nothing if not romantic. The extent to which events on the football field matter – how much they engage and enthuse – was made clear by the euphoria that Arsenal's dramatic Championship win at Anfield provoked. There is then, irony in the fact that the manager behind the team that provided us with a moment of such drama and romance, is one of the game's most hard-headed realists. Amidst the disbelief that greeted the final whistle at Anfield, I doubt if George Graham bothered to pinch himself.

The 44-year-old Scot was an elegant inside-forward in Arsenal's last Championship-winning side, and after a tough managerial apprenticeship at Millwall is now approaching his fourth season at Highbury. The public face is one of aloofness bordering on the arrogant. In reality it is a mask that hides a fiercely protective nature towards his club and his players. According to one of his senior players, he is softer, more relaxed than his public image suggests. He is not unaware of that image, but unlike his good friend up the road at Spurs, Terry Venables, he finds the public relations side of his job at best a distraction, at worst distasteful. His is not the superficial amiability or throwaway quote beloved of the media. As he candidly and somewhat modestly admits, 'I'm no good at PR'.

We were talking at Highbury just ten days after the Anfield triumph, the atmosphere around the famous marble halls still buzzing in the aftermath, but Graham clearly had his feet firmly back on the ground. That he cares passionately about the game is obvious, but talking to him is rather like picking your way through the minefield of a political interview. He is always courteous, but at the same time cagey and defensive, eager to steer the conversation into avenues he feels appropriate. The only time the veneer of diplomacy breaks somewhat are in his asides against his *bête noire*, the tabloid Press. But first conversation turned to that most memorable of nights still so fresh in the memory. Was the euphoria largely down to where and how Arsenal ended that eighteen-year wait?

'Well, the victory wasn't just about those few seconds at Anfield, it was about being the most consistent team over the whole season. That's why it means so much, why it's the summit of every manager's ambition. The impact was because it was so unexpected to go up to Anfield and win. They had gone four-and-a-half months without losing a game whilst we had had a few hiccups, and to go to without question the best and most consistent League side in the history of the game when they are on top form and win 2-0 was a tremendous achievement.'

After the Wimbledon game there had been a feeling amongst the fans that it had slipped away. Was this shared at the club, at least deep down?

'No, I don't think so. I certainly made sure in training that we didn't think that way. We went there in a positive frame of mind.' In fact, Graham believes that needing to win had worked in Arsenal's favour. Tactically, things had worked to plan. 'In the first half we played nice sensible football. I was hoping we might score one but the most important thing was not to concede a goal. 0-0 was crucial at half-time, otherwise we were looking at three or four goals to win. Maybe Liverpool were more pleased than us at that stage but I wasn't too worried. I knew if we got an early goal in the second half, as we did, the onus would be on them. Then they tried to protect what they had, which really suited us. I was quite surprised really. Especially that the media never latched on to that, no mention of how they played. Can you imagine the stick Arsenal would have got if they had done that?'

Unlike many people, Graham had actually maintained that it would go all the way to the last couple of games. As far as he was concerned, Arsenal's great points lead had been a fixation that was never true: 'Everybody forgot about the four games Liverpool had in hand. If we had played the same amount of games there would have been more truth in it.' That is not to suggest that he wouldn't have preferred to win it by a bigger margin. Unlike the romantics among us, winning the title three or four games earlier would have provided him with more professional satisfaction, even if it had denied us the great sporting moment that Anfield produced. When the final margin is so close, how big a part does luck play? 'I'm not a great believer in luck,' he swiftly asserts. 'You make your own. I think it was Gary Player who said that the harder he practised, the luckier he got. We work very hard at Arsenal. If there is any luck going I'd say it is deserved.'

Clearly it rankles that anybody should deny his side credit. Likewise, he doesn't underplay his own role. 'Yes, you have a big influence because all your ideas and philosophy, the things you believe in, get through to the team and the way it plays and the way the club is run.' Obviously, Graham belongs to that breed of manager whose influence pervades the whole club. He admits to enjoying the different facets of the job, leaving training and putting on his managerial cap.

'I love working with the players. Coaching is one of my strengths and it gives me great satisfaction. At a club like Arsenal your time is valuable. I've only got a set time with the players in the morning so, whatever I'm putting across, I want their undivided attention. My role is like that of a teacher; I give them suggestions and it is up to them to use them as they see fit.' Somehow it is difficult to imagine any of his players actually over-looking one of his suggestions. Don Corleone's phrase, 'I'm going to make you an offer you can't refuse' immediately springs to mind! Unaware of any understatement, Graham continues the schoolteacher analogy: 'Obviously certain players don't receive information as easily as others. It's like kids; the bright ones pick things up straightaway, some take a little longer, and some fall by the wayside because they just haven't got it. But I would like to think that any team I have coached, any players, have learned a lot.' Again the almost Calvinist work ethic emerges: 'That is more important than the enjoyment of it because I want players to improve, and I want to improve myself as well.'

Here, conversation naturally turns to Graham's great tactical innovation of the season, the introduction of the sweeper system for the final run-in, a move as bold in its timing as its implementation. Clearly its success had given him a great deal of pleasure – during no part of our conversation was he more animated. At the same time, this was tinged with a sense of bit-terness that such a bold initiative hadn't been recognised. 'I thought it was very important. I was absolutely delighted, not just for myself but for the players, for the way they responded to changing a complete system which had worked well for two-and-a-half years. And yes, I could see a few of them thinking, why are we doing this? We proved a point, I think: went five games unbeaten, scored ten goals with only one against, and that an own goal. It was a great run. We keep on criticising Bobby Robson, or the so-called media do, for not experimenting, but as soon as somebody tries a change everybody thinks it is negative.' This is an allusion to the accusa-tions of negativity that greeted the move, many from people that should know better. It still rankles: 'The anti-Arsenal, the anti-George people, they said it was defensive. But I introduced the system because we have two excellent attacking full-backs, and would have introduced it sooner if Steve Bould hadn't been injured. We in fact played three at the back, never five, as people said. Unfortunately, when you play that way somebody has to drop out up front, but it all fitted to plan because Brain Marwood got injured badly. As a club we didn't get the credit for trying it so late in the season at such a vital point.'

Certainly the statistics refute the argument that Arsenal's success was based merely on a sound defence. As Graham is happy to point out, 'The most important thing to me next to winning it was finishing top goal-scorers; that gave me a hell of a lot of pleasure.' Unusually, a larger pro-portion of their goals were scored away from Highbury. Why had most of Arsenal's best performances been away? 'Well, in fact, the majority of the Championship contenders had better records away from home: Norwich's was superb, so was Liverpool's. You find that teams that are not as good as you, when they attack you on their home ground they are much more vulnerable, while at home against poorer sides it is hard to break them down.' Why, though, was this a recent phenomenon? 'Teams are getting more organised, they are also much fitter. If you put these two things together there is always a possibility you can stop teams winning. But when the onus is on teams to attack you on their home grounds it is a different ball game.'

Another of the characteristics of Arsenal's side was its youth, many of its young players home-grown talent. 'Our youth system is one of the things we are most proud of at Highbury. The big successful clubs are normally the ones who buy because they can afford it. At Arsenal they tried that and it didn't work. When you are brought into a club very young you develop a love for the club – now obviously when they become profes-sionals there is a financial aspect as well, but deep down there is still that feeling.'

Clearly Graham has an almost paternalistic concern for his young charges, and he displays an acute awareness of their vulnerability. 'You must do things nice and gradually; young players come on quickly, then blow up quickly. The thing to do is get them out of the team before they go off, because then they lose all their confidence. We all want consistency, but we have got to remember they are just young men. We want immacu-late adults and performances to match, but they still haven't reached maturity.' While quick to squash speculation about the beginning of a Graham dynasty at Highbury, he relishes enthusing about the future of his young team. 'The nice thing about this team is that it has got another 40 per cent in it. They are still young and they have already won the Cham-pionship on merit, they can certainly do it again. In your mid-20s you begin to hit your peak and if you think of Rocastle, Thomas, Adams, Merson, etc., they can only get better .. that is a lovely prospect.'

It has often been said that the failure of the Double side – a team that Graham describes as more resilient but less exciting than the current line-up – was its inability to build on that initial success. Was that a danger this time around? As usual, the response gives short shrift to an off-the-cuff analysis: 'It's easy for people to say build on it, but you can't build without better players. I want to improve my squad, but if you are going to replace a player it has to be with somebody better – whether it is 50 per cent or 5 per cent, it must be better. If those players are not available then we have to stick with what we've got'.

Of course, Graham has never been one for brandishing the chequebook willy-nilly and he avoids easy speculation about transfers. Likewise he avoids polemics with other people in the game. His dislike for such practices genuinely provokes his chagrin.

'There is a disappointing and growing tendency for football people to criticise one another in the media. Those in authority: managers, chairmen, directors, have a big part to play in stamping it out, I'm very strong on that.' At this stage I was about to venture that opinions on football were nothing if not subjective, and therefore bound to generate some controversy. Given that Graham gives the impression he would like to shoot dissenters, I desisted. He continues, 'Michael Thomas and Tony Adams came in for a lot of criticism individually that lacked dignity. For that reason I was particularly pleased for them at Anfield.'

As we neared the end of our chat, talk turned to the future again. He had now achieved his ambition of becoming only the fifth manager to lead Arsenal to the title – an experience he emphatically places above doing it as a player. Was the pressure off now? 'No, in any profession if you want to stay at the top you must handle the pressure, it is part of your ability. The salary rewards, status, etc., all stem from that. Anyway, it's nice pressure. It's lovely, we're at the top, we should be enjoying it. I hope we are going for the Championship in the last game next year.'

When George Graham says he wants to win it 'again and again' you have to take it seriously. Clearly he won't be satisfied with anything less than making a deep and lasting impression on the game. Who would bet against it?

FOOTBALL LEAGUE 88/89

Final League position: Champions
Average home gate: 35,593

Wimbledon	(a) 5-1	Smith 3, Marwood, Merson	
Aston Villa	(h) 2-3	Marwood, Smith	
Tottenham Hotspur	(a) 3-2	Winterburn, Marwood, Smith	
Southampton	(h) 2-2	Marwood (penalty), Smith	
Sheffield Wednesday	(a) 1-2	Smith	
West Ham United	(a) 4-1	Smith 2, Thomas, Rocastle	
Queens Park Rangers	(h) 2-1	Adams, Smith	
Luton Town	(a) 1-1	Smith	
Coventry City	(h) 2-0	Thomas, Adams	
Nottingham Forest	(a) 4-1	Smith, Bould, Adams, Marwood	
Newcastle United	(a) 1-0	Bould	
Middlesbrough	(h) 3-0	Merson 2, Rocastle	
Derby County	(a) 1-2	Thomas	
Liverpool	(h) 1-1	Smith	
Norwich City	(a) 0-0		
Manchester United	(h) 2-1	Thomas, Merson	
Charlton Athletic	(a) 3-2	Marwood 2 (1 penalty), Merson	
Aston Villa	(a) 3-0	Smith, Rocastle, Groves	
Tottenham Hotspur	(h) 2-0	Merson, Thomas	
Everton	(a) 3-1	Merson, Smith, Richardson	
Sheffield Wednesday	(h) 1-1	Merson	
West Ham United	(h) 2-1	Groves, Smith	
Millwall	(a) 2-1	Marwood, Smith	
Queens Park Rangers	(a) 0-0		
Coventry City	(a) 0-1		
Luton Town	(h) 2-0	Groves, Smith	
Millwall	(h) 0-0		
Nottingham Forest	(h) 1-3	Smith	
Charlton Athletic	(h) 2-2	Rocastle, Davis	
Southampton	(a) 3-1	Groves, Rocastle, Merson	
Manchester United	(a) 1-1	Adams	
Everton	(h) 2-0	Dixon, Quinn	
Newcastle United	(h) 1-0	Marwood	
Norwich City	(h) 5-0	Winterburn, Smith 2, Rocastle, Thomas	
Middlesbrough	(a) 1-0	Hayes	
Derby County	(h) 1-2	Smith	
Wimbledon	(h) 2-2	Winterburn, Merson	
Liverpool	(a) 2-0	Smith, Thomas	

FA Cup 88/89

Third Round:		Third Round replay:	
West Ham United	(a) 2-2 Merson 2	West Ham United	(h) 0-1

League Cup 88/89

Second Round 1st leg:		Third Round:	
Hull City	(a) 2-1 Winterburn, Marwood	Liverpool	(a) 1-1 Rocastle
		Third Round replay:	
Second Round 2nd leg:		Liverpool	(h) 0-0 (after extra time)
Hull City	(h) 3-0 Merson, Smith 2	2nd replay:	
		Liverpool (Villa Park)	1-2 Merson

Appearances

	League	FA Cup	League Cup	Total
John Lukic	38	2	5	45
David Rocastle	38	2	5	45
Nigel Winterburn	38	2	5	45
Tony Adams	36	2	5	43
Alan Smith	36	2	5	43
Michael Thomas	33+4	2	5	40+4
Brian Marwood	31	2	5	38
Kevin Richardson	32+2	2	3+2	37+4
Lee Dixon	31+2	1	5	37+2
Paul Merson	29+8	2	4	35+8
Steve Bould	26+4	1	5	32+4
David O'Leary	26	2	0	28
Paul Davis	11+1	0+2	2	13+3
Perry Groves	6+15	0+2	1+1	7+18
Martin Hayes	3+14	0	0+4	3+18
Niall Quinn	2+1	0	0	2+1
Gus Caesar	2	0	0	2

Goal-scorers

	League	FA Cup	League Cup	Total
Alan Smith	23	0	2	25
Paul Merson	10	2	2	14
Brian Marwood	9	0	1	10
Michael Thomas	7	0	0	7

	League	FA Cup	League Cup	Total
David Rocastle	6	0	1	7
Tony Adams	4	0	0	4
Perry Groves	4	0	0	4
Nigel Winterburn	3	0	1	4
Steve Bould	2	0	0	2
Paul Davis	1	0	0	1
Lee Dixon	1	0	0	1
Martin Hayes	1	0	0	1
Niall Quinn	1	0	0	1
Kevin Richardson	1	0	0	1

Season's Review 1989/90

The Big Hangover

After the last-gasp exploits of Anfield and the ensuing festivities, the 89/90 season proved to be a case of the extended hangover that just wouldn't go away. Though the Gunners were still in with a mathematical chance of holding on to their title as late as mid-April the harsh reality is that a successful defence never really looked like a serious possibility, as the form of key players dipped alarmingly.

Somewhat surprisingly, George Graham chose to ignore the received wisdom about fresh blood maintaining momentum, and the new season kicked off without a single new face at Highbury. Graham had gone on record as saying he expected the youngsters who formed the backbone of the Championship-winning side to keep on improving. Maybe if Arsenal had faced the prospect of a European campaign he would have been more willing to reinforce his squad. As it was, the end of the European ban on English clubs was still a tantalising season away and Arsenal would not have to worry about competing on another front. Still, when a hectic pre-season schedule produced injuries to Steve Bould and Paul Davis, the decision to rely on 'more of the same, please' was already appearing complacent. Most of the players started the new season looking as if they were wearied by a recently finished campaign rather than invigorated by the prospect of a new one – thanks to the club apparently being more interested in exploiting new-found commercial possibilities in the wake of the Championship triumph rather than in making sensible preparation for maintaining standards on the park.

After a three-game tour of Sweden, three games at Wembley in the Makita International Tournament and the Charity Shield, and a long haul to Miami for the Zenith Data Challenge (!) against Independiente of Argentina, the season proper (*sic*) started horribly with a 4-1 defeat in a comedy of errors at Old Trafford. Arsenal's on-field antics were strictly in line with the pre-match farce provided by Chariman-never-to-be Michael Knighton's ball-juggling in front of the Stretford end. When the convalescent Adams was forced to make an early exit, 'North Sea Gus' Caesar re-emerged from the confines of the reserves to strike fear, not into the hearts of United's forwards, but into the hearts of the Arsenal fans who had travelled north hoping to see the Gunners carry on where they had left off at Anfield. If John 'the penalty-king' Lukic had not been in inspired form – his third penalty save at Old Trafford was just one of several outstanding interventions – Arsenal's start could have been even more demoralising. Just 90 minutes into the new League season, a crowing Old Trafford taunted the travelling Arsenal fans as if they were already the champions-elect. As it was, the game heralded yet another false dawn for United. Unfortunately, it would prove an all-too-reliable pointer of what Arsenal's season held in store – a bad case of the away-day blues. A striking dip in the away form that had swept Graham's team to the title meant that Arsenal's Championship defence never got out of first gear – at the death, a mere four away wins and a whacking ten defeats would make for depressing reading.

Despite the generally uninspiring football on display and amidst a somewhat half-hearted jostling for position before their rivals eventually stepped up a gear, the Gunners' typically steady home form saw them established as leaders by Christmas. They actually remained unbeaten at home until succumbing to Chelsea in mid-March but, unfortunately, the long distance travails just wouldn't go away. The Boxing Day defeat at Southampton (see footnote to season) proved to be the start of a run which yielded only two points from seven away-games and which saw eternal title-rivals Liverpool, and a David Platt-inspired Aston Villa, threaten to cast Arsenal adrift. Graham's men had earlier managed to raise their game to beat Liverpool at Highbury in the League Cup (only to bow out feebly in the very next round at Second Division Oldham) but that was a rare moment to savour amidst the mediocrity (almost as rare as the Alan Smith goal that saw off Dalglish's team that night). Given Arsenal's woeful away form, the six weeks between late January and early March without a single game at Highbury didn't help much either. That League impasse was marked by a very un-Arsenal-like surrender to Queens Park Rangers in the FA Cup – a listless performance in a 0-0 draw at Highbury followed by a tame surrender in the two-goal defeat at Loftus Road. In fact, both Cup exits were characterised by the total lack of resilience that had been an omnipresent virtue of Arsenal under Graham, even on the bad days. All hope of another successful season was finally abandoned in the space of one gloomy week in mid-April that saw Arsenal incapable of overcoming either of their two main rivals at Highbury, and thus surrendering any chance of holding on to the title.

Winning the Championship is obviously difficult enough, but as an oft-quoted managerial cliché has it, 'retaining it is even more difficult'. But notwithstanding the anticipated problems of motivation and keeping players on their toes against opponents who are after the top-dog's scalp, Arsenal's dip in fortunes was particularly alarming. So what exactly went wrong? George Graham blamed individuals for not repeating their form of the previous year, claiming that it was impossible to carry so many out-of-sorts players, a contention that was undoubtedly true, but one that begged a couple of leading questions. Wasn't it Graham's role to motivate the players? And if key figures went through long periods without performing, wasn't it the manager's job to make sure there were adequate replacements waiting in the wings?

The defence as a unit maintained the same high standards. Fourteen clean sheets in 38 games and the second-best goals-against tally was practically a carbon copy of the previous term, although individually there were more lacklustre performances and even the normally steadfast Nigel Winterburn had the occasional off-day. The ever-present Lee Dixon was probably Arsenal's most consistent performer; seemingly oblivious to the surrounding malaise, he had now firmly established himself as one of the best full-backs in the country. His speed of recovery on the rare occasions he was beaten, his bite in the tackle and his unadulterated enthusiasm made him a formidable opponent for forwards who ventured down his flank. Dixon also relished the chance to get forward and, at times, especially when Graham opted for a five-man defence, his role was more akin to that of an out-and-out midfielder. He also became a regular on the score-sheet after assuming his fruitful role of penalty-taker against Norwich in November. But you know that a team is struggling for ideas when it relies on players getting forward from the back to create danger, and scoring goals proved to be a major problem all year.

Alan Smith, the First Division's top marksman the previous term, failed to put any kind of scoring run together and managed only ten League goals all season, though in his defence he could point to the dearth of reasonable service. David Rocastle, so influential in 88/89, was only performing in patches and seemed incapable of taking defenders on as of old. Most worryingly, he was beginning to display the horizontal tendencies that would soon plague his game. The distinct lack of penetration down the so recently productive flanks was compounded by the long-term absence of Brian Marwood. The inspirational Yorkshireman missed half the season through injury, and how the team missed him! No player has ever made such an impact at Highbury in such a short period of time as Marwood did: either side of his pivotal role in the 88/89 Championship triumph he made only 22 appearances, but in George Graham's first 8 years at the club, no other attacking player has come even close in terms of effectiveness down the flanks.

One of the most prominent features of the Arsenal make-up since Marwood departed to play out his career in discreet fashion at the likes of Sheffield United, Swindon and Barnet, has been the failure to adequately replace him. Marwood was similar in style to the ex-Nottingham Forest winger, John Robertson – neither player was gifted with blistering pace, but they shared a consummate ability to drift just one side of defenders before knocking the ball quickly and accurately into the box, all before their hapless marker could even think about making a tackle. Defenders generally knew what was coming but stopping it was another thing all together. Just as the Scot was an unsung but key figure in Forest's League and European Cup-winning sides, Marwood was all-important to Arsenal's 1989 title triumph. He didn't arrive in the big time at Arsenal until he was 28, and it was his undiluted motivation, after having spent a career in less glamorous surroundings at Hull and Sheffield, that was perhaps the key to his success. Unfortunately, as veteran status beckoned, he became increasingly injury-prone and was unable to maintain his initial impact. Marwood's spot of Highbury glory came late and was fleeting, but it was unforgettable.

As the chances dried up in that first post-Championship-winning season, Alan Smith, in particular, must have realised how lucky he had been the previous campaign to count on Marwood. Alongside the struggling (and isolated) centre-forward, Paul Merson looked anything like the exciting prospect of the previous year and, despite the odd flash of brilliance (how he contrived to lob the giant Ogrizovic from such an impertinent angle at Coventry is still a puzzler), began to display the erratic form and infuriating indolence that was to later become his trade mark. On the whole, the individual inspiration which had produced so many memorable goals in winning the Championship was conspicuous by its absence.

With the main striking pair in the doldrums, Arsenal's lack of cover up-front became alarmingly clear. The conclusions to be drawn from Perry Groves' twenty starts were emphatic and undeniable. Groves was a useful squad man who provided a valid option as a late substitute to run at tiring defences, but his limitations were simply too pronounced to make him a genuine first choice. His commitment deserved more than the considerable stick he invariably got from his own fans but, if the truth be told, he really was a frustrating player. Groves had the pace to operate on the flanks, but as a wide-man he was invariably let down by deficient ball skills and his inability to cross accurately; and as an out-and-out striker, he was just too lightweight and profligate in front of goal. As for the more gifted Martin Hayes, he again demonstrated that he lacked the mental or physical dura-bility to complement his undoubted talents (what a great player the more tenacious Groves would have been if he had Hayes' natural ability!) and the unavoidable conclusion is that his 24 goals in the 86/87 season were simply a flash in the pan. Given the way Hayes' career has nose-dived spectacularly at Celtic and Swansea, George Graham is a firm candidate for honourable hard-man status after squeezing £600,000 out of his fellow Scots for Hayes as the season closed.

The sufferers in the Highbury congregation realised things were getting really desperate when, for one (blissfully) short period, Graham resorted to the up-front pairing of the off-form Alan Smith and the awkward-looking Niall Quinn, in a battering-ram combination that was as aesthetically un-appealing as it was ineffective. (Perhaps it was a desperate attempt by Graham to recreate the Radford/Kennedy partnership that had operated so successfully in front of him in the Double year?). Thankfully, Quinn's de-parture to Manchester City for £750,000 in March put paid to that crude experiment and, to be fair to the Irishman, given an extended run of first-team football in a team that played to his strengths, he proved to be a much better player than his North London critics suggested. Arsenal's striking problems compared unfavourably with Liverpool's embarrassment of riches up-front. In reality, you could have taken any combination from Smith, Merson, Groves, Quinn or the still raw Kevin Campbell, and they would have looked pretty sick alongside a rampant John Barnes, Peter Beardsley and the back-on-Merseyside Ian Rush.

It was not only the service from the flanks that was deficient, though. Michael Thomas – despite a promising early spell of goal-scoring form – was still failing to stamp his mark on the midfield anything but sporadi-cally, and was displaying a continuing tendency to go AWOL for extended spells (presumably without the permission of General Graham of Barged-die). Kevin Richardson performed as soundly as ever in the engine-room of midfield, but it was still asking too much of an essentially supporting player to shoulder the creative burden. Richardson was too often forced to assume a playmaker's role that was not really his forte, and his inability to really thrive in a creative function made him unpopular amongst some of the fans. However, his consistency and pluckiness won him grudging admir-ation from the more perceptive Highbury regulars. So it was something of a surprise to the player, and just about everybody else at the club when, come the summer, George Graham accepted an offer for the Geordie from the Spanish club, Real Sociedad. As ever, Paul Davis was Arsenal's best hope of providing the creative touch, but in the wake of his pre-season thigh operation he didn't make a League appearance until Boxing Day and subsequently he would struggle to re-adjust to the pace of first-team football. David Platt's outstanding season, as Villa went to the line with Liverpool, only served to highlight the gaping hole at the heart of Arsenal's ranks.

Given these obvious weaknesses it was surprising that George Graham's only foray into the transfer market during the season was to pick up Colin Pates from Charlton. Pates was a solid enough centre-half, but a move from Chelsea to the Valley hardly suggests your career is on the up-and-up and he was by now fast approaching veteran status. His subsequent lack of opportunities in the first team certainly make his signing a bit of a mystery. Graham's decision at the beginning of the season to stick with the same squad that had won the Championship was perhaps understandable – bearing in mind its youthful nature and the logical belief that a hardcore of players could only get better, it wasn't an unreasonable bet. What is inexplicable is that as the season progressed, and faced by the mediocre form of so many of the players paid to make and take goals, his only signing was as cover for the one part of the team that continued to perform up to standard. It was only when Arsenal were finally cast adrift from the title race after their disappointing week in April, that Graham recognised that, yes, maybe he should have strengthened the squad, and that, yes, he would need to draft in new faces for the following season.

On the positive side, the season would best be remembered for David O'Leary's record-breaking 622nd Arsenal appearance in a memorable 4-3 victory over Norwich at Highbury in November. The normally composed and shot-shy Irishman marked the occasion with a rare double: a vigorous display of anger (provoked by the roving elbows of Malcolm Allen) and his first League goal for more than six years. Unfortunately, O'Leary's unusual attack of pique was not the only explosive moment in an ill-natured game. An injury-time brawl led to Arsenal receiving a £20,000 fine and a black mark in the FA's book; a spot of 'previous' that was to have more serious consequences the following season.

In the meantime, there was the small matter of the World Cup in Italy. O'Leary would play a memorable part in Ireland's campaign as his decisive goal in the penalty shoot-out against Romania capped a memorable Indian summer of a long and distinguished international career. Somewhat surprisingly, though, he was a Gunner-alone in Italy, Bobby Robson having decided he could do very nicely, thank you, without the help of George Graham's all-English cast of Highbury heroes. In the end, Arsenal's disappointing season deprived the likes of Tony Adams, Alan Smith, Brian Marwood, Michael Thomas and David Rocastle of a chance to make an impact on the biggest stage of all, and not a single Arsenal player featured in England's memorable campaign. How different it might have been if the World Cup had been held just a year earlier.

Footnote: Southampton FC. When scholars sit down to write the bicentenary history of Arsenal, the likes of Tottenham, Liverpool and Manchester United will no doubt loom large as late-twentieth-century rivals of major standing. But, hey, don't forget Southampton. A less fancied name they may be, but since George Graham arrived at Highbury, no team has been on hand for so many historical occasions. Surely some mistake? Read on:

★ 27 December 1986: Arsenal's Centenary celebrations at Highbury see Bob Wilson doing his PR bit on the pitch with 28 legendary players (and a microphone). Oh, and a goal from budding legend (not) Niall Quinn in a 1-0 win.

★ 21 November 1987: The party-poopers from the South Coast put an end to Arsenal's record-breaking run of victories with a 1-0 win at Highbury.

★ 9 April 1988: Arsenal mark Alan Shearer's first full appearance with a present – Gus Caesar and Michael Thomas at centre-back. The ungrateful whippersnapper scores three times in a 4-2 victory at the Dell. At seventeen, he's the youngest player ever to score a First Division hat-trick.

★ 17 September 1988: Paul 'the Cobra' Davis sees red (and white stripes) and puts Glenn Cockerill in intensive care.

★ 28 September 1991: Here's where the Gunners start to get their own back. Ian Wright. League debut. The Dell. A hat-trick. 'Nuff said.

★ 2 May 1992: The North Bank's farewell. Ian Wright says goodbye with a hat-trick and grabs the Golden Boot of Japan-bound Gary Who?

★ 13 March 1993: Arsenal 4, Soton 3. The Gunners' £500,000 signing Jimmy Carter scores twice. His only goals for Arsenal. At £250,000 each, that's a bit stiff, don't you think, George?

★ 19 March 1994: Anders Limpar turns it on in a 4-0 mugging of the Saints at the Dell (George still drags him off, though!). A couple of days later, the 'Super-Swede' is packed off to Everton.

BY GEORGE ...

'I've warned before, occasional hiccups will happen during a long season. I hope the scoreline at Old Trafford was just a hiccup.'
George holds his breath after first day crash against Manchester United.

'One of the hallmarks of Liverpool's consistent success is that they've always improved their squad while they've been at the top. I aim to do the same for Arsenal.'
George in contradictory vein at beginning of season
(Arsenal signed no one).

'I'm not going to jump on the transfer merry-go-round and spend huge fees for players who are no better than those we have already.'
Back in more familiar mode (October 1989).

'Most of our squad are the same players who clinched the title last season. They haven't become ordinary in a few months. So I still believe we can finish the season with a flourish. One goal in seven games has obviously caused our fans tremendous frustration. I know many of you would like to see me throw Kevin Campbell in for our closing matches. It's important to pick the right moment. I don't want to toss Kevin in at the deep end, so he's burdened with unrealistic expectations because of his youth and reserve team record. I'm looking at his long-term potential, not just the next two months. I could say the same about the transfer market. I'm prepared to spend big if a quality player becomes available. There aren't many up for grabs. I'm not interested in short-term buys. I want players who can give us years of good service.'
Shortly after signing veteran centre-half, Colin Pates.

BARCLAYS LEAGUE 89/90

Final League position: 4th
Average home gate: 33,672

Manchester United	(a)	1-4	Rocastle
Coventry City	(h)	2-0	Marwood, Thomas
Wimbledon	(h)	0-0	
Sheffield Wednesday	(h)	5-0	Merson, Adams, Thomas, Marwood, Smith
Nottingham Forest	(a)	2-1	Merson, Marwood
Charlton Athletic	(h)	1-0	Marwood (penalty)
Chelsea	(a)	0-0	
Manchester City	(h)	4-0	Groves 2, Thomas, Merson
Tottenham Hotspur	(a)	1-2	Thomas
Everton	(a)	0-3	
Derby County	(h)	1-1	Smith
Norwich City	(h)	4-3	Dixon 2 (1 penalty), O'Leary, Quinn
Millwall	(a)	2-1	Thomas, Quinn
Queens Park Rangers	(h)	3-0	Smith, Dixon (penalty), Jonsson
Liverpool	(a)	1-2	Smith
Manchester United	(h)	1-0	Groves
Coventry City	(a)	1-0	Merson
Luton Town	(h)	3-2	Smith, Merson, Marwood
Southampton	(a)	0-1	
Aston Villa	(a)	1-2	Adams
Crystal Palace	(h)	4-1	Smith 2, Dixon, Adams
Wimbledon	(a)	0-1	
Tottenham Hotspur	(h)	1-0	Adams
Sheffield Wednesday	(a)	0-1	
Charlton Athletic	(a)	0-0	
Queens Park Rangers	(a)	0-2	
Nottingham Forest	(h)	3-0	Groves, Adams, Campbell
Manchester City	(a)	1-1	Marwood
Chelsea	(h)	0-1	
Derby County	(a)	3-1	Hayes 2, Campbell
Everton	(h)	1-0	Smith
Aston Villa	(h)	0-1	
Crystal Palace	(a)	1-1	Hayes
Liverpool	(h)	1-1	Merson
Luton Town	(a)	0-2	
Millwall	(h)	2-0	Davis, Merson
Southampton	(h)	2-1	Dixon (penalty), Rocastle
Norwich City	(a)	2-2	Smith 2

FA Cup 89/90

Third Round:
Stoke City   (a) 1-0 Quinn
Fourth Round:
Queens Park Rangers(h) 0-0

Fourth Round replay:
Queens Park Rangers(a) 0-2

League Cup 89/90

Second Round
  1st leg:
Plymouth Argyle   (h) 2-0 Smith, og
Second Round
  2nd leg:
Plymouth Argyle   (a) 6-1 og, Thomas
                              3, Groves,
                              Smith

Third Round:
Liverpool   (h) 1-0 Smith
Fourth Round:
Oldham Athletic   (a) 1-3 Quinn

Appearances

	League	FA Cup	League Cup	Total
John Lukic	38	3	4	45
Tony Adams	38	3	4	45
Lee Dixon	38	3	4	45
Alan Smith	37+1	2	3+1	42+2
Nigel Winterburn	36	2	4	42
Michael Thomas	35+1	2+1	4	41+2
Kevin Richardson	32+1	3	4	39+1
David O'Leary	28+6	3	4	35+6
David Rocastle	28+5	2+1	4	34+6
Perry Groves	20+9	3	1+2	24+11
Paul Merson	21+8	1+2	2+1	24+11
Steve Bould	19	3	0	22
Brian Marwood	17	0	1	18
Martin Hayes	8+4	0	2	10+4
Paul Davis	8+3	2	0	10+3
Kevin Campbell	8+7	0	0	8+7
Niall Quinn	6	1	2	9
Siggi Jonsson	0+5	0+1	1	1+6
Gus Caesar	0+2	0	0+1	0+3
Kwame Ampadu	0+2	0	0	0+2
Colin Pates	0+1	0	0	0+1

Goal-scorers

	League	FA Cup	League Cup	Total
Alan Smith	10	0	3	13
Michael Thomas	5	0	3	8
Paul Merson	7	0	0	7
Brian Marwood	6	0	0	6
Tony Adams	5	0	0	5
Lee Dixon	5	0	0	5
Perry Groves	4	0	1	5
Niall Quinn	2	1	1	4
Martin Hayes	3	0	0	3
Kevin Campbell	2	0	0	2
David Rocastle	2	0	0	2
Paul Davis	1	0	0	1
David O'Leary	1	0	0	1
Siggi Jonsson	1	0	0	1

Season's Review 1990/91
One Step Beyond

That most durable of myths, sustained by generations of hyperbole – both from the pens of ignorant hacks and by insular thinkers from within the game itself – that maintains that the English top flight is the best in the world, may finally have been scotched in recent years by more assiduous coverage of overseas football. Yet despite the unquestionable technical superiority on show in the Italian, Spanish, Dutch and French Leagues, only the churlish would deny that our football is still the most competitive, with unrivalled strength in depth. The notion of an easy game barely exists in England; even teams struggling at the bottom of the table are rarely satisfied with dignity in defeat against stronger opposition, as is invariably the case elsewhere. Taken within this context, Arsenal really didn't get the credit they deserved for their formidable achievement, against considerable odds, of losing just one game in the 90/91 Championship-winning season.

For the record, only Preston North End have gone a whole season without losing a single game, and that was as long ago as 1888/89 and in a 22-game season, thus making comparisons redundant. In modern times, only Leeds United's record of two defeats in 68/69 comes close. Quite simply, by coming within just 90 minutes of carrying their colours throughout a whole League season, George Graham's Arsenal surpassed the achievements in a single domestic campaign of all the legendary sides of English football. Not one of the all-conquering Liverpool sides, nor Busby's Babes, nor Revie's Leeds, nor the Double sides of either Arsenal themselves or Bill Nicholson's Spurs, ever came so close to an unbeaten campaign. Arsenal's 23-game unbeaten start to the season has been topped twice: Leeds in 73/74, and Liverpool in 87/88, both held out 29 games before conceding their first defeat, but both would go on to lose more games over the whole season. That Arsenal were similarly just a game away from an attempt at an unprecedented second Double, adds yet further merit to the achievement.

So why the muted response? Surely Arsenal's astonishing season deserved to be greeted by rapturous applause rather than the somewhat grudging praise that was the reality? Of course, much was made of the blow dealt to Liverpool's chances by Kenny Dalglish's unexpected departure from Anfield in February. But while it may be true that neither Ronnie Moran nor Graeme Souness were able to steer the Anfield ship back on course amidst the resulting turmoil, Liverpool's self-inflicted crisis was at most a minor footnote to Arsenal's season. In comparison, the response of George Graham's team to their own considerable setbacks was far more positive – team-spirit and determination to win the title seeming to grow in direct relationship to adversity. And the handicaps were considerable: the eventual winning margin of seven points would have been nine if not for the two points deducted by the Football Association after the collective rush of blood at Old Trafford. And while Liverpool may have lost a manager, for eight games at a crucial point in the season Arsenal had to make do without their highly influential captain, Tony Adams. The potentially demoralising 6-2 reverse at the hands of Manchester United in the League Cup was taken firmly in the stride – just three days later Arsenal faced League-leaders Liverpool, at Highbury, in a game they simply could not afford to lose. Pressure, what pressure? The Gunners just picked themselves up, dusted themselves off and proceeded to comprehensively outplay Kenny Dalglish's team in a convincing 3-0 win. The Press still did their best to take the gloss off the victory: 'CON MAN – Anders has Kenny's lads in a rage' ranted the *Daily Mirror*, 'LIMPAR IS A CHEAT' railed the *Sun*, paraphrasing Liverpool's Glen Hysen. Rather than concentrate on Arsenal's commendably professional reaction to their midweek setback or take Dalglish to task for putting out a team full of defenders against understandably wary opposition, the tabloids preferred to revive the early season controversy about Limpar's tendency to dive.

The Highbury debacle against United – Arsenal's worst home defeat in seventy years – might have proved cataclysmic for a team built on flimsier foundations, but there were absolutely no recriminations from George Graham. He was convinced that Arsenal's approach was the right one and he wasn't about to change well-established habits because of one fluke result. His oft-repeated message at Colney over the next couple of days left no room for doubt (or the doubters): 'OK, Arsenal might have conceded as many goals in ninety minutes as in the previous seventeen League and Cup games, but you don't become a bad side overnight,' argued Graham. That long unbeaten run was the real Arsenal, he insisted. He then reminded his players of a very relevant precedent: in the 70/71 Double-winning season, Graham the player had been part of the team that suffered a 5-0 hammering at Stoke City. On that occasion, Bertie Mee and Don Howe had made sure that the off-day and the resulting media onslaught served as an incentive to spur the players to greater heights. In the wake of that now infamous defeat in the Potteries, Arsenal accumulated 25 out of 28 points in a winning run that laid the foundations for the Championship triumph.

In the Double-winning season the smart money was on Leeds right until the death. Twenty years later, Arsenal's triumph would become obvious much earlier. But despite having plenty of time to prepare the eulogies, the Press singularly failed to do justice to Arsenal's 90/91 achievement. If the cynics think this is simply a gratuitous echoing of George Graham's own, at times over-sensitive, attitude to the media, just compare the hysterical over-reaction that greeted Manchester United's long-awaited 1993 Championship. Graeme Souness grumbled that Liverpool had in fact lost the title, a bizarre claim given Arsenal's overall statistics and the fact that Graham's men did the Double over the Merseysiders, and an ungenerous reaction that did him no credit. Once again an Arsenal victory on Merseyside was decisive. Paul Merson's classic counter-attacking goal at Anfield in March dealt Liverpool their first home defeat of the season and only their second since 'Mickey did it' back in 1989. More damagingly for the hosts, it was their third defeat in nine days in the wake of Dalglish's departure. That victory left Arsenal three points ahead – hardly a decisive margin on paper with another twelve games to go – but given the chasm in form and confidence there were few subsequent takers on Liverpool. If Souness's petulant attitude was echoed by a lukewarm Press, luckily, from within the game, praise was generally more forthcoming. Typical was Alex Ferguson's assessment: 'People ask if they are worthy champions. But they have lost only one game all season in the League, so what else must they do to prove it? The club is built on solid foundations and even though some people think that the team only has discipline and tactical awareness, they have, in my opinion, enough flair for any side.'

The lack of media acclaim had a lot to do with the supposedly 'unexciting' and 'unattractive' characteristics on which Arsenal's success was forged. Resilience, character, and team-spirit were the favoured buzzwords used to describe Graham's team, labels which were brandished at times as if they were insults rather than positive characteristics. As has often been the case, the very same qualities that inspire so much admiration for English football on the Continent, earned barely disguised contempt at home. In fact, 'English' football should normally read 'British' but the sheer *Englishness* of George Graham's Arsenal made them a

193

notable exception. Far from being the cosmopolitan mixture of English, Scots, Irish and Welsh, with the occasional dash of something a little more exotic that is the norm for most leading English club sides, Arsenal's most typical 90/91 line-up boasted ten 'Lions of Saint George' and Anders Limpar. In contrast, some of Liverpool's all-powerful sides of the 70s and 80s were struggling to field a single Englishman and, to cite another illustrious example, where would the legendary Manchester United side of the swinging sixties have been without George Best, Denis Law, Paddy Crerand et al.? Admittedly, Arsenal's top-dog himself was a Scot but, then again, so were Matt Busby and Bill Shankly (not to mention Alex Ferguson and Kenny Dalglish, Graham's biggest rivals amongst contemporary managers). Given the homogenous hue of the passports and the team's magnificent season, it was strange that only Lee Dixon was an England regular in 90/91 – Tony Adams did manage two caps and Alan Smith one, but after that you could stop counting.

The all-English core of Alan Smith, Paul Merson, Lee Dixon, Tony Adams, Steve Bould and Nigel Winterburn – all stalwarts of the 1989 side – and the newly-returned Paul Davis, provided a well-integrated backbone to the side. But as in that previous title-winning year, the introduction of fresh blood provided the side with vital early season impetus. In character and style, Anders Limpar was about as different from Brian Marwood as you can get but, like his predecessor, he offered penetration down the flanks which caught opponents off their guard in the opening months. Despite an indifferent spell in Italy with Cremonese, the Swede arrived at Highbury exuding confidence, flair and imagination, attributes which prompted the normally taciturn George Graham to describe him as a 'unique talent'. In his end-of-season analysis Graham would claim that, 'until Christmas, Limpar was breathtaking'. And he wasn't exaggerating. Goals like the wonderful solo effort at Elland Road in the FA Cup were the work of an audacious and gifted player. Whether it was because he was unused to the vigours of the long English season, or simply because he was naturally prone to the inconsistency that Graham would later berate, the 'Super-Swede's' form dipped in mid-season. On a personal level, Graham never seemed able to establish a satisfactory relationship with Limpar, and their public slanging matches over the player's desire to represent his country were an early sign of impending storms. At one stage, Graham accused a half-fit Limpar of jetting off to play for Sweden without permission, though the player denied being injured and insisted it was simply a case of the club going out of their way to renege on contractual obligations. Limpar would later argue that he had never been looking for star treatment and that a lot of the problems could have been avoided if Graham had just sat down and talked to him. Unfortunately, the tiff was to prove anything but fleeting, but no one can deny that Limpar provided the surprise element early on that was central to Arsenal's good start in their second Championship assault.

Graham's other big signing was David Seaman – at £1.3 million the most expensive British goalkeeper ever. As if the price-tag didn't guarantee enough pressure, the big man also faced the problem of winning over the hearts and minds of fans who, in the main, had vociferously opposed the departure of his predecessor John Lukic, an authentic cult figure at Highbury. Seaman's response was flawless. On the rare occasions that some bold opposition forward actually managed to breach that Chinese Wall of a defence he would come face-to-face on the other side with the intimidating presence of the burly Yorkshireman, standing as firm and imposing as they come. The only black mark against Seaman's year arrived in the first-ever FA Cup Semi-Final at Wembley and, worst of all, against the old enemy from across North London. As the goalkeeper would admit after the game in his typically forthright manner, he was to blame for at least one goal – Gary Lineker's second – and possibly another one too – Paul Gascoigne's free-kick (formidable, but, gee, he was a long way out). Not that recriminations were in order. If it hadn't been for Seaman's, at times, single-handed resistance against Leeds in the Fourth Round saga, particularly in the first goalless tie at Highbury, Arsenal would never have reached Wembley in the first place.

Coming so close to the fabled Double was the biggest disappointment of Arsenal's season, and the defeat against Spurs provided George Graham's detractors with a rare chance to have a dig at him with an adverse result on their side. After the game, there was lots of talk of Terry Venables having outwitted his friend and rival with a five-man midfield, but in reality Arsenal's downfall had little to do with tactical manoeuvres. To start with, too many Arsenal players had an off-day: Seaman, as he admits, plus defenders who were caught napping early on and forwards who lacked spark. But above all the balance was tipped by an inspired half-hour from a half-fit but irrepressible Paul Gascoigne. It would be churlish to deny that such prodigious talent deserved to win on the day, but the inspiration of the anarchic Gascoigne hardly represents a tactical victory for Venables. Even then, as the talismanic Geordie's legs understandably went in the second-half and forced him to retire from the fray, a 25-minute pounding of Spurs' rearguard by a willing if uninspired Arsenal team could have turned the game around before Lineker's conclusive strike. The Gunners had gone into the game having won the three previous all-London Semi-Finals. Spurs, for their part, had won six consecutive Semis. On the day, something had to give and, unfortunately for the Double dreamers, it was Arsenal.

If the new faces (with the exception of Andy Linighan, who only started seven games all season, and only those when Adams was detained at Her Majesty's Pleasure) were decisive early on, in the latter stages of the season the Highbury conveyor belt threw up fresh faces from the ranks to provide a much-needed injection of youthful vigour and enthusiasm. During the close season, reserve team boss, Stewart Houston, had stepped up to first team duty after the departure of Graham's long-time assistant Theo Foley to Northampton. At the same time, the manager's team-mate from the Double-winning side, George Armstrong, returned to Highbury to look after the reserves. Many outsiders were surprised that youth team coach, Pat Rice, was not promoted in the reshuffle, but the omission was anything but a slight – at a club that sets such store by its youth team policy, the role of coach to the youngsters is considered second in importance only to the manager's job itself. Apart from a brief sojourn at Watford in the latter part of his playing career, Rice has spent the best part of thirty years at Highbury since joining the club straight from school in Islington, and nobody understands better than he does the importance of instilling good habits at an early age. What is more, it is a job that he relishes. In constant liaison with Graham, it is Rice's job to ensure that the youth team is a carbon copy of the first team, not just in the tactical sense, but in creating that all-important bonding between the players and the notion that playing for Arsenal really does represent something special. George Graham himself is well-schooled in the art of coaching youngsters, given his experience at Crystal Palace and Queens Park Rangers, and if Pat Rice was maintained as youth team coach it is because the manager believes that his old teammate is the ideal person to make sure the youngsters get off on the right foot.

Of the new breed, the powerful Kevin Campbell – yet another product of the fertile South London breeding ground that had thrown up Davis, Rocastle, and Thomas – provided a more than useful foil to the more cerebral Alan Smith in the final third of the season. In his own words, his job was to 'ruffle a few feathers', and ruffle he most certainly did. Nine crucial goals and some powerhouse performances were a significant contribution at the death. Less spectacular, but equally effective, was David Hillier, who slotted comfortably into midfield for the flagging Michael Thomas and immediately demonstrated an admirable refusal to be intimidated by even the biggest of names when asked to do a marking job. And who knows? If a battered shin courtesy of Southampton's Jimmy Case had not prevented the youngster sitting on Paul Gascoigne in the Semi-Final, Arsenal's season might have taken an even more glorious turn. (George Graham's one considerable gaffe against Spurs – and one that his players had tried to talk him out of prior to the game – was to assign to Thomas the Hillier role in midfield. As the players feared, Thomas proved he was simply not cut out for a man-to-man marking job and he failed miserably to control Gascoigne.)

Thomas and the injury-jinxed David Rocastle were more peripheral figures than in the previous Championship year, and this time around it was Paul Davis – the veteran of the so-called 'Three Degrees' – who was most influential, re-establishing himself as the cool ruler and gifted playmaker that Arsenal had so missed in his previous two jinxed campaigns.

Of the other 'old-hands', Alan Smith's 22 goals ensured him a place in history as the First Division's top scorer in two separate Championship-winning seasons. This was despite a slow start – after scoring on the opening day Smith didn't find the back of the net again until the Southampton game in November. Not that his contribution was purely about scoring; with his more laidback, less overtly aggressive approach than is the norm in traditional English centre-forwards, 'Smudger' once again led the line in intelligent fashion, a master at holding the ball up with his back to goal and at bringing team-mates into the game with his deft touches. One of Smith's many unnoticed qualities was his ability to finish equally well with both feet (ask yourself, is he left- or right-footed? Can't answer, can you?) and, combined with his ability in the air, it made him an opponent that defenders were never comfortable having to mark. His partner up-front, the distinctly right-footed Paul Merson, weighed in with an anything but unlucky thirteen strikes. After a disappointing second full year in the side, when he attracted as many headlines for his penchant for a tipple and a bet as for his on-field exploits, Merson recaptured the form that had made him look such a prospect in the first Championship-winning year, and he was soon pushing for a place in the England set-up.

But despite the invaluable contributions of Smith, Limpar, Merson and Davis, the key to success was again to be found at the heart of an almost unbreachable defence, as Arsenal came within two goals of equalling Liverpool's 78/79 record of just sixteen goals conceded in a season. It was not until Manchester United's Steve Bruce converted an otherwise meaningless last-minute penalty amidst the title celebrations in the penultimate game, that David Seaman finally saw Ray Clemence's enviable record snatched from his grasp. Even when Tony Adams, always the most headline-grabbing member of the mean-machine, was missing behind bars his absence barely registered on the defensive Richter Scale – a mere six goals were conceded in that mid-winter spell as Andy Linighan and/or David O'Leary slotted easily into the well-oiled unit.

Sometimes Graham put out a side with four men at the back, sometimes five but, whatever the formation, the end result was inevitably the same: an astonishing 24 clean sheets in the League left the Gunners' nets almost as unruffled as the unflappable Seaman. The goalkeeper himself, plus Lee Dixon, Nigel Winterburn and Steve Bould, were all present in Arsenal's 50 games over the length of the season. And while Seaman's formidable contribution has already been acknowledged, he would be the first to admit that even the best goalkeepers are only as safe (or as vulnerable) as the men in front of them. If the previous title hadn't done enough to convince the doubters, a fresh Championship triumph confirmed beyond doubt that the £1 million which Graham had spent on Dixon, Winterburn, and Bould at the beginning of his reign (yes, that's barely £1 million for all three) was the best bit of business he had ever done. At full-back, Dixon's attacking qualities had helped to earn him a regular place in the England team while Winterburn's unwavering consistency and positive attitude had been fundamental in establishing Arsenal's famed resilience.

However, those in the know at Highbury were unanimous in nominating their key man – 90/91 was very much the year of the criminally underrated Steve Bould. Alongside the more aggressive and impetuous Tony Adams, the contribution of the more measured Bould has sometimes gone unnoticed outside Highbury. It reflects particularly badly on successive England managers that the qualities that would have served the centre-half so well on the international stage – great positional sense, uncomplicated but intelligent distribution of the ball, an ice-cool temperament (when 'Bouldie' gives an opponent a kick, it's simply because he has weighed up the situation and calmly decided that's the right thing to do) and, when necessary, the aerial ability you expect of a man who stands 6 feet 4 inches tall – failed to earn him international recognition until the belated call-up by Terry Venables.

The highest compliment that you can pay Bould is to state unequivocally that the more celebrated Adams looks only half the player without the calm assurance of his partner. George Graham has suggested that if Bould hadn't missed the second half of the defeat at Chelsea (he picked up a knock on the ankle just before the break, and David Hillier was forced into an unfamiliar centre-back position for the second 45 minutes) Arsenal might have gone the whole campaign unbeaten. 'Bould has been our outstanding player' was the end-of-season verdict from the boss, a sentiment echoed by the fans who later voted him Arsenal's 1991 Player of the Year. Bould had certainly come a long way after an inauspicious start in the top flight; the key man in the Gunners' record-breaking campaign had been part of the Stoke City outfit that registered a record 31 defeats in the 84/85 season (it will probably surprise no one that one of Stoke's three victories that year was against Don Howe's listless Arsenal!). That is not to suggest that the returning Tony Adams wasn't welcomed wholeheartedly; after an eight-game absence, more than 7000 fans turned up at Highbury to ensure him a rousing reception in a reserve game against Reading in February. A week later, Adams was back in the first-team fold against Shrewsbury in the FA Cup and in as formidable mood as ever.

Despite the excellence of several individuals, Arsenal's triumph was mostly about the collective response to the aforementioned setbacks. In this respect, the all-pervasive influence of Graham just can't be denied. As BBC pundit and Arsenal-crazy Bob Wilson put it, 'Graham has used adversity to increase team-spirit.' Those few seconds of madness at Old Trafford in October led to a swift reaction from the club itself, anxious to maintain its Old Etonian image, at least as far as etiquette went. Before the Football Association had time to act, five players – Davis, Limpar, Rocastle, Thomas and Winterburn – had been docked two weeks' wages and George Graham himself had been fined £10,000. 'The name of Arsenal has been sullied,' said the club's chairman, Peter Hill-Wood. 'The ultimate responsibility for the conduct and misbehaviour of the team lies with the manager, and that is why a fine has been imposed on George Graham.'

What amounted to a public ticking-off must have been a bitter pill to swallow for a man who prides himself on his absolute dedication to the club, but at the end of the season Hill-Wood put things into perspective when he hinted that a lesser man than Graham might well have been sacked, citing his enormous respect for the manager as decisive in counselling restraint. Such a reaction would have been exaggerated in the extreme, but the very way in which Graham took the blow – with enormous dignity and without a single word of public dissent – demonstrated why he is so highly valued at the club. The Manchester flare-up also signalled the beginning of a witch-hunt orchestrated by certain sections of Fleet Street that saw the anti-Arsenal, anti-Graham campaign raised to the level of a personal crusade. Even sectors of the quality Press jumped on the bandwagon – the normally reasonable Patrick Barclay, writing in The Independent, urged the FA to fine the club £1 million in the wake of the incident. Eventually, the FA deducted two League points and fined the club £50,000 for bringing the game into disrepute: the fact that the match was being beamed live to 64 different countries could hardly have encouraged leniency amongst the purveyors of the squeaky-clean, old-school-tie brigade image at Lancaster Gate.

The Press campaign may have been over the top, but to a certain extent Arsenal did only have themselves to blame. Graham's detractors accused him of creating a 'them and us' gang mentality at Highbury – they claimed that any team which lays its reputation on the altar of commitment will inevitably become embroiled in problems and that Arsenal's unbridled aggression would inevitably boil over into the kind of unsavoury incident witnessed at Old Trafford. A lot of the talk of professionalism, and of a supposed siege-mentality at Highbury, was redolent of the controversy Don Revie's Leeds once attracted. When the FA met to mull over the Old Trafford affair there was also the little matter of Arsenal's 'previous' to be taken into account. The infamous ruckus against Norwich had been followed by an unfortunate incident at Villa Park, when a gang of Arsenal players surrounded the referee in intimidating fashion to protest the legality of a Derek Mountfield goal. On that occasion, four players were fined £1000 each by the club and an angry Peter Hill-Wood had been forced to concede that 'it was very silly and totally unacceptable'.

That kind of behaviour was certainly not a one-off. Arsenal had by now gained a potentially damaging reputation amongst referees; their constant bickering and the mob-handed questioning of decisions was hardly likely to earn them the benefit of the doubt. Arsenal fans have always been out on a limb, but this was a period of particularly striking isolation. As Nick Hornby summarised memorably in the Arsenal's fans' bible, *Fever Pitch*: 'Each of these transgressions isolated the club and its devotees further and further from the lip-pursing, right-thinking, Arsenal-hating mainland; Highbury became a Devil's Island in the middle of North London, the home of no-goods and miscreants.'

Whether George Graham actually reflected on the criticism is doubtful – and though over the top in form, in substance there was more than an element of truth to the accusations – what is beyond doubt is that he used the poisoned arrows of his detractors to rally his troops. The two points deducted in the wake of Old Trafford left Arsenal eight points adrift of a still ominous-looking Liverpool. Far from wavering, Arsenal's sprint for the title started in the very next game, with a 4-0 win over Southampton. Likewise, Graham used the hysterical Press reaction to Tony Adams' imprisonment for drink-driving at the end of December to gee-up his players still further.

That Graham in particular, and the club in general, were slammed for supporting Adams during a difficult period speaks volumes for the hypocritical agendas of certain sectors of the popular Press. The player's problems may indeed have been self-inflicted, but they hardly warranted such approbation. What did the Press expect? That Arsenal would see him locked up in jail and promptly throw away the Highbury keys as a Christmas present? Amidst predictable headlines about blown careers the gentlemen of the Press (teetotallers to a man, of course!) demanded that Adams should never play for England again. George Graham, meanwhile, stood up in court to praise Adams' professionalism and leadership – and while no one condones his misguided off-field behaviour, only the malicious would deny that Adams is impeccably professional when defending the colours of his club. The club's reaction to the jail sentence was to state unequivocally that Adams' captaincy was not under threat and that his £2000-a-week salary would not be affected. His team-mates, who had been taking the mick out of him mercilessly as he set off to court, were stunned by the verdict. Paul Davis, the man who led the team in his absence said, 'I won't mind handing over to Tony. He was a great captain before – he'll be even better now'.

If deciding to pay Adams the full whack in his absence was perhaps questionable, Arsenal's overall posture was commendable. For their part, the FA had obviously never heard the one about not kicking a man when he is down and, with Adams left musing on the errors of his way in Chelmsford jail, they fined him £1000 for an incident which had taken place at Loftus Road the previous November. On that occasion, Adams had reacted to incessant jibes from the QPR supporters by giving them the two-fingers when Kevin Campbell's goal sealed a memorable comeback after Arsenal had been behind for most of the match. The now depressingly familiar 'donkey' jibes had been the backdrop to every Adams away-day since the frank, bold and free *Daily Mirror* had picked up on the reaction of the Old Trafford crowd to the player's own-goal the previous April, and subsequently decided to pin a pair of donkey's ears on a photo of him. It is not Adams' style to mock but, deep down, he must have felt inordinate satisfaction at seeing his critics off – something he had done in conclusive fashion by the time he paraded the Championship trophy around Highbury in May as captain of the League champions. (How that must have hurt the self-confessed Spurs fan who is chief football writer at the *Mirror*!)

They say that he who laughs last laughs longest, and, at the end of such a magnificent season, George Graham could also allow himself a rare and well-deserved moment of self-congratulation. 'It's beginning to look as though I could be a better manager than I was a player – and that's not to say I was a bad player.' This time there was no grandstand finish *à la* Anfield 1989: on a sunny May Bank Holiday Monday, Liverpool succumbed to Nottingham Forest in the afternoon, converting Arsenal's later fixture against Manchester United into the mother of all Highbury celebrations. By the time the players arrived at the ground, the party had already begun and Alan Smith's hat-trick to set up the 'Golden Boot' would eventually round off the day in perfect fashion. The party continued the following Saturday with a 6-1 demolition job of Coventry, when Anders Limpar bade goodbye to a memorable first season at Highbury with a hat-trick, while Smith's solitary goal was enough to see him edge ahead of Lee Chapman as the First Division's top scorer.

Despite the grudging praise and the snide allusions to the nature of Arsenal's triumph, few were in doubt that this was the beginning rather than the end – of something big. The first time that Arsenal won the League title twice in three seasons was at the start of the 30s, and subsequently the team (or, more accurately, the club) that Herbert Chapman built had gone on to dominate the decade and forge the legend of Arsenal. Would George Graham's Arsenal go on to dominate the 90s in similar fashion? Two League titles in three years meant that the notion of a Graham dynasty was very much on the agenda.

BY GEORGE ...

'We have granted Colin Pates' transfer request. Colin wants to settle down at centre-back again, and with so many centre-halves in the club, we've agreed to let him leave.'

Surely not, George? (September 1990).

'I accept my responsibility. We all need to bear in mind not only the good of our clubs but also the good of the game.'

The week after the battle of Old Trafford, October 1990.

'I can only look upon it as an aberration, taken against our magnificent start to the season. As a player, I remember similar events in our Double campaign. We crashed 0-5 at Stoke, then went down to a shock home defeat by Crystal Palace in the League Cup a few weeks later ... we've never exactly been the darlings of the media. I'm sure Wednesday's scoreline will have delighted a lot of people outside Highbury. So now is the time for us to show that our seventeen-match unbeaten start was the real Arsenal.'

After the 2-6 defeat at home to Manchester United in the League Cup
(28 November 1990).

'I can't remember any player of such high quality having to suffer so much extreme, unfair, criticism; not to mention taunts from opposing fans all round the country. He's handled all that. And I'm sure he'll cope with this latest episode and come back even stronger.'

Reacting to Tony Adams' jail sentence, 26 December 1990.

'We have this thing called resilience – we won't lie down.'

After a goalless draw at Spurs, January 1991.

'When you pay the best, you get the best. Seaman is a colossus.'

Putting the Indian sign on David Seaman before the Spurs Semi-Final.

'The title is won over 36 games and there are times when your performance is not to the standard you would want, and so you have to dig in and refuse to lie down. You may have to concede a little flair to achieve that consistency.'

After the 0-0 draw at Sunderland left Arsenal
on the brink of winning the title.

203

'I'd like to include a special mention for Steve Bould. I've called him a colossus and that's the right word, because he's been toweringly consistent. If he hadn't had to go off at half-time against Chelsea we might have come through the season unscathed.'

On the Man of the Season.

'I reckon we're a lot better equipped to defend our title – both mentally and in squad strength – than we were two years ago. Playing in Europe will be a tremendous challenge. We are certain to learn a great deal from pitting our wits against different players, different coaches and different tactics. There's no doubt we should all improve.

Looking forward, May 1991.

BARCLAYS LEAGUE 90/91

Final League position: Champions
Average home gate: 36,878

Wimbledon	(a)	3-0	Merson, Smith Groves	Derby County	(h)	3-0	Smith 2, Merson
Luton Town	(h)	2-1	Merson, Thomas	Sheffield United	(h)	4-1	Dixon (penalty), Smith 2, Thomas
Tottenham Hotspur	(h)	0-0					
Everton	(a)	1-1	Groves	Manchester City	(a)	1-0	Smith
Chelsea	(h)	4-1	Limpar, Dixon (penalty), Merson, Rocastle	Tottenham Hotspur	(a)	0-0	
				Everton	(h)	1-0	Merson
				Chelsea	(a)	1-2	Smith
				Crystal Palace	(h)	4-0	O'Leary, Merson, Smith, Campbell
Nottingham Forest	(a)	2-0	Rocastle, Limpar				
Leeds United	(a)	2-2	Limpar 2	Liverpool	(a)	1-0	Merson
Norwich City	(h)	2-0	Davis 2	Leeds United	(h)	2-0	Campbell 2
Manchester United	(a)	1-0	Limpar	Nottingham Forest	(h)	1-1	Campbell
Sunderland	(h)	1-0	Dixon (penalty)	Norwich City	(a)	0-0	
				Derby County	(a)	2-0	Smith 2
Coventry City	(a)	2-0	Limpar 2	Aston Villa	(h)	5-0	Campbell 2, Smith 2, Davis
Crystal Palace	(a)	0-0					
Southampton	(h)	4-0	Smith 2, Merson, Limpar				
				Sheffield United	(a)	2-0	Campbell, Smith
Queens Park Rangers	(a)	3-1	Merson, Smith, Campbell	Southampton	(a)	1-1	og
				Manchester City	(h)	2-2	Campbell, Merson
Liverpool	(h)	3-0	Merson, Dixon (penalty), Smith	Queens Park Rangers	(h)	2-0	Dixon (penalty), Merson
				Sunderland	(a)	0-0	
Luton Town	(a)	1-1	Smith	Manchester United	(h)	3-1	Smith 3 (1 penalty)
Wimbledon	(h)	2-2	Merson, Adams				
Aston Villa	(a)	0-0		Coventry City	(h)	6-1	Limpar 3, og, Smith, Groves

FA Cup 90/91

Third Round:				3rd replay:			
Sunderland	(h)	2-1	Smith, Limpar	Leeds United	(a)	2-1	Merson, Dixon
Fourth Round:				Fifth Round:			
Leeds United	(h)	0-0		Shrewsbury Town	(a)	1-0	Thomas
Replay:				Sixth Round:			
Leeds United	(a)	1-1	(after extra time) Limpar	Cambridge United	(h)	2-1	Campbell, Adams
2nd replay:				Semi-Final (Wembley):			
Leeds United	(h)	0-0	(after extra time)	Tottenham Hotspur		1-3	Smith

League Cup 90/91

Second Round:				Third Round:			
Chester City	(a)	1-0	Merson	Manchester City	(a)	2-1	Groves, Adams
Chester City	(h)	5-0	Groves 2, Adams, Smith, Merson	Fourth Round:			
				Manchester United	(h)	2-6	Smith 2

Appearances

	League	FA Cup	League Cup	Total
Steve Bould	38	8	4	50
Lee Dixon	38	8	4	50
David Seaman	38	8	4	50
Nigel Winterburn	38	8	4	50
Paul Merson	36+1	8	4	48+1
Alan Smith	35+2	8	4	47+2
Paul Davis	36+1	6+1	4	46+2
Anders Limpar	32+2	5	2	39+2
Michael Thomas	27+4	8	2	37+4
Tony Adams	30	3	4	37
Kevin Campbell	15+7	4+2	0+4	19+13
Perry Groves	13+19	3+1	4	20+20
David Rocastle	13+3	0	2	15+3
David O'Leary	11+10	5+1	0+1	16+12
David Hillier	9+7	3+1	2	14+8
Andy Linighan	7+3	3+1	0	10+4

	League	FA Cup	League Cup	Total
Siggi Jonsson	2	0	0	2
Andy Cole	0 + 1	0	0	0 + 1
Colin Pates	0 + 1	0	0	0 + 1

Goal-scorers

	League	FA Cup	League Cup	Total
Alan Smith	22	2	3	27
Paul Merson	13	1	2	16
Anders Limpar	11	2	0	13
Kevin Campbell	9	1	0	10
Lee Dixon	5	1	0	6
Perry Groves	3	0	3	6
Tony Adams	1	1	2	4
Paul Davis	3	0	0	3
Micky Thomas	2	1	0	3
David Rocastle	2	0	0	2
David O'Leary	1	0	0	1

Season's Review 1991/92
The Wright Fantastic!

I f Arsenal's haughty progress through the 90/91 season had been smooth and practically flawless, the 91/92 campaign was bumpy to a fault, though as it turned out, barely less entertaining. Following on from the previous season's exploits was always going to prove an awesome task, but nobody could have predicted the veritable Jekyll and Hyde nature of Arsenal's season: the first half characterised by staggering inconsistency and sloppy defending; the second, by some of the most scintillating attacking football ever seen at Highbury, or anywhere else for that matter. If the extent of the schizophrenia was surprising enough in itself, the fact that neither of the two 'Arsenals' exhibited the characteristics that normally spring to mind where George Graham's sides are concerned, was equally perplexing, though at least there was little of the 'comical antagonism and adversity' off the pitch of the previous year.

The pre-season jostling threw up a couple of interesting vignettes: first, in the shape of the return of erstwhile idol Charlie Nicholas to Highbury for Paul Davis's testimonial (an appearance which Charlie marked with a cracking goal in front of a still-compliant North Bank) and, second, in an interesting reconnaissance against the Italian champions Sampdoria in the Makita Trophy. Gianluca Vialli's stunning volleyed goal was a hint of the sort of quality that was likely to cross Arsenal's path in Europe. The previous spring, Manchester United had successfully ended the first year back in Europe for English clubs, after five years of post-Heysel exile, by beating the Spanish champions-elect Barcelona to win the European Cup-Winner's Cup – a scalp that must have encouraged George Graham to believe his side were in a strong position to have a serious crack at Europe's premier trophy. For a club of its size and stature, Arsenal have made little impression on the wider European stage and the Scot was well aware that this was his chance to carve himself a unique niche in the Highbury history books. If further incentive were needed, Graham's own memories of the competition were coloured by his unfortunate own-goal (ironically, given his strengths as a player, with his head) that saw Arsenal succumb to Johan Cruyff's Ajax in the 1972 Quarter-Final. 'It will be great to play famous teams and see famous faces, and the tactical challenge of it appeals to me,' said Graham of the impending European assault. The feeling was that this was the one which Field-Marshall Graham really wanted to win in the 91/92 campaign.

For the second time in three years, Graham decided to defend the Championship with the same squad of players that had won the title. Despite the negative predecent of the 89/90 term, the bookmakers approved and Arsenal were quickly installed as favourites, the first time in ten years that Liverpool's pre-season pole position had been usurped. But once again the reigning champs were brought rapidly down to earth with a bump. If it hadn't been for Paul Merson's deflected shot on 90 minutes, Queens Park Rangers would have done in the opening game of the new season what no team had managed over the whole Championship-winning campaign – which was to leave Highbury with three points in the bag. That opening day wobble was followed by two defeats in four days: a lame performance in a 3-1 reverse at Goodison followed by a comedy of errors at Villa Park where the otherwise steadfast Nigel Winterburn was again tormented by his own particular bogey man, Villa's Tony Daley.

After just three games, Arsenal were left contemplating more defeats than they had suffered in the whole of the previous season. (A poor start has been an ever-present feature of Arsenal's post-war Championship defences: in 49/50, four out of the first five games were lost; in 53/54, the first eight winless matches produced six defeats; in 71/72, Bertie Mee's team lost three of their first five games; and George Graham's men started their previous defence in the 89/90 campaign with that 4-1 thrashing at Old Trafford.)

In the fourth game, Arsenal finally chalked up their first win by defeating a witless Luton side that arrived at Highbury goalless and like lambs to the slaughter. A few days later, Manchester City proved to be equally tame opposition, but in both cases the result was far better than the stuttering performances. The City game was at least memorable for a crazy ricochet of a goal by Anders Limpar; after Tony Coton had made a great save from Paul Davis's acrobatic diving header, Michael Thomas hit the rebound against the bar from a tight angle on the right. Before Coton in the City goal could breathe a sigh of relief, Limpar smacked the rebound home emphatically from a daft angle on the left. Even dafter was Lee Dixon's own-goal in the next home game against Coventry – the full-back's back pass floated over the head of a bemused David Seaman before the opening minute was up and paved the way for Arsenal's first defeat at Highbury since April 1990.

Dixon's goal may have been the winner in the egg-on-the-face stakes, but it was typical of the kind of defensive mistakes that would plague the first half of the season. The ankle injury sustained by Steve Bould in his least favourite tournament, the Makita (a pelvic injury sustained when heading the winner in the 1990 edition had seen him out of action in that season for five months), and Tony Adams' troublesome groin, saw the tight wedge at the heart of Arsenal's defence torn apart, and the resulting musical chairs at the back produced mayhem. The ever-changing centre-back combinations proved to be uniformly insecure: David O'Leary was now regularly getting caught out for pace, Andy Linighan was still worryingly accident-prone (the fans had christened him 'Goal a Game' Linighan because of his habit of donating a goal to the opposition every game) and Colin Pates must have felt like a blind man thrown to the lions, groping around amidst such chaos after two years spent wallowing in the reserves.

The slapstick was obviously contagious; when either Adams or Bould did play, they proved as fallible as the rest. One of the main features of Arsenal's season was the extraordinary number of goals conceded after mistakes in the centre of the defence left grateful opponents unmarked in the box. Unfortunately, the surprise of finding themselves in such an unaccustomed position against possibly the most parsimonious defence on earth, didn't prevent Robert Wilson, Mo Johnston, Lee Chapman et al. from gleefully accepting the free gifts. Behind the back four, the previously impeccable David Seaman was also struggling to maintain his 90/91 standards and in some of the early games (Everton, Aston Villa and Sheffield United immediately spring to mind) he looked positively lethargic. A series of conspicuous errors throughout the season should still be seen in the context of his generally steady form, but even so they were frequent enough to threaten his position as the long-term heir to Peter Shilton. In the end, Seaman's fumbling performance in his one full international of the season, against Czechoslovakia in March, meant he also lost out on the number two spot for the summer's European Championships – Crystal Palace's Nigel Martyn eventually got the nod to shadow Chris Woods.

The out-of-sorts Lee Dixon was another player totally incapable of reproducing his outstanding form of previous campaigns, and the full-back's poor form proved so durable that it would eventually produce cruel taunts from his own fans. The memorable, if exaggerated, East Stand chant of 'If Lee Dixon plays for England, so do I!' first reared its head during the dismal New Year's Day showing against those perennial Highbury party-poopers, Wimbledon. 'He should be right-back behind the goal' was another jibe that Dixon regularly had to endure from his touchline critics. It was certainly where most of his crosses seemed to end up, they would add. The Wimbledon game also saw a memorable slanging match between Nigel Winterburn and the punters in the Lower East after the full-back's sloppy back pass gave the Dons a goal, though Winterburn's tetchy response should be seen within the context of his admirable resistance to interlopers on his patch *per se*. That incident aside, he was the only member of the defence to fend off the general malaise, this despite the fact he was carrying a knock for most of the season that would require a hernia op as soon as the summer arrived. In the end, Arsenal's famed defensive obduracy was only restored when the Adams/Bould partnership was reunited once and for all against Manchester United at the beginning of February. It is no coincidence that this fixture marked the beginning of Arsenal's seventeen-game unbeaten run-in to the season. It had become clear that with Adams and Bould missing, Arsenal were as vulnerable as the next team in defence; and all the second-rate cover in the world at centre-back couldn't change that.

However, to lay all the blame for the goals against statistics on the defence would be unfair: that Arsenal played much of the season with a 4-2-4 formation also had predictable repercussions in the 'goals against' stakes. Defenders as exceptional as Adams and Bould could perhaps compensate for a lack of cover in midfield, but in their absence the attacking tendencies of nominal midfielders like Merson and Limpar was always going to create an excessive burden for a defence populated by mere mortals. As George Graham experimented early on with Rocastle and Davis in a two-man midfield, the risks implicit in the system soon became apparent as, at times, the duo found themselves outnumbered and outhustled. Back in his old youth-team role in centre midfield, Rocastle initially struggled, but with customary grit he would swiftly play himself back into form and, eventually, back into the England fold. After eighteen months in the international wilderness, Rocastle was recalled for England's decisive European Championship qualifier against Poland in November. The autumn arrival of Ian Wright, his childhood friend from South London, was another boost for Rocastle and a breathtaking goal at Old Trafford in October (he left Bryan Robson and Paul Ince red-faced and spreadeagled on their backs, before cheekily lobbing the giant Peter Schmeichel from 30 yards) was vintage 'Rocky' – the goal of a talented *and* tenacious footballer. Manchester United manager, Alex Ferguson, marvelled at the player's audacity: 'I don't think the goalkeeper had any chance. You've got to hand it to Rocastle. That was a brilliant piece of imagination and improvisation.'

Paul Davis wasn't so lucky; asking a 30-year-old to play a harrying, chasing game in a two-man midfield was surely asking too much, especially when that player had never been an exceptional athlete, even in his younger days. Not that Davis had to put up with the situation for long – after a public slanging match with George Graham he was banished to the reserves at the end of October and made only one more appearance all season. That row was out of character for both the resolutely uncontroversial Davis (who eventually asked for a transfer from his beloved Arsenal) and the manager who so admired him. Fortunately, time and circumstances would bring Davis back into the fold, even if the two never quite kissed and made up.

With Michael Thomas hedging his bets on the future and Siggi Jonsson on the point of retiring because of persistent back trouble, young David Hillier again stepped into the midfield breach. Hillier was less naturally talented than the likes of Davis and Thomas, but he was infinitely more suited to the tracking down of opponents that Arsenal's formation demanded. As it was, even the tigerish qualities of Hillier and 'Rocky' were not enough to prevent them being swamped in midfield on the bad days. Thomas eventually moved on in December, to Liverpool of all places, and while the fans were sad to see the hero of Anfield leave the club, in truth, his last year at Arsenal had been disappointing on and off the pitch – in the latter case, mostly due to his agent's constant scamperings to plant stories in the Press about supposed interest from Italian clubs. Quite rightly, George Graham would not be held over a barrel when it came to more money and when, surprise, surprise!, the Italian interest never materialised, in jumped Liverpool. Once Thomas had left, he did little to endear himself to Arsenal devotees by criticising George Graham in the Press. Despite Graham's supposedly strained relationship with his players, it was a rare case of serious public disdain from one of his ex-charges, though Thomas's musings on the manager's dictatorial temperament were uncannily similar to Kevin Richardson's memorable 'Gadaffi' barb! Michael Thomas's ignoble parting shots for cash would eventually earn him a fine from the FA and, though the gist of his accusations – 'I found his style of football so unattractive. It was too direct. I might as well have been a long-distance runner rather than a First Division footballer' – may have contained more than a grain of truth, criticising the manager who had displayed so much faith in him was little short of treasonable.

By the time Thomas was defecting up north, there was already another South Londoner on the pay-roll eager to write his name in the Arsenal record books. It would be tempting to split Arsenal's season into a before-

and after-Ian Wright – tempting, but not strictly accurate. Wright's arrival from Crystal Palace for a record club fee of £2.5 million was a major surprise; in George Graham's five years at Arsenal the club had been linked with just about every available and rated British player going, but not one really big name had actually signed on the dotted line. Graham's track-record in the transfer market had provoked a litany of received wisdoms about him, most of which alluded either to his Napoleonic delusions of grandeur or his Presbyterian stinginess: he didn't like stars and wouldn't or couldn't integrate them into the team; there was only room for one big name at Highbury and that was Graham himself; he had negotiated massive increases in salary for himself but wouldn't pay the wages to attract top players to the club; and many other oft-aired clichés.

Once Crystal Palace chairman Ron Noades had made unfortunate comments about black players for a TV documentary, the word on the London grapevine had it that peer pressure would ensure Ian Wright's days at Palace were numbered. Wright may not wear his origins on his sleeve in an overtly political sense, but he is a resolutely black *and* British superstar, the polar opposite of a more manufactured establishment figure like the supine Frank Bruno. Wright is similar to Linford Christie, his only peer in the black superstar stakes, in that he adapts happily and naturally to new environments. But at the same time, he is not about to forget where he came from. As a role model for young blacks, it was always going to be difficult for Wright to turn a blind eye to Noades' *faux pas*.

In purely sporting terms, Wright was an exciting and individual talent, but he was anything but individualistic – the key to Graham's interest. The manager was convinced Wright would prove an asset on and off the field and, when the word got to him that the circumstances were ripe, he acted swiftly and surreptitiously. Before the Press got wind of the impending bombshell, a positively beaming Wright was being paraded at Highbury in the red and white of Arsenal. He was hardly a stranger to his new teammates either: Rocastle was from the same South London estate, Campbell and Thomas were fellow cronies in London's so-called 'Black-pack' network and the likes of Seaman, Dixon, Adams and Smith were already familiar with Wright's exuberant presence from their England duties.

If the execution of the signing came as a surprise, the precise moment when Graham finally chose to splash out on a forward also raised a few eyebrows. It may be difficult to believe it now, but when Wright first arrived at Arsenal, a typical question on the Highbury terraces was 'Do we really need him?' After struggling to score early on, the team had struck a rich vein of goals and in the three games prior to Wright's arrival Arsenal

213

had thumped no less than fifteen past Crystal Palace, FK Austria Memphis and Sheffield United. Kevin Campbell was really beginning to look the part, mugging defences into submission in uninhibited style, and Alan Smith was banging in the goals with something like his old abandon – four goals and a night in the limelight against the Austrians was a thoroughly deserved reward for the unsung Smith. Alongside them, Anders Limpar and Paul Merson were both capable of making and taking chances; and all of these players, with the exception of Smith, were considerably younger than Wright. And after all, wasn't £2.5 million a lot of money to pay for a 28-year-old?

Although Campbell initially made way for Wright, the long-term loser was another home-grown striker still on the fringes of the first team. Andy Cole had been Arsenal's reserve team top scorer in 90/91 and his involvement in the pre-season games against Panathinaikos and Sampdoria suggested that he was on the verge of making a breakthrough. Wright's arrival effectively ended any realistic hope Cole had of breaking through into the first team, and later in the season he was shunted off to Second Division Bristol City, where he made the briefest of pit stops before arriving at Newcastle. We all know what happened next! At the time, Cole's departure barely caused a blip beyond the Highbury grapevine, and with Wright arriving in a blaze of goals, the in-the-know doubters were immediately silenced. Ian Wright's subsequent contribution to the Highbury cause has been immense, but amongst Arsenal fans it still rankles to see Cole free-scoring at Newcastle and, given Campbell's subsequent progress, it is difficult to avoid the conclusion that Graham let the wrong forward go.

Wright's signing had other negative side-effects, too: David Rocastle may have been delighted to see his old sparring partner from South London arrive at Highbury, but any chance of 'Rocky' playing wide again disappeared overnight. Limpar, Merson and Groves were already competing for the wide places in Arsenal's attack and now Campbell would sometimes be forced wide as well. Graham's subsequent signing of Jimmy Carter for £500,000 from Liverpool at the beginning of October provided yet more short-term competition down the flanks, even if the Islington-born winger would barely cause a ripple in the long-term. Wright's arrival at the end of September also signalled the effective demise of Alan Smith as a regular goal-scorer at Arsenal. At that point in the season, Smith had already scored seven goals in the League, but he would only manage four more all season, a strike-rate that was to become ingrained – in 92/93 he would score 3 League goals in 31 games, in 93/94, 3 in 25. Much has been made of Wright and Smith's incompatibility up-front, and there is no doubt they do like a different kind of service – Smith is in his element when the ball is played into his feet, laying the ball off wide and getting on the end of crosses, while Wright prefers the quick ball down the middle that allows him to escape defenders with his lightning pace. But the chalk and cheese argument is not conclusive; having the big man flick and the little man pounce is a hardy perennial of British football and the hugely successful Wright/Bright combination at Palace was not markedly different in make-up to the Wright/Smith pairing. As it was, Smith, who after all was England's centre-forward at the time of Wright's arrival (finally getting the chance to play alongside his ex-Leicester partner Gary Lineker, he would score a crucial winner for England against Turkey just a couple of weeks later), would never be a prolific scorer again at Arsenal.

Returning to the before- and after-Wright scenario, the away-day at Southampton undoubtedly witnessed the birth of a Highbury legend as the travelling North Bank chorused 'What a waste of money' in response to an unforgettable three-goal blast – a performance that must surely rank as the best-ever Arsenal League debut. It wasn't, however, the turning point of the season. Despite hitting a rich seam of goals early on – including a memorable Limpar-assisted four-goal haul against Everton – Wright was on the scene for Arsenal's goalless November and for the dismal Christmas and early New Year run that effectively ended any hopes of retaining the Championship. His goals would undeniably play a major part in Arsenal's fabulous run-in but, in reality, he was one of several players who would hit sparkling form at the same time and make Arsenal an unstoppable unit. Unfortunately for everybody concerned at Highbury, Wright's eye for a goal was missing for the biggest game of Arsenal's season, the hugely disappointing European Cup defeat against Benfica. Graham had added Wright and Carter to his squad with one eye on a possibly chaotic fixture list, but Arsenal's new main-man would not be available until the third game of the semi-final group stage. As it turned out, the strain of competing on multiple fronts never arose and Wright never got the chance to make an impact on the European Cup.

Arsenal's excellent performance in Lisbon gave no hint of the disaster to come. Graham would later admit that Sven-Goran Eriksson threw his initial plans out of gear by the inclusion of Isaias, a player the Swedish coach had cunningly kept under wraps in the games that the manager and his cohorts had watched. The Brazilian forward loved to run at defenders from deep, and it was one such surge after a searching through-ball from Stefan Schwarz no less, which broke Arsenal's off-side trap and found Isaias storming through to put the Portugese ahead. Graham's answer was to get

Paul Merson to tuck-in deeper and put Paul Davis on Isaias. That took the sting out of Benfica and Kevin Campbell's unstoppable shot – in his own words, 'that was hard!' – did the rest. A 1-1 draw in Lisbon left Arsenal as favourites in the tie and rubbing their hands at the prospect of a nest-egg in Europe; with a relatively weak line-up of clubs in the 91/92 European Cup, on-field glory and off-field riches surely beckoned.

They say a week is a long time in politics; unfortunately for Arsenal it was soon to prove a discouragingly long time in football. The Gunners' disastrous seven days began with a timid surrender to Coventry in the League Cup. The perceptible, if unvoiced reaction to that defeat – 'it could prove to be a blessing in disguise' – was indicative of where Arsenal's real aspirations lie, and that attitude was reinforced when George Graham rested Adams, Davis, and Campbell for the subsequent League game against West Ham. The result? Another home defeat against weak opposition, but who's counting, we've got Benfica on Wednesday!

In front of an expectant Highbury, a fired-up Arsenal made all the running in the first half: Campbell hit the woodwork before Colin Pates, making his European debut at thirty, grabbed his five minutes of fame. What at the time promised to be a crucial goal turned out to be a mere anecdote – the centre-half's one and only goal for Arsenal. With Alan Smith and Kevin Campbell up front together, there was always the temptation to hump aimless balls in their direction and hope for the best – especially against Continental opposition who were supposed to crumble on cue against such tactics. In the second half, Arsenal duly abandoned any more subtle efforts to break down increasingly resistant opponents and the long punt forward saw David Seaman practically assume the role of Arsenal playmaker. The ploy only served to nullify Arsenal's wide-men and allowed Eriksson to shift his troops 10-15 yards deeper and defend on the edge of the penalty box. Against a tiring Arsenal, the Portugese were able to capitalise on the extra space in midfield whenever the ball broke loose to launch their own swift counter-attacks. Both of Benfica's injury-time goals derived from midfield breaks in acres of space, although it initially took a touch of pure class from Sergei Yuran to create Kulkov's equaliser and ensure the extra period.

Later, Graham would insist that Arsenal had been the better side over 90 minutes, claiming that Benfica's superiority and eye-catching goals in extra time had clouded people's judgement. And if Smith hadn't missed an extra-time sitter when the scores were still level (how he would have liked to swop just one of his Austrian strikes for that one) or if Tony Adams hadn't sliced against the post from point blank range with Benfica just a goal ahead, things might indeed have been different. Neither would many argue with Graham's contention that an on-form Arsenal would have won. Benfica's subsequent poor performance in their Semi-Final group certainly added weight to Graham's argument that they were not a particularly good team. Still, nothing could change the result. If the financial implications of losing out on the jackpot of a guaranteed six more games were irreversible, at least in purely sporting terms Graham would put the experience to good use. In Arsenal's next European campaign, the manager would demonstrate conclusively that he had learned one valuable lesson – if you give European teams space in midfield you are likely to pay a heavy price. Better to smother the opposition with a 'mass of tangled bodies', as Don Howe once memorably christened the more typical midfield of the English game.

There is a school of thought which reckons that those seven days, and particularly the Benfica disappointment, tore the heart out of Arsenal's season. While not prone to over-dramatisation, George Graham did admit it knocked the stuffing out of his team. Some of the players, though, argued that the side had not really been playing that well anyway. In the weeks that followed, Arsenal's form was indifferent at home and poor away. Depending on which side of the fence you were standing, the Benfica game was the catalyst, or simply a stopping-off point along the way.

With performances degenerating from mediocre to downright bad, the Christmas and New Year holiday fixtures yielded just one point and saw League pacemakers Leeds and Manchester United threatening to pull away at the top. But the worst was still to come. Arsenal travelled to North Wales on the first Saturday in 1992 for a Third Round FA Cup tie at Wrexham which seemed, to all intents and purposes, a formality. After all, Arsenal were still the reigning champions and Wrexham had finished 92nd and last in the previous campaign. Under the tutelage of George Graham, Arsenal were anything but the band of over-paid nancy-boys of bygone years who tended to lie down and die on a cold and inhospitable afternoon against spirited opposition from further down the League. With time running out at the Racecourse Ground, things were going according to plan; Arsenal were one goal ahead and Wrexham didn't look remotely likely to pull level. Then with only eight minutes to go, a bolt from the blue in the shape of Micky Thomas's ferocious free-kick (awarded for a non-existent foul by David O'Leary) began to threaten the pre-ordained script. Amidst general disbelief, a monumental hash-up involving O'Leary and Tony Adams – the last two players you would expect to get nervous in the circumstances – left Steve Watkins wriggling through to put the disbelieving Welshmen ahead. There was still time for Jimmy Carter to bundle the ball in the back of the net in a last frenzied attack, but the goal was disallowed (to this day no one has satisfactorily explained why) and Arsenal had been bundled out of the Cup. Forget Swindon 69 and 79, Walsall 83 or York 85, this was an upset to compare with Walsall's 1933 elimination of Herbert Chapman's all-conquering Gunners. It may have been a fluke – Arsenal had enough chances to win the game several times over and the ending was as much Benny Hill as Billy's Boots – but who was going to let that get in the way of a good story? Certainly not the Arsenal baiters in the Press: 'The pits' taunted the *Mail on Sunday*; 'Micky Mouse Arsenal' mocked the *News of the World*.

George Graham could live with the ridicule, and it would take a lot more than a hiccup in the Cup – however embarrassing – to shake the foundations he had built at Highbury, but there was no getting away from the unpalatable truth: with the Christmas decorations still gracing the Marble Halls, the Wrexham defeat had left Arsenal's season – a season that had promised so much – in tatters. Failure to score in the next three League games, with Wright and Smith still failing miserably to gel and the 4-2-4 formation looking as unbalanced as ever, meant that Manchester United arrived in North London on the first day of February, a massive twenty points ahead of the eighth-placed and out of contention Gunners – an advantage shared by the eventual champions, Leeds.

For the second time in the season, David Rocastle conjured up a splendid goal against United (as it turned out, his very last for Arsenal), this time courtesy of a lightning counter-attack propelled by Ian Wright. A point that day against a United side whose end-of-term attack of nerves was still some way off, was the beginning of a seventeen-game unbeaten run-in to the season during which Arsenal would play their most attractive football under George Graham.

So what came right all of a sudden? As has inevitably been the case since Graham arrived at the club, the foundations of a long unbeaten spell were to be found at the back. After just three games together all season, the United game marked the aforementioned Adams/Bould reunion, and Graham's classic pairing at the back would hold the defensive fort in their own inimitable fashion for the rest of the season. If anybody still had their doubts about the collective and individual merits of Adams and Bould, they were surely dispelled now. The skipper had fully recovered from his hernia problems and was in as authoritative mood as ever, while Bould's knack of taking the heat out of compromising situations had not been affected by his lay-off. In midfield, Rocastle and Hillier were still battling away against the odds, but they were now helped immeasurably by the fact that Arsenal's attack was leaving First Division defences punch-drunk – opposing midfielders now had their work cut out simply trying to stem Arsenal's forward flow. There were no significant changes on the drawing board; quite simply Wright, Limpar and Merson all hit unreal form at the same time. When that combination of talent was on song there wasn't a defence in England that could live with them.

However, it was Kevin Campbell, generally out of favour since the arrival of Wright, who first opened the floodgates in a historic game against Sheffield Wednesday in February. In that match, Arsenal were struggling to overcome an in-form Wednesday until a rampant Campbell stepped into the fray for a limping Smith and set about inspiring the Gunners to rattle in a record-breaking six goals in eighteen breathtaking minutes. And what goals! Goals that would grace the Maracana, let alone Highbury: Campbell's own lightning turn and volley for the second goal was the first of a cluster of spectacular strikes that simply flew past the hapless Chris Woods. Paul Merson's gloriously lazy chip with the outside of his right foot from the edge of the box was the pick of a stunning repertoire.

The rest of the season was an authentic catalogue of classic goals. It had often been argued that the ability to shape quality goals out of mundane play was a prominent feature of Arsenal's game and, in the past, particularly during the first Championship-winning season, this had indeed been the case. But for three short months of bona fide brilliance it most certainly wasn't; the football was sparkling and the goals were even better. If one team has ever scored more spectacular goals in such a short space of time we'd like to see the evidence.

Whether slotting in alongside Alan Smith, playing wide on the flanks or functioning as an attacking midfielder, Paul Merson had already enjoyed a fine season amidst the insanity, but in Arsenal's late late show he would now hit new peaks of creativity. When the mood takes him, 'the Merse' is a throwback to a bygone era of English footballer, the heir to precocious talents à la Osgood, Marsh, Worthington and Bowles; almost lazily talented, but capable of inventing something out of nothing. Certainly no current player in the English game lobs or volleys with comparable verve and aplomb: a masterpiece of a lob against Crystal Palace from unspeakably wide on the right was just one of a succession of impossible goals in a richly productive spell. A bags-full-of-confidence Merson finally made his mark on the international stage, too, marking his first full appearance against Czechoslovakia, in Prague, with an uninhibited performance and a debut goal.

Anders Limpar, the Swede with the looks, skill and temperament of a more Latin stereotype, was in equally creative mood, his jinking runs and searching passes a constant source of goals. Ian Wright, in particular, thrived on the service of Arsenal's 'Superswede'. In its 79 years as the 'Home of Football', Highbury can have witnessed fewer goals more special than Limpar's daringly conceived and stunningly executed 40-yard lob which was the apotheosis of an authentic demolition job of Liverpool. That 4-0 ictory – and six or seven goals would not have flattered Arsenal on the day – confirmed that the previous imperious Merseysiders were at long last hitting the kind of extended slump that afflicted the rest of the footballing populace. Kevin Campbell will never please the purists as much as a Merson or Limpar, but given his opportunities after a frustrating period biting his nails, many a bruised defender discovered that a determined and confident 'Souper Kev' is just about the most difficult player around to knock out of his stride. And to his eternal credit, Campbell is a praiseworthy example of a muscle-bound striker who hustles opponents off their game without ever resorting to the underhand shenanigans, or sheer nastiness, that some of Britain's bigger names of similar physical attributes often employ. And one left-foot volley hit with extraordinary venom past Crystal Palace's Nigel Martyn was a goal to compare with anything that went on around it in Arsenal's spectacular late show.

And last, but most certainly not least, the goal-machine himself, Ian Wright! Wright! Wright! Bubbly, irrespressible, impetuous, wholehearted, belligerent, aggressive, feisty, inspirational, unpredictable – you pays your money and takes your choice. But really only one epithet could have done Wright full justice in that memorable run-in – UNSTOPPABLE!

George Graham, for one, wouldn't have changed Wright for the world. 'I still think Ian can add a little subtlety to his game and hold the ball better. He also needs to harness his aggression. But I never want him to lose that special quality, because it's that determination that carries him into areas where it really hurts. He has tremendous courage for a relatively small striker and his infectious enthusiasm rubs off on everyone around him.'

In Arsenal's inspired late rush, Wright was like a kid at Christmas. With Messieurs Merson, Limpar, et al., providing such silver platter service, the goals just flowed: being the bane of Tottenham does you no harm in the Highbury popularity stakes and Wright's late equaliser at White Hart Lane (added to his strike in the corresponding fixture at Highbury) was greeted with predictable joy. The game at Oldham earlier in the season had attracted headlines for all the wrong reasons. After being taunted and derided for 90 minutes and then spat at as he left the field, it was hardly surprising that Wright lost his rag; that he had to face a Football Association disciplinary hearing after being on the end of what was clearly racially-motivated abuse was a disgrace and yet another example of the FA's inveterate hard-line approach to Arsenal. In the return fixture, Wright let his boots do the talking; a clinical finish after a sweet interchange between Limpar and Hillier proved that the good guys do come out on top sometimes. That goal was followed by two 'this is my ball and I'm going to score' Wright specials against West Ham and the subsequent visit to Norwich produced a mad rush of a sprint from inside his own half that saw Wright overtake a speeding 'Rocky' to put the lid on a textbook counter-attack. A brace of goals in the aforementioned dismantling of Liverpool's reputation demonstrated that Wright was not in awe of big names either.

But despite the team's breakneck form in that long unbeaten run and a late dash for the line worthy of Sebastian Coe at his peak, by the time Southampton arrived for the last home game, Arsenal had been forced to throw in the towel in the race for a UEFA Cup spot. A draw at Chelsea in the penultimate fixture – marked by yet another brilliant goal, Lee Dixon's swerving lob from outside the box *à la* Merson – was not quite enough to peg back a Sheffield Wednesday team that had proved admirably resilient in the aftermath of their Highbury thrashing. As the 91/92 season drew to a close, Trevor Francis's side always did just enough to keep the chasing Gunners at bay, though revenge was not too far off. The Southampton game was still a memorable occasion; nearly 38,000 packed into Highbury to create an unforgettable atmosphere, more akin to a Championship-winning celebration than the last rites to what was, on paper at least, an unsuccessful season. In reality, the fans were galvanised not only by the exciting times of late and the promise of good times ahead, but by the opportunity to pay homage to Highbury's perennial twelfth man – the North Bank. Despite the heartfelt protests of generations of fans who had served their Arsenal apprenticeship on the sprawling steps, the terracing was about to be demolished to allow the construction of a new all-seater stand. The supporters, and at least one player, were determined to give the old faithful a rousing send-off.

As he entered the fray on that last day of the season, Ian Wright was neck-and-neck with Gary Lineker in the race for the 'Golden Boot'. Lineker, who was playing his last game for Tottenham in the game at Old Trafford, boasted a slight advantage, with 27 goals to Wright's 26. For just 90 minutes, surely even George Graham would have accepted that it was more about the individual than the team. Highbury had put on its Saturday best for a special occasion and the Prince of Dreams was not about to let his adoring congregation down. Before his own personal recital began, Wright's joyous reaction to Smith's goal provided a noteworthy vignette that said more about him as a person than a thousand tabloid hatchet-jobs and demonstrated precisely why he is so popular amongst his team-mates. Nobody loves to score more than Wright, but unlike many top strikers he could never be accused of being selfish; few players get more pleasure from their team-mates doing the business or celebrate their goals more genuinely and enthusiastically. At a time when he could have been forgiven for just wanting to get on with it as soon as possible, Wright's reaction to Smith's 85th-minute strike was as effusive and extended as ever.

Wright had already got off the mark himself with a penalty earlier in the half, but as the minutes ticked away in the second half and with the news filtering through from Old Trafford that Gary Lineker had scored, it was beginning to look as if the dream was going to remain just that. Fortunately, nobody had bothered to tell Wright. His second goal was the kind of thing you might see in the school playground or on Hackney Marshes, but in the Premier League? With 89 minutes on the clock, David Seaman clutched a cross out of the air one-handed and threw the ball like a bullet to Wright, who was lingering with intent, but still nearer to his own goal than Tim Flowers'. As Wright was later to express it in his own inimitably infectious Sarf London ragga-speak: 'He just threw it and I just said, this is it, man, I'm going for a goal.' And go he most certainly did. Such was his determination that the redoubtable Terry Hurlock, of all people, hesitated before making a half-hearted challenge in no man's land and was shrugged aside with ease. Swept along on a tide of bravado, Wright sprinted deep into Southampton territory, cut inside Kevin Moore and slammed the ball past Flowers with all the strength left in his body.

But there was more to come. Barely a minute later, Alan Smith's pass found Wright totally unmarked on the penalty spot with just Flowers to beat and the history books beckoning. Maybe he was still up in the clouds after his previous effort, maybe nerves got the better of him, or maybe he was just plain shattered – but for once Wright contrived to get it all wrong and the ball bobbed agonisingly off his shin. But fortune favoured the brave, the miskick threw Flowers off-balance, the ball trickled home and somehow Wright had his hat-trick. Maybe, just maybe, the collective efforts of generations of North Bankers did the trick as they willed the ball into their net for one last time and finished the days of the famous end with a flourish. Rarely can a goal that meant so little in the greater scheme of things have been celebrated with such joyous abandon.

As consolation prizes go, Wright's 29 League goals – 24 of them in just

30 games for Arsenal after his arrival from Palace – was entertainment of the highest order. But as the players paid a long and touching farewell to the North Bank to ironic choruses of 'Boring, boring Arsenal', the word 'if' was inevitably on most lips – if only the season could have gone on a couple more weeks, Arsenal would surely have been champions. As it was, the irregular first half of a schizophrenic season was too much of a handicap at the death. Still, with a settled defence back in place and Arsenal ending the term as top-scorers, the promise for the following season was immense.

Given Arsenal's prolific end to the season and the accepted logic of picking in-form players, it was a mystery why only Alan Smith – who was not really a central figure in Arsenal's late burst anyway – and Paul Merson made Graham Taylor's England squad for the European Championship Finals in Sweden that summer (Lee Dixon would have gone as well if he hadn't sustained a freak knee injury after tripping over outside his house just before the final squad was named). If the general absence of Gunners was inexplicable, Taylor's decision to leave Ian Wright at home was simply bizarre, though perhaps not surprising given the precedents. Wright had in fact been Taylor's first new cap after taking over from Bobby Robson in 1990, but over the length of this season, his very best, the in-form striker had made just one brief England appearance, and that as a late substitute in a friendly against Hungary. In the end, leaving Wright at home was a decision Taylor must have regretted, as England – unable to cope with Gary Lineker hitting the dry patch that would end his England career in controversial fashion – managed only one goal in three games and were dispatched swiftly home with their tails between their legs. As that summer's memorable 'Gary Who?' campaign flooded London's hoardings in celebration of Nike-man Wright's snatching of the 'Golden Boot' from the departing Lineker-san, Taylor was faced with an omnipresent and uncomfortable reminder of his most inexplicable of decisions.

BY GEORGE . . .

'Tonight we're leading England back into the European Cup so I hope the whole country will be right behind us. That *would* be a new experience for Arsenal!'

'It was a great night to admire the strengths of English football: pace, skill at speed, determination, resilience. We imposed our style on them, and some of our football was excellent. If we could play like that every game, my life would be ideal.'

Before and after the 6-1 thrashing of FK Austria Memphis
(September 1991).

'5-2 is too cavalier. I would have preferred 2-0 or 3-0.'
After the bagful-of-goals victory over Sheffield United.

'It's a tough draw. Last season Benfica played 38 games like us and lost only one, the same as us. They only conceded 18 goals, the same as us, but they scored more goals than we did, 89 to our 74. I don't know a lot about them.'
On mysterious European opponents, Benfica.

'I was very pleased with our performance in the Estadio da Luz. The atmosphere was very intimidating, and Sven-Goran Eriksson surprised us with his tactics early on ... we also had to come to terms with some different interpretations of the laws from what we're used to at home ... our performance showed all the good things about our side. Our attitude and spirit was tremendous. Our display was a combination of hard work, skill and organisation and we earned our reward. We're an adventurous side and that increases the pressure on the back players. But our defence did a superb job, well-marshalled as always by Tony Adams. In Britain, we're good at knocking ourselves. Let's look on the positive side. That was a performance that should make us all proud of British football.'
After taming the Lions of Lisbon in their own den.

'It's difficult to be passionate twice a week. I thought Coventry were hungrier than us.'
After the defeat at Coventry ushered in the longest week.

'You'll find most championship-winning teams are built on tight defences.'
Classic George, November, 1991.

'In terms of skill, the Continentals have got a big head-start on us ... it's very unusual that you see sides against Arsenal look fitter than us on the pitch. They looked fitter. If we'd been fresh and played at something like our best, we could have beaten Benfica.'

After Benfica put paid to European ambitions at Highbury.

'It was a see-saw contest and must have made for great entertainment for the millions watching on TV. We played some cavalier stuff. But we didn't get the result. That sums up so much of our season so far. I'm not going to shut up shop and go for a defensive approach. Forget any talk about "Boring Arsenal". You don't win two titles in three years by boring opponents into submission. I'm delighted with the constant threat our forwards pose. We always look like scoring. But we need to be tighter, too.'

After 3-2 defeat at Forest ...

'Come to Highbury for thrills. Ian Wright's finishing was terrific. His scoring record has been excellent. Do I enjoy high-scoring games? Yes. If we win them! If not, you wonder how you could have scored so many goals and come away with nothing. I felt a bit like that after our defeat at Forest.

... and Ian Wright's four-goal mugging of Everton in the next game.

'I heard our fans singing "What a load of rubbish". That's fair, we *were* rubbish. After today the players should question their ability, effort, application and attitude.'

After Boxing Day crash at bottom-placed Luton.

'This is the biggest low of my managerial career. Now we must get back to work. That's the only way to react to last Saturday's defeat at Wrexham. It will be a test for all of us, because we've become used to success. But we have no God-given right to succeed. We've had to work hard for our Championships. Now we must sort things out again on the training field. We haven't become a bad team because of one result.'

After Welsh KO.

'Believe me, he is the player every club in the country would love to have.'

After Tony Adams' inspired comeback against Forest.

'Ian Wright was a bit wound up against Palace. He was so eager to score against his own club. Ian is one of the game's great enthusiasts. With most

players, it's a case of winding them up before a match. With Ian the opposite applies. He's so determined, you need to relax him before the kick-off.'

On the still irrepressible Ian Wright.

'Our recent form has been encouraging. I just wish the season could go on
for another month! Congratulations to Leeds and Howard Wilkinson for
winning the title. But we want it back next season. And I can tell Howard
from experience: it's harder to retain the title than win it.

'Looking back, the injuries to Steve Bould and Tony Adams did have a
big effect. Losing to Benfica in the European Cup hit us too. It took us a
while to get over that disappointment. But we've been more consistent in
the past three months. If we can recapture the defensive meanness that was
the hallmark of our 1991 title success, then we'll be very hard to beat.
We're already the First Division top-scorers. We have bags of flair. I'd love
us to win the Championship with people talking about our attacking
power. I wouldn't swap our attacking players with anyone. Just look at the
names – Paul Merson, Anders Limpar, Ian Wright, Kevin Campbell and
Alan Smith!'

At the end of a long season.

BARCLAYS LEAGUE 91/92

Final League position: 4th
Average home gate: 31,914

Queens Park Rangers	(h) 1-1	Merson
Everton	(a) 1-3	Winterburn
Aston Villa	(a) 1-3	Smith
Luton Town	(h) 2-0	Smith, Merson
Manchester City	(h) 2-1	Smith, Limpar
Leeds United	(a) 2-2	Smith 2
Coventry City	(h) 1-2	Adams
Crystal Palace	(a) 4-1	Campbell 2, Smith, Thomas
Sheffield United	(h) 5-2	Smith, Dixon (penalty), Groves, Rocastle, Campbell
Southampton	(a) 4-0	Rocastle, Wright 3
Chelsea	(h) 3-2	Dixon (penalty), Wright, Campbell
Manchester United	(a) 1-1	Rocastle
Notts County	(h) 2-0	Smith, Wright
West Ham United	(a) 0-1	
Oldham Athletic	(a) 1-1	Wright
Sheffield Wednesday	(a) 1-1	Bould
Tottenham Hotspur	(h) 2-0	Wright, Campbell
Nottingham Forest	(a) 2-3	Merson, Smith
Everton	(h) 4-2	Wright 4
Luton Town	(a) 0-1	
Manchester City	(a) 0-1	
Wimbledon	(h) 1-1	Merson
Aston Villa	(h) 0-0	
Queens Park Rangers	(a) 0-0	
Liverpool	(a) 0-2	
Manchester United	(h) 1-1	Rocastle
Notts County	(a) 1-0	Smith
Norwich City	(h) 1-1	Merson
Sheffield Wednesday	(h) 7-1	Campbell 2, Limpar 2, Smith, Merson, Wright
Tottenham Hotspur	(a) 1-1	Wright
Oldham Athletic	(h) 2-1	Wright, Merson
West Ham United	(a) 2-0	Wright 2
Leeds United	(h) 1-1	Merson
Wimbledon	(a) 3-1	Parlour, Wright, Campbell
Nottingham Forest	(h) 3-3	Dixon (penalty), Adams, Merson
Coventry City	(a) 1-0	Campbell
Norwich City	(a) 3-1	Wright 2 (1 penalty), Campbell
Crystal Palace	(h) 4-1	Merson 3, Campbell
Sheffield United	(a) 1-1	Campbell
Liverpool	(h) 4-0	Hillier, Wright 2, Limpar
Chelsea	(a) 1-1	Dixon
Southampton	(h) 5-1	Wright 3 (1 penalty), Campbell, Smith

227

European Cup 91/92

First Round:
FK Austria Memphis (h) 6-1 Smith 4,
                             Linighan,
                             Limpar
FK Austria Memphis (a) 0-1

Second Round:
Benfica   (a) 1-1 Campbell
Benfica   (h) 1-3 (after extra
                       time) Pates

FA Cup 91/92

Third Round:
Wrexham   (a) 1-2 Smith

League Cup 91/92

Second Round:
Leicester City (a) 1-1 Wright
Leicester City (h) 2-0 Wright,
                       Merson

Third Round:
Coventry City (a) 0-1

Appearances

	League	FA Cup	League Cup	Europe	Total
David Seaman	42	1	3	4	50
Paul Merson	41+1	1	3	4	49+1
Nigel Winterburn	41	1	2	4	48
Lee Dixon	38	1	3	4	46
David Rocastle	36+3	1	3	4	44+3
Tony Adams	35	1	3	4	43
Alan Smith	33+6	1	2	4	40+6
Ian Wright	30	0	3	0	33
Kevin Campbell	22+9	1	2	4	29+9
David Hillier	27	1	0	0	28
Anders Limpar	23+6	0	1	3	27+6
Steve Bould	24+1	0	0	0+1	24+2
Andy Linighan	15+2	0	1+1	2	18+3
Paul Davis	12	0	2	3	17
David O'Leary	11+14	1	0+1	1	13+15
Colin Pates	9+2	0	2	2	13+2
Michael Thomas	6+4	0	2	1+1	9+5
Perry Groves	5+8	0+1	1+2	0+4	6+15
Jimmy Carter	5+1	1	0	0	6+1
Pal Lydersen	5+2	0	0	0	5+2
Ray Parlour	2+4	0	0	0	2+4
Stephen Morrow	0+2	0	0	0	0+2
Neil Heaney	0+1	0	0	0	0+1

Goal-scorers

	League	FA Cup	League Cup	Europe	Total
Ian Wright	24	0	2	0	26
Alan Smith	12	1	0	4	17
Kevin Campbell	13	0	0	1	14
Paul Merson	12	0	1	0	13
Anders Limpar	4	0	0	1	5
Lee Dixon	4	0	0	0	4
David Rocastle	4	0	0	0	4
Tony Adams	2	0	0	0	2
Stephen Bould	1	0	0	0	1
Perry Groves	1	0	0	0	1
David Hillier	1	0	0	0	1
Michael Thomas	1	0	0	0	1
Ray Parlour	1	0	0	0	1
Nigel Winterburn	1	0	0	0	1
Andy Linighan	0	0	0	1	1
Colin Pates	0	0	0	1	1

Season's Review 1992/93

Up for the Cups!

The 92/93 season was the year of 'and it's Ian Wright, Ian Wright FC . . .' of terrace-chant legend, as at times Arsenal came uncomfortably close to becoming a one-man team, especially when it came to scoring goals. But while the indefatigable Wright deservedly grabbed most of the headlines, it was also, somewhat paradoxically, the year of the unlikely hero. Stephen Morrow, a quietly-spoken Belfast lad, who off the field looks more like a bookish undergraduate than a professional footballer, emerged out of nowhere to score the winner in the League Cup Final (his first-ever goal for the Gunners) before fate, and Tony Adams' exuberance, conspired to send him straight back into obscurity via a hospital ward.

In the FA Cup, Andy Linighan, though a better-known name than Morrow, proved an even more unlikely hero. In the three years following his arrival from Norwich for £1.2 million, the big centre-half, thwarted by the formidable Adams/Bould tandem, had rarely managed to shake off the tag of bit player, only making the starting line-up when injuries, suspensions or Her Majesty's pleasure, deprived George Graham of either member of his first-choice pairing. When he did play, a somewhat cumbersome gait, and the air of a man who has arrived at a party uninvited and doesn't quite know what he is doing there, had palpably failed to win over the Highbury faithful. But at the season's end, it was Linighan's battling display in the FA Cup final replay that saw the famous old trophy back at Highbury for the first time since 1979. Ignoring the pain of a broken nose courtesy of Mark Bright's roving elbow, Arsenal's odd-man out – a popular figure at the club if not on the terraces – soldiered on in typically brave fashion to grab the all-important last-gasp goal. For one night at least, the man whose too-sexy-for-my-shirt vanity is a constant source of amusement in the dressing-room, could bask in some wider glory. After the game, Tony Adams revealed exactly how bad things had got for his partner at the back: 'Andy used to tell me that he ought to be called "Boo Linighan" because boos were all he seemed to get from our fans,' adding with relish, 'but he'll deservedly be a hero now.'

So, on paper at least, it was another historic season, with Arsenal becoming the first-ever side to win the FA and League Cups in the same season and, in the process, enabling George Graham to add another 'done that' to his already impressive curriculum vitae by completing a unique hat-trick of domestic trophies as Arsenal manager. But whatever the history books record for posterity, the harsh reality is that the 92/93 Arsenal was almost certainly the weakest team since Graham had arrived at the club, and it was only saved from obscurity by the continuing exploits of the feisty Ian Wright – without his 15 goals in the two Cup competitions, Arsenal were, quite simply, on the road to nowhere.

Just why Arsenal were so disappointing in the League remains something of a mystery. The previous campaign had ended with the Gunners in prolific goal-scoring form and they entered the starting gate as pre-season favourites to win the inaugural Premier League. But like the fancied horse that falls at the first hurdle, they never really got going – the tally of three wins in their first nine games served as a reliable taster to the end of season return of a mere 15 victories in 42 games. Loose talk of retaining the title did abound until Christmas (not bad for White Hart Lane perhaps, but immensely disappointing *chez* George) but only the really gullible were fooled. In the end, an immensely disappointing tenth position was not simply the worst performance under Graham's stewardship, but a performance only beaten twice (in the negative sense) since the manager himself played in the Double-winning side back in 70/71. Quite how a side goes from being the top scorers in the Division to the lowest in the space of only one season is anybody's guess.

The first day of the season is always one of high hopes up and down the country, and with Arsenal 2-0 up and buzzing against Norwich as the players strolled off the pitch for that first half-time cuppa, Highbury was an authentic 'house of fun'. But any illusions that Graham's men would carry on where they had left off the year before, lasted only for those first 45 minutes. Norwich's four goals in the second half didn't only put paid to Arsenal's opening day ambitions, although they guaranteed an early obituary for the attacking abandon of the new model Gunners. In truth, George Graham had probably never been too convinced by the shift in physiognomy; as the previous season ended he had commented: 'The run has not fooled me, we've played fantastic attacking football but we need to strengthen. We definitely need two or three new faces to give everybody a lift.' Not for the first time the new faces didn't materialise, but his immediate reaction to the Norwich setback suggested that we would soon be seeing a more familiar Arsenal: 'I still think we have the most exciting set of forwards in the country, but we've got to get the balance right between attacking and knowing when to dig in.' That was George-speak for forget the 4-4-2 formations, the seven-goal wins and general fun all-round – clean sheets are what I want!

With the Gunners soon firing blanks up-front as the born-again advocates for the defence ruled, it was a good job that the Norwich debacle turned out to be a one-off, and that the defence – with the inspirational Tony Adams leading from the front in swashbuckling fashion – was soon proving as obdurate as ever. For most Arsenal fans, putting the record straight against Tottenham in the FA Cup Semi-Final was the highlight of the season, and oh, what sweet revenge the winner must have meant to Arsenal's very own 'Captain Fantastic'! The game was a tighter, more cagey affair than two years before, something that suited Arsenal down to the ground. Vinnie Samways did have one early chance for Spurs after Adams made an uncharacteristic hash of a back-pass, but after that you could stop counting.

In the second half, Arsenal always looked the most likely, and the Ians, Selley and Wright, both might have opened the scoring. With the game about to enter its last ten minutes and a leg-sapping extra half-hour beckoning, Ray Parlour's youthful vigour took him forward on one last probing run, forcing Justin Edinburgh to bring him down just outside the box. For once, free-kick specialist Paul Davis stepped aside, leaving it to Paul Merson to size up the situation before curling the ball beyond the Spur's defence to the far post where Tony Adams came charging in unmarked to thud a textbook header downwards and beyond Thorsvedt. Two years of jibes were about to be banished to the ancient history books and the sweetest of winning goals prompted an immediate rash of T-shirts around Highbury, sporting the legend, 'Donkey Won the Derby!' That decisive header at Wembley was practically a carbon copy of Adams' goal at Ipswich in the Quarter Finals – though on that occasion the skipper was sporting a bloodstained bandage on his forehead for dramatic effect – and once again demonstrated how important his presence was when the going got tough. Not before time, Adams was beginning to receive the plaudits that had been denied him for so long outside the confines of Highbury – four days before the Semi-Final he had practically been proclaimed a national hero after a storming game for England in a World Cup Qualifier in Turkey. There was still time for Lee Dixon to get himself sent off after an ill-advised body-check on an admittedly theatrically wronged Edinburgh (an ongoing and uncharitable *tête-à-tête* with the tetchy Nayim had already earned the full-back a yellow card in the first half) but Spurs never seriously looked like equalising. Despite the referee's efforts to prolong the game straight into the *Guinness Book of Records*, Arsenal hung on to secure another Wembley date and a chance to win the FA Cup – the only domestic trophy that George Graham had yet to win as manager.

Tony Adams' late goal did nothing to dispel the now standard talk about Arsenal's name being on the Cup. Nightmares about another Wrexham may have briefly crossed the collective Arsenal psyche when the Third Round draw had paired Arsenal with legendary giant-killers Yeovil back in January, but a ruthless performance and an Ian Wright hat-trick proved to be an early statement of FA Cup intent and the West Country minnows never looked like adding to their sixteen League scalps. The omens were promising, too: Arsenal's run to the Cup Final in the Double year also started with three goals on the sloping pitch at Yeovil.

But it was the Leeds tie in the next round that first produced the inevitable clichés about FA Cup destiny. In the first game at Highbury, Arsenal were two down and struggling badly at half-time; only a stunning 25-yard shot from Paul Merson after a typical jink inside Chris Fairclough with just nine minutes to go kept the Gunners in the competition. 'It could have gone anywhere, into the net or killed someone in the back of the stand' was the wry reaction of 'the Merse' to his life-saving and spectacular goal. In the replay at a seething Elland Road, Arsenal again came back from the dead; Ian Wright, back in the side after a three-game suspension, equalised with just three minutes left on the clock before hitting the winner in extra time, on a night when the hapless John Lukic was in unusually generous mood against his old team-mates. After that against-the-odds achievement, Arsenal's run to the Semi-Final was relatively straightforward: relegation-bound Nottingham Forest were cannon-fodder for an inspired Ian Wright at Highbury and, with all due respect, Portman Road was never going to prove the daunting arena that Elland Road had been.

Arsenal's Cup run threw up plenty of excitement and goals but thrills and spills in the League were sparse. Despite the long-term absence of Steve Bould – the rearguard's Mr Reliable missed the last third of the season with a thigh injury – the defence was again the team's strongest department by a distance, and only League champions Manchester United conceded fewer goals over the season. Not that George can ever get enough centre-halves! At the beginning of February, Martin Keown, a defender who left the club as a boy for just £200,000, returned as a man and a fully-fledged International – though, at £2 million, a damn sight more expensive too.

Understandably, Keown's arrival exposed Graham to accusations of criminal negligence for letting him go in the first place. Despite the decision to shore up the defence further, the crux of Arsenal's problem was at the other end; an appalling return of just 40 goals was the club's lowest-ever in the top flight, and the lowest of *any* team in the much-hyped Premier League. To put it mildly, it was a highly disappointing performance for a club of Arsenal's stature with a squad that included so many gifted forwards. Basically, if Ian Wright didn't score, Arsenal were not only up the proverbial creek without a paddle, they were missing the canoe as well.

Perhaps the arrival of the exuberant Wright had led to a subconscious shift of attitude on Alan Smith's part, in particular. The latter's role in Arsenal's wonder years is unquestionable, and in the game against Coventry in November he joined the select band of players to have scored 100 goals or more for Arsenal – an achievement only John Radford (149) and Frank Stapleton (108) could boast in the last 25 years. But maybe the less assertive side of Smith's nature had begun to take command, as he, like everybody else, assumed and accepted that the weight of goal-scoring responsibility would now fall on Wright's more assertive shoulders. It may be true that Arsenal changed their approach as Wright became the focal point of the attack and that Smith could no longer rely on decent service from the flanks (rather than getting on the end of things in the box, Smith would often find himself stranded in deeper positions trying to flick the ball on for his new partner), but that is still only half the story. Certainly, Smith never looked anything like the sharp-shooter of old, and a meagre 3 goals in 31 League games was a poor return for a striker of his goal-scoring pedigree. By the end of the season, even George Graham, a staunch fan of his long-time centre-forward, was forced to admit that Smith had been out-of-sorts.

If 'Smudger' was a shadow of his old self, Kevin Campbell practically shifted into reverse, blundering around like a hod carrier on ice, now looking ponderous where before he once looked so powerful. By now, the youngster had earned himself the unflattering nickname of 'the Frank Bruno of Highbury' – i.e. he looked the part but never became Champ. Admittedly, his performances against Millwall and Derby as Arsenal's League Cup run got underway were decisive, but against better quality opposition he struggled to make an impact and his woeful lack of touch began to provoke serious doubts about his long-term ability to live up to the expectations those goal-scoring feats as a youngster had once generated. Not that you could ever reproach 'Souper' for a lack of effort in a good cause – just ask Ian Wright – but the harder he tried, the worse things seemed to get.

As for Paul Merson, nobody could ever accuse him of trying too hard! 'The Merse' was back in infuriatingly erratic mode and his attitude at times seemed to border on the non-committal. Most damningly, his fitness looked anything but that of a top-flight professional. Merson's gait as he stood around in the centre-circle after the slightest exertion – hands on hips, red-faced, gasping for air – wouldn't have looked out of place in a Sunday morning pub team. The erstwhile hero of the lads had fallen so far from grace, and in such a short space of time considering his heroics of the previous campaign, that treacherous whispers became an item on the terraces at Highbury – if it was true that Glasgow Rangers were willing to pay silly money for such a 'fanny merchant' then maybe George Graham should cash in his chips for the gap-toothed one before it proved too late. In the end, there was the saving grace of the odd match-winning performances when it really mattered, most notably his 'Man-of-the-match' effort at Wembley in the League Cup Final, and the quality of his goals. However, rewind-the-video efforts like the wickedly swerving volley in the latter game (please ignore Brian Moore's over-the-top protestations the next time you watch this one in slow motion – there was absolutely *no* deflection), the aforementioned cracker against Leeds that kept the Gunners in the FA Cup, a gloriously irreverent chip against Chelsea, or a Platiniesque free-kick at Ipswich, were not backed up by the more mundane strikes of a prolific scorer. Even allowing for the fact that Merson has always been a scorer of great goals rather than a great scorer, the increasingly rare glimpses of his abundant natural talent were starting to try the patience of even his biggest fans. Not for the first time, the end of term report on 'the Merson person' would read 'must try harder'.

George Graham's patience with Merson – season after season he has been a fixture in the side despite his inconsistency – was yet again in stark contrast with his attitude to Anders Limpar. Limpar is a similarly gifted player who doesn't always do himself justice – though, if pressed to choose, most seasoned Arsenal watchers would probably argue that he was more consistent than Merson – but Graham never displayed anything like the same patience with the Swede. At times, the manager even went so far as to break his own strict rules about washing dirty linen in public, and criticised the player for his lack of application. And while other players could spend whole seasons playing badly and still not get the heave-ho, Graham would drop Limpar at the slightest opportunity. For once, Graham's standards were patently not the same for everybody; and God knows what it must have done to the Swede's confidence, knowing that one bad game would inevitably earn him the big freeze. Not that he did himself many favours; the cameos as substitute were often breathtaking, but when in the team for 90 minutes, Limpar would flit around in eye-catching enough fashion, but he would rarely impose himself on the game. Graham's attitude to the Swede was best demonstrated by his failure to turn to him in the six most crucial games of the season: Limpar didn't manage to get on the pitch for a single minute of Semi-Final or Final action in either Cup competition. Whatever the reasons for his fall from grace, Limpar's failure to make the long-term impact at Highbury which his talent warranted was a continuing disappointment to Arsenal devotees.

Both Limpar and Merson could have taken a leaf out of Ian Wright's book on attitude. Wright had by now become the *bête noire* of opposing fans and the media alike. With malicious intent or not, many tended to confuse his unbridled enthusiasm with aggression, pointing to the 'silly bugger' celebrating as evidence of a supposedly provocative nature. But in reality there is no edge to Ian Wright; quite simply, few professional footballers approach each game with such glee, and none get such a kick out of scoring. As a youngster, Wright was repeatedly told he was too small to make it in the professional game and, after being rejected by several League clubs, he left school and started to make a living as a plasterer and bricklayer. When he was nineteen, Brighton came knocking at his door, but some vibrant performances on trial still weren't enough to get him in the game full-time. Back playing semi-professional football with Greenwich Borough, Wright probably thought that his chance had passed him by. Luckily, Crystal Palace invited him for one last trial and the circumspect but discerning Steve Coppell liked what he saw. At the ripe old footballing age of 21, the raring-to-go player finally got the chance he had always dreamed of. Wright had a glimpse of the scrap-heap and not surprisingly didn't like what he saw. Consequently, nobody appreciates their place at the top more; and if he soaks it for all he can get, who can blame him? Being black and playing for Arsenal – a combination guaranteed to provoke the bigots on the one hand and the under-achievers on the other – hardly helps, either. Suffice to say that when a Lee Sharpe or a Mick Quinn does a silly dance or celebrates effusively there are less complaints; but, then again, few players get as much chance to celebrate as Wright and most teams don't win as often as Arsenal. And the celebrating is not just about playing to the gallery, either; we're talking here about a player who gets such a kick out of scoring that he celebrates hitting the net in training as if he'd just scored the winning goal in the Cup Final!

Wright recognises that his critics often pick on him as a way of getting at Arsenal: 'I love the club and I hate it when their reputation suffers through me.' A vivid demonstration of this witch-hunt mentality was provided by the outrageously over-the-top reaction to an innocuous clash with Tottenham's David Howells in December. Against the backdrop of an almost hysterical Press campaign, Wright was eventually charged with misconduct by the FA and banned for three matches. Suffice to say that with punches like that White Hart Lane effort, Arsenal's budding pugilist could be in serious danger of spending his life trapped in a paper bag.

Maybe Wright could be accused of somewhat spiteful over-celebrating after scoring against his old team, Crystal Palace (as he invariably does), but given the reasons he left the club, that doesn't take a lot of figuring out either. Even then, when Wright kisses the crest on his Arsenal shirt, it has little to do with the gratuitous boasting immediately after changing clubs which we see from other big-name players who shall remain nameless – it is simply a genuine appreciation of where he's arrived after such a long and tortuous journey to the top. Wright's unfailingly positive attitude is best summed up by his remarks before the FA Cup Final: 'I just love football. If you can win something at the end of it, that's the icing on the cake. I just love the game, and I love the important games more. On Saturday I won't think about anything else but winning. I'll visualise myself doing well, doing good things. It's easy to visualise yourself scoring a goal, but you have to make sure other things are right as well. Steve Coppell always used to say to me: see the game in your mind, see yourself doing good things.' Paul Merson describes Wright's pre-match enthusiasm like this: 'You should see him in the dressing-room before a game. He's potty – shouting, dancing, on fire.' On the surface, the supposedly dour George Graham, a man who keeps his cards close to his chest if ever there was one, and the ebullient Ian Wright, a man who wears his heart loudly on his sleeve, may seem poles apart, but they both know what it is to struggle to make ends meet and they are both winners. As the player himself puts it: 'I'll do anything to win. I want to win so much that I'm on the edge, but I'm never malicious. That's just not me.' Nobody at Highbury, least of all the gaffer, is complaining about Wright's record or his approach to the game. On the contrary, George Graham would just love to have a squad full of players with the same attitude.

If, Wright apart, the forwards were firing blanks, it was hardly down to criminal profligacy. Given the lamentable service, you needed to be a genius à la Wright to get even a sniff of goal. And if a subtle or telling pass from midfield was about as typical as a clean sheet on the other side of North London, in the goal-scoring stakes the midfielders proved uniformly impotent, too. In the Premier League, Jensen, Hillier, Parlour, Morrow,

Selley, and Davis seemingly conspired to go the whole League season without scoring. And if those free-spirited blighters Parlour and Hillier hadn't gone and spoilt it all by scoring a whole goal each, the midfield slack-pack would indeed have managed a goal-free season, an astonishing feat by any standards. Graham shuffled his resources continuously in search of the right blend, but the truth is that you could have picked any two from the above and the lack of discernible creative nous would still have been unmistakable.

David Rocastle, the most effective attacking midfielder in Graham's reign at the club, had now gone, surprisingly off-loaded to Leeds in the close season. Graham has subsequently admitted that letting go a player he not only admired professionally, but was fond of personally, was perhaps the hardest decision he has had to make since arriving at the club. As a symbol of Arsenal's youth policy, 'Rocky' was an extremely popular figure at the club and on the terraces, but the fact remains that a combination of injury and weight problems, and a corresponding loss of pace and confidence, meant that he had never quite lived up to his early promise. Still, while never repeating the form of the first Championship-winning season, Rocastle had remained a key figure in Graham's planning and the season before his move he had played in no less than 47 matches. Surely he must have been doing something right? Maybe Graham simply believed the offer of £2 million from Howard Wilkinson was too good to refuse. It was either that or an overnight change of mind, which is hardly the Scot's style.

Whatever the reasons for his departure, Rocastle's ability to link up with the forwards was missed and left Graham's squad bereft of midfielders with naturally attacking instincts. With Paul Davis on hold for the big games – he didn't make his debut until March and only played six League games all season – Graham was eventually forced to concede that his midfield was indeed in need of an injection of quality new blood. In the end, the old hand Davis would play in all three Cup finals and the Spurs Semi-Final, his incisiveness only serving to throw the surrounding famine of ideas into stark relief. He also maintained his knack of decisive free-kicks at Wembley: goals by Paul Merson and Ian Wright following assists by dead-ball Davis, maintained a tradition established by Charlie Nicholas and Martin Hayes in earlier Finals. Many Arsenal fans wondered why Graham didn't play Davis more often, even if his legs weren't up to a full season. The motives behind the midfielder's extended absences probably went back to his very public falling-out with Graham the previous season. To outsiders, it may look as if Paul Davis is the only player to have challenged the Highbury Don's authority and hung around to tell the tale. In reality, while the player never quite became a *persona non grata*, Graham could never totally forgive and forget his 1991 heresy and from then on he would only use his most gifted midfielder when his presence was indispensable (Graham may be stubborn but he's not stupid enough to throw stones at his own glasshouse).

The new breed of Arsenal midfielders were not bad players (although it would be fair to say that there was hardly a budding Liam Brady among them either), it was just a question of balance – too many willing Indians in need of a chief. Things could have been worse; at the beginning of the season Graham had been prepared to pay £2.5 million for Crystal Palace midfielder, Geoff Thomas. Fortunately for Arsenal, Ron Noades upped the ante and Thomas stayed where he was.

The case of John Jensen, Arsenal's only midfield reinforcement in the wake of Rocastle's departure, was most eloquent. Arriving from Brondy for £1 million after helping Denmark to win the European Championship, the Dane immediately struggled with the dual burden of coming to grips with the pace of English football and living up to the false expectations created by his blockbuster of a goal in the Final against Germany. As a destroyer, Jensen is fine, and if he had a Brady or a Hoddle to feed after winning the ball, great, but as a genuinely creative influence or goal-scorer he is a non-starter. Asking him to assume the role of main playmaker in midfield was a piece of miscasting redolent of the earlier misconceived use of Kevin Richardson. Still, 'J.J.' is certainly wholehearted enough and, after a much-needed rest, Graham brought him back to make a decisive contribution to the FA Cup Final triumph. The Dane finished the season more happily as he played a vital part in shutting down Sheffield Wednesday's more creative midfield in a role that he was more suited to, and in a hint of what was to come in Arsenal's forthcoming Euro-campaign.

On the plus side, as ever, Graham was prepared to give youth a fling on the biggest stage, and in the FA Cup Semi-Final the eighteen-year-old Ian Selley and twenty-year-old Ray Parlour ran their hearts out to sterling effect, though Selley would not make the FA Cup Final line-up and Parlour was unable to reproduce his form from that first occasion. In Arsenal's second Wembley date of the season, the League Cup Final, it was action-replay time as another Ray Parlour surge earned a decisive free-kick, this time the one that led to Paul Merson's opening goal. But it was another product of the Highbury youth factory who would hog the next day's headlines: Steve Morrow gleefully accepted the chance given to him by Carlton Palmer to bang home his first-ever goal for the club and secure a place in the Arsenal history books. It's just a shame that as the rest of the players were going up to collect their medals, the youngster was being stretchered off with his arm broken in two places – the result of falling off Tony Adams' back after some boisterous celebrations. The accident certainly took the gloss off the ensuing celebrations; rarely can a captain have walked up the Wembley stairs to pick up a trophy in such downbeat mood as Adams. Thankfully, no long-term damage was done, and the youngster got the rousing reception he deserved when be belatedly climbed up to the Royal Box to collect his winner's medal shortly before the FA Cup Final kick-off – not bad, really, for a player who started the season with more appearances for Northern Ireland than Arsenal. In his days being shunted off on-loan to Reading, Watford and Barnet he would surely have settled for this better-late-then-never glory!

The League Cup Final was an open and attractive game abounding in goalmouth incident, but just 27 days later, the FA Cup Final between the same sides (the first time the same two clubs had made both Finals) was anything but a classic although, amidst the subsequent Press-slaying, it was conveniently forgotten that it takes two to tango. Wednesday had gone into the first Final on the back of a run of fluent form and were strongly fancied. Never better than when pitched into the role of underdogs, this suited Graham's men down to the ground. But by the time of the big one, Arsenal had assumed the role of favourites; not only did they hold the psychological edge after their League Cup triumph, but the guaranteed UEFA Cup place meant the game was not going to make or break their season. On the down side they went into the match with serious doubts about Ian Wright's fitness; the striker had broken his toe in the match against Nottingham Forest just a month earlier and was still not 100 per cent fit. In the end, he was forced to hobble off early in both games, but that still didn't stop him proving to be the scourge of Wednesday and, in passing, keep up his great scoring record in FA Cup Finals. Three years earlier, despite being only half-fit, Wright had come off the bench to score twice for Crystal Palace against Manchester United, a tally he was about to double. His 21st-minute goal in the first game, like Adams' effort against Spurs in the same scenario, was a header straight out of the textbook; after pulling away from forward-cum-defender-cum-God-knows-where-I-am-supposed-to-be-playing, Paul Warhurst, Wright's header from Linighan's knock-on was incisive and unstoppable. The less said about the rest of a dire game the better; suffice to mention that (a) David Hirst equalised in the 62nd minute of what even George Graham admitted was a Wednesday-dominated second half and (b) the ensuing extra-time saw neither side seriously threaten to break the deadlock.

The replay wasn't much better, and though Graham made noises about the tiredness of the players after the long hard English season, fatigue was just one of several contributing factors to the non-event. The rain that swirled around Wembley; the familiarity-breeds-contempt status of the fixture, and the anti-climax of a fourth trip to Wembley in quick succession were equally insidious conspirators. Only 62,267 spectators turned up for the replay – an unthinkably miserable turn-out just a few years ago in any Cup Final, let alone one featuring London's top side, and a measure of the extent to which the Wembley experience has been devalued by the unholy alliance between opportunity-grabbing Wembley Stadium Limited marketing men and compliant FA officialdom.

Again, 'Wright on cue', our hero gave the Gunners the lead on the half-hour, this time with a truly memorable goal. For once, Arsenal's very own 'odd couple' combined effectively; after Smith's measured flick, Wright was simply too quick off the mark for Palmer and Warhurst and his gloriously subtle touch at speed over Woods provided a fitting climax. The 30th and final goal of Wright's memorable season was the finish of a truly great goal-scorer. But history was to repeat itself in the second half as Wednesday got on top of the listless Gunners, and Chris Waddle's somewhat fluky goal in the 68th minute was enough to take the game into extra-time again. Almost despite the efforts of the combatants, tired legs produced a degree of excitement and inevitably chances came and went on both sides, but the decisive goal still failed to materialise. Wembley's first-ever penalty lottery in a Cup Final looked unavoidable until the dramatic final denouement provided by Chris Woods' frankly pathetic attempt to stop Andy Linighan's 119th-minute header. A fitting finale to a damn poor show.

Despite the subsequent media onslaught about ill-gotten gains, Arsenal had demonstrated, yet again, that whatever the epoch, they are nothing if not durable. Linighan's goal was just the latest in a long line of late winners that had secured last-gasp victory for the Gunners on the big occasion: Ray Kennedy on the night Arsenal clinched the League at White Hart Lane in 1971; Alan Sunderland's miraculous FA Cup winner in 1979 against Manchester United – after Arsenal themselves had untypically done their best to snatch defeat out of the jaws of victory; Paul Vaessen's header against Juventus in the 1980 Cup-Winners' Cup Semi-Final in Turin; David Rocastle's League Cup Semi-Final winner at Spurs in 1987 on the night when the durability of Graham's Arsenal first became apparent; and, of course, Michael Thomas's 'it's up for grabs now' Championship winner in 1989.

One man, David O'Leary, had played a part in all but the first of the above and, for him at least, the Sheffield Wednesday replay proved a memorable occasion. Just three days after 22,000 fans had paid tribute to him in a farewell match at Highbury, he bowed out as a Gunner after eighteen years in the first team. In heart-rending fashion, he did a lap of honour around Wembley with the FA Cup held high. Coming on twice as substitute for Ian Wright was certainly a bizarre note on which to finish! Nigel Winterburn and Lee Dixon must have been equally chuffed by the FA Cup glory: Winterburn had missed out on Wimbledon's 1987 giant-killing of Liverpool by leaving the Dons for Highbury just days before the Final and his medal was a fitting reward for an unsung hero. As for Lee Dixon, he would have been mightily relieved to get a second shot at Wembley glory after his FA Cup Semi-Final sending-off had seen him miss the League Cup Final through suspension.

For once, the maxim 'winning isn't everything, it's the *only* thing' seemed entirely appropriate, though on the night justice was most certainly done, especially after Mark Bright's foul deed in the first half, when the Wednesday centre-forward broke Andy Linighan's nose with a rogue elbow. How Bright stayed on the pitch after that is anybody's guess – maybe the fact that it was out of character saved him. If the referee, Keiren Barratt, had missed the incident, fair enough, but the resulting yellow card means he presumably saw what happened. So why wasn't the card red? Still, Bright would get his come-uppance in no uncertain fashion. In the second half he missed two absolute sitters that might have put the game beyond Arsenal and, most poetically of all, he was comprehensively outjumped by Linighan for the late winner.

A unique brace of victories in the Cups may have produced a verdict of all's well that ends well, but that couldn't hide the fact that for most of the season Arsenal's performances were about as muted as the North Bank mural. An insidious combination of the building work that kept the famous end out of action all season, a certain amount of resentment felt by the fans in the wake of the Bond controversy, the anomalies of the ticket registration system designed to alleviate the problems caused by the reduced capacity, and the lacklustre football on offer, combined to produce a measly 24,403 average attendance in the League. The atmosphere at Highbury often resembled a morgue and by the latter stages of the season it was clear that the team were going through the motions between Cup games – hardly an attitude that encouraged wavering supporters to hand over hard-earned cash. The League season fizzled out insipidly in the run-in to the FA Cup Final as a practically unrecognisable Arsenal played five League games in just ten days, the makeshift line-ups boasting the presence of several hereto unknown youngsters – most notably the young Scot, Paul Dickov, who demonstrated his promise with a couple of cracking goals – and fringe players like Jimmy Carter, Mark Flatts, and the Cup-tied Martin Keown. The only late episode worthy of a headline was an Ian Wright-led demolition of Crystal Palace on the last Saturday of the season that sent the South London outfit crashing out of the Premier League. How Palace must hate Arsenal! A 5-1 aggregate defeat in the League Cup Semi-Final and that last day disaster were the bitter culmination to years of humiliating defeats against their bogey team from across the river.

In the last game of the season, Tottenham defeated a shadow Arsenal side at Highbury to secure their first League Double in nearly twenty years, a result that edged them ahead of Arsenal in the final League table. But for once, the attitude among Arsenal fans was 'so what?' With the FA Cup Final just four days away they could afford to be magnanimous.

When all is said and done, if you are going to have an average League season, winning both Cups and earning a crack at Europe is not a bad consolation. However, to grasp the subtle, and to be perfectly honest, hardly positive transformation that had taken place at Highbury since the Championship triumph in 1991, you only need hark back to the words of the *Guardian* sage, David Lacey, after the FA Cup Semi-Final against Spurs in that same season. He wrote: 'Arsenal are a team built to last the rigours of the League programme rather than resist the explosions of Cup ties.'

Things had certainly changed. George Graham prides himself on his tactical flexibility and would have been pleased to outwit Trevor Francis in the one-off Wembley games – in the League Cup, surprise choice Steve Morrow stifled Wednesday playmaker John Sheridan, while the 'Footballer of the Year' Chris Waddle had arguably his three quietest games of the season entangled in Graham's spider's web – but the Scotsman will certainly have judged Arsenal's season over the 42 League games. After all, Graham had always insisted that the real litmus test was the League: 'You can win a Cup by winning six or seven games. It's winning the Championship that makes you the best team.' The fact that some Arsenal fans would express disappointment at the season as a whole was a measure of the great expectations that the manager had furnished. As the season closed, Graham would have been vigorously planning to get Arsenal back on the Lacey-defined track.

BY GEORGE ...

'It's been an interesting summer. I made one major signing, John Jensen. I wanted to make more. It wasn't to be. The Geoff Thomas deal didn't come off. But as I've said before, I'm still looking for another quality midfield player.'

Haven't we heard that one before somewhere?

'I hope we'll be recognised for our attacking play. That would make a change for an Arsenal side! With the firepower in our line-up it's really a case of keeping them supplied.'

An August premonition, perhaps?

'Every manager I know would like to win 6-0 playing entertaining football, but we don't want to be out of a job ... Our fans have to realise that my priority is winning matches rather than playing pretty football ... I wouldn't want to be bottom of the table, but playing football.'

Summer optimism turns to autumn realism
(after 1-0 win at Forest in October).

'Every year since I came to the club there has been a crisis ... even when we won the Championships. I have to make sure that the players who go out for Arsenal have the necessary self-desire.'

December 92.

'People are telling me we need midfield players but don't they think I know that? The problem is that there are very few around of the quality we want, and the ones that could be available are being tagged with ridiculous prices.'

Is this starting to get boring? February 93.

'Tony Adams has been a star at Arsenal for six years now. Yet suddenly in one week he is a hero and that surprises me only because he has been my hero ever since he came into the side.'

After Adams' match-winning Semi-Final goal against Spurs.

'In our profession, there's an opposition. And in any confrontation you try to look at your opponents' strengths and weaknesses. And my philosophy has always been that you've got to know their strengths and nullify them, and then try to impose your strengths on them. It's no use saying: "Oh, they've got wonderful players." Like Chris Waddle. It amuses me when I am actually criticised for nullifying Waddle and John Sheridan. I laughed when I read Brian Glanville saying that George Graham had ruined the game! How naive and innocent for such an experienced journalist to say that I had ruined the game. It's my job to nullify the opposition, and I thought, "I'll get some credit for this." But I was criticised for it. That's when I said: "Let's just forget about the Press in future and just get on with winning some more trophies." '

On negative Press reaction to the League Cup Final victory.

'I am proud of my track record here. My decisions are not often wrong.'
April 93, after Spurs' Semi-Final.

FA PREMIER LEAGUE 92/93

Final League position: 10th
Average home gate: 24,403

Norwich City	(h) 2-4	Bould, Campbell
Blackburn Rovers	(a) 0-1	
Liverpool	(a) 2-0	Limpar, Wright
Oldham Athletic	(h) 2-0	Winterburn, Wright
Sheffield Wednesday	(h) 2-1	Parlour, Merson
Queens Park Rangers	(a) 0-0	
Wimbledon	(a) 2-3	Wright 2
Blackburn Rovers	(h) 0-1	
Sheffield United	(a) 1-1	Wright
Manchester City	(h) 1-0	Wright
Chelsea	(h) 2-1	Merson, Wright
Nottingham Forest	(a) 1-0	Smith
Everton	(h) 2-0	Wright, Limpar
Crystal Palace	(a) 2-1	Merson, Wright
Coventry City	(h) 3-0	Smith, Wright, Campbell
Leeds United	(a) 0-3	
Manchester United	(h) 0-1	
Southampton	(a) 0-2	
Tottenham Hotspur	(a) 0-1	
Middlesbrough	(h) 1-1	Wright
Ipswich Town	(h) 0-0	
Aston Villa	(a) 0-1	
Sheffield United	(h) 1-1	Hillier
Manchester City	(a) 1-0	Merson
Liverpool	(h) 0-1	
Wimbledon	(h) 0-1	
Oldham Athletic	(a) 1-0	Linighan
Leeds United	(h) 0-0	
Chelsea	(a) 0-1	
Norwich City	(a) 1-1	Wright
Coventry City	(a) 2-0	Campbell, Wright
Southampton	(h) 4-3	Linighan, Merson, Carter 2
Manchester United	(a) 0-0	
Middlesbrough	(a) 0-1	
Ipswich Town	(a) 2-1	Smith, Merson
Aston Villa	(h) 0-1	
Nottingham Forest	(h) 1-1	Wright
Everton	(a) 0-0	
Queens Park Rangers	(h) 0-0	
Sheffield Wednesday	(a) 0-1	
Crystal Palace	(h) 3-0	Wright, Dickov, Campbell
Tottenham Hotspur	(h) 1-3	Dickov

FA Cup 92/93

Third Round:

Yeovil Town	(a) 3-1	Wright 3

Fourth Round:

Leeds United	(h) 2-2	Parlour, Merson

Fourth Round Replay:

Leeds United	(a) 3-2	Smith, Wright 2 (after extra time)

Fifth Round:
Nottingham Forest (h) 2-0 Wright 2
Sixth Round:
Ipswich Town (a) 4-2 Adams, Wright (penalty), og, Campbell
Semi-Final (Wembley):
Tottenham Hotspur 1-0 Adams

Final (Wembley):
Sheffield Wednesday 1-1 Wright (after extra time)
Replay (Wembley):
Sheffield Wednesday 2-1 Wright, Linighan (after extra time)

League Cup 92/93

Second Round:
Millwall (h) 1-1 Campbell
Millwall (a) 1-1 Campbell (after extra time) Arsenal won on penalties 3-1 (Hillier, Campbell, Smith)
Third Round:
Derby County (a) 1-1 Campbell
Replay:
Derby County (h) 2-1 Wright, Campbell

Fourth Round:
Scarborough (a) 1-0 Winterburn
Fifth Round:
Nottingham Forest (h) 2-0 Wright 2
Semi-Final 1st leg:
Crystal Palace (a) 3-1 Wright (penalty), Smith 2
Semi-Final 2nd leg:
Crystal Palace (h) 2-0 Linighan, Wright
Final (Wembley):
Sheffield Wednesday 2-1 Merson, Morrow

Appearances

	League	FA Cup	League Cup	Total
David Seaman	39	8	9	56
Tony Adams	33+2	8	9	50+2
Paul Merson	32+1	8	9	49+1
Ian Wright	30+1	7	8	45+1
Lee Dixon	29	8	7	44
Nigel Winterburn	29	8	7	44
Kevin Campbell	32+5	4+3	5+4	41+12
Alan Smith	27+4	5+2	7	39+6
David Hillier	27+3	4+1	7+1	38+5
John Jensen	29+3	4	3	36+3
Andy Linighan	19+2	7	4	30+2

GEORGE GRAHAM: THE WONDER YEARS

	League	FA Cup	League Cup	Total
Steve Bould	24	1	5	30
Ray Parlour	16+5	4	3+1	23+6
Stephen Morrow	13+3	2+2	4+1	19+6
Anders Limpar	12+11	2	4	18+11
Martin Keown	15+1	0	0	15+1
Jimmy Carter	11+5	1+1	1	13+6
Ian Selley	9	3	1	13
Paul Davis	6	3	2	11
David O'Leary	6+5	1+3	2	9+8
Pal Lydersen	7+1	0	1	8+1
Mark Flatts	6+4	0	1	7+4
Neil Heaney	3+2	0	0	3+2
Alan Miller	3+1	0	0	3+1
Colin Pates	2+5	0	0	2+5
Scott Marshall	2	0	0	2
Paul Dickov	1+2	0	0	1+2
Gavin McGowan	0+2	0	0	0+2
Perry Groves	0+1	0	0	0+1

Goal-scorers

	League	FA Cup	League Cup	Total
Ian Wright	15	10	5	30
Kevin Campbell	4	1	4	9
Paul Merson	6	1	1	8
Alan Smith	3	1	2	6
Andy Linighan	2	1	1	4
Jimmy Carter	2	0	0	2
Anders Limpar	2	0	0	2
Paul Dickov	2	0	0	2
Tony Adams	0	2	0	2
Ray Parlour	1	1	0	2
Nigel Winterburn	1	0	1	2
David Hillier	1	0	0	1
Stephen Morrow	0	0	1	1

Season's Review 1993/94
Smells Like Team-Spirit

K een student of Arsenal history that he is, George Graham knew that for all the success of his first seven years as Arsenal manager there was one arena where he had failed to make a reputation for the club which befitted its status – Europe. The defeat against Benfica in the Champions' Cup in 1991 was an open wound yet to heal, with most commentators convinced that Arsenal would have gone very close to winning Europe's premier club trophy had they overcome the Portuguese champions that year.

In the 93/94 season, the Cup-Winners' Cup looked the strongest European competition on paper, with the likes of Real Madrid, Torino, Paris Saint-Germain and Ajax vying with holders Parma, who had demolished Antwerp 3-1 at Wembley a few months earlier to lift the trophy.

Despite the thoroughbred nature of the field, however, the feeling around Highbury was that Graham had learnt some painful lessons in his first European sortie as manager and had devised a gameplan to eliminate the mistakes of the previous campaign. Domestically the Premiership was the obvious number one target. Arsenal's pedigree under Graham (two titles in seven seasons) meant that most Arsenal fans considered a realistic tilt at the Championship a matter of course, particularly as the team had failed to challenge convincingly in the previous two seasons.

Disappointingly, transfer movements in and out of Highbury during the close season did little to boost the confidence of the faithful, demanding a serious onslaught on champions Manchester United and free-spending Blackburn Rovers. After a long and distinguished Highbury career spanning nearly twenty years, David O'Leary moved to Leeds, having enjoyed a magnificent swansong at Wembley in the FA Cup Final. The almost universally acclaimed need at Highbury was a creative midfielder (later in the season, George Graham even had a T-shirt commissioned with the slogan 'I know we need a midfield player') was for a (creative) midfielder to provide more ammunition for the Gunners' under-achieving strikeforce and another forward or winger to provide some width and take some of the onerous goal-scoring duties away from Ian Wright. In the 92/93 campaign Wright had scored 30 goals in all competitions, with no other player getting into double figures, and the whole midfield contributing a measly two goals for the entire campaign.

As a consequence, Arsenal finished as lowest scorers in the Premier League and fans anxiously awaited the pre-season flourishing of the chequebook to stop the rot. Unfortunately, the only top-quality midfielder available during the close season was young Irish midfielder Roy Keane of Nottingham Forest. Arsenal were supposedly in the hunt but it was clear from the offset that Keane preferred Manchester United, not least because the wages there would be almost twice what he could be guaranteed at Arsenal.

Instead, George plumped for Eddie McGoldrick, the Crystal Palace utility midfielder/forward-cum-occasional sweeper who had performed creditably in the Palace side which was relegated at the end of the 92/93 season. However, McGoldrick looked more like a good addition to the squad than the answer to the Gunners' particular problems.

With no additional arrivals, despite the usual platitudes from Graham about Arsenal 'always being in the market for quality players', the Highbury *cognoscenti* could already sense, before a ball had even been kicked, that Arsenal would not mount a serious challenge for the League Championship, despite a rumoured change in Graham's game plan. The word circulating around Highbury was that George, perhaps sensitive to the muted (and, in the case of *The Times*' David Miller, downright hostile) media reaction to the domestic Cup successes of 1993, intended to kick off with a more progressive passing game. This plan lasted approximately 60 minutes of the season's opener against Coventry at Highbury. The occupants of the newly opened all-seater North Bank stand recoiled in shock as Coventry's rotund striker Mick Quinn helped himself to a day one hat-trick. It was 3-0 to Coventry. Graham's reaction, no doubt spoken through clenched teeth, was that 'we had a lot of quality players out there but the majority of them didn't live up to their reputations.'

With suitable actions to back up his strong words, Graham dropped the 'creative' Limpar and Merson and replaced them with the more prosaic McGoldrick and Parlour for the local derby two days later at White Hart Lane, which was televised live by Sky.

The result was a midfield of more shape and purpose, and a much better Arsenal performance rounded off by Wright's instinctive header from the edge of the 6-yard box in the 87th minute. For the first time this season it was 1-0 to Arsenal. Victory aside, the game had thrown up some interesting cameos which were to develop later during the campaign.

Limpar's omission after the first game spelt the beginning of the end of the Superswede's career at Highbury. Since his pivotal role in the Championship-winning team of 90/91, his influence had waned with each season, a fact reflected by the number of games he started compared to the frustration of sitting on the bench – 90/91: 39 (starts) and 2 (sub); 91/92: 27 and 6; 92/93: 18 and 11; and 93/94: 11 and 1. His much-publicised rows with Graham over representing Sweden were at the heart of the problem, Graham being noted as a manager who manifestly places club before country – 'Players have to learn that it is their clubs they play for first and foremost!' As Brian Marwood commented after his sole England cap against Saudi Arabia, 'George puts Arsenal first. As a Scot he doesn't ever seem interested in the England side, let alone anybody else.' Ironically for Limpar, his club and country wrangles came to nought as he was not used once by Tommy Svensen in Sweden's charge to the Semi-Finals of USA 94.

Limpar's problems, however, were not totally limited to his perceived 'right' to represent his country when he deemed fit. In truth, his performances in subsequent seasons never lived up to the high standard he established in 90/91 and 91/92. This was highlighted in the League Cup Second Round second leg match against Huddersfield at Highbury when he failed to beat a journeyman lower division full-back all evening. Limpar supporters, and there were still many at Highbury when he finally departed for Mike Walker's Everton in March 1994, would argue that Limpar was a classic victim of Graham's suspicion of unpredictable players.

The Limpar-conspiracy-theorists conclude that this constant threat to his place in the side undermined his confidence and, ergo, his performances. History will probably look more favourably on George Graham, as Limpar, like so many others, has done little since he left Highbury to prove Graham wrong.

Paul Merson, the other player dropped for the Spurs game, is another frustratingly inconsistent player, although one who has enjoyed Graham's patronage and patience both on and off the pitch. Merson's early-season lethargy was also a concern for Graham and fans alike, prompting the fanzine *One-Nil Down, Two-One Up* to devote the front cover of their second issue of the season to the question, 'MERSON – Should he stay? ... or, should he go?' Merson eventually recovered to play a (muted) role in the European adventure although many still felt he was a (bulky) shadow of the young colt who burst on the scene in 88/89. Even when Merson returned against Leeds on 24 August with a goal and an assist, Graham commented 'I thought he played spasmodically.'

Merson was immediately linked with a £4 million move to Glasgow Rangers but George Graham was unmoved, commenting, 'Paul can work a lot harder. I have been his biggest advocate here when he has fallen out with certain people. But if he is not producing it, he'll be out the same as other players.' Graham's willingness to drop two internationals after one game of the season is testament to his ruthlessness when it comes to doing what is right for Arsenal. The fact that the team could bounce straight back in two days to win a difficult derby away from home is also a comment on the strength of the squad Graham had assiduously cultivated over the past few seasons.

The margin of victory at Spurs could have been much greater, however, were it not for the profligacy of Wright's main (and preferred) striking partner Kevin Campbell.

Campbell's main assets are pace and power, with a natural striker's instinct for the rare space in a crowded penalty area. In the latter half of the 91/92 season Campbell had also became a prolific marksman, seemingly able to 'score for fun' during a remarkable spell which persuaded George Graham he could do without the services of one Andy Cole. Kevin Campbell had arrived. However, the goals dried up in 92/93, with only 9 coming from 53 appearances, and some began to question his finishing ability. The match at White Hart Lane did little to dispel the creeping doubts about Campbell as he missed a clutch of half-chances which should have secured the game long before Wright's late header. It is perhaps his relationship with Wright that is the key to Campbell's inability to fulfil the potential of his first few seasons. As Wright sprinted to the gleeful Arsenal fans massed at the Park Lane end after the final whistle, to receive the adulation of the travelling Gooners, Kevin Campbell stood next to him, pointing at Wright almost in awe, as if to say 'this is the man'. Wright and Campbell are famous for their post-goal 'bogling' celebrations, but the inescapable conclusion at White Hart Lane was of a younger man in awe of the finished item. It is difficult to assess the psychology of such finely tuned professionals but the general feeling is that the respect and affection Campbell obviously has for Wright has precluded him from developing the selfishness that the really top strikers need.

Having said that, Campbell gets his fair share of chances; it is more a question of the conversion rate. Gerd Muller once said that he scored 75 per cent of his goals without knowing the precise positioning of the goalkeeper and the goal itself. 'It's a matter of instinct.'

Campbell's nineteen goals in 93/94 was his best haul in Arsenal's colours, and included the winner against Paris Saint-Germain in the European

Cup-Winners' Cup Semi-Final. However, in many crucial League games, when Arsenal might have hauled themselves back into contention in the title race, the chances fell to Campbell and were spurned. The basic instinct once again seemed to be missing.

The victory over their nearest rivals had put Arsenal back on track after the shock Coventry defeat and they went unbeaten over the next six League games to haul themselves into second position in the table, level on points with Manchester United. Next on the League agenda? A trip to Old Trafford.

Before the clash of the Premiership's top two at Old Trafford, Arsenal travelled to Denmark to begin their European odyssey against humble Odense. It was to prove to be Arsenal's worst performance in Europe all season as they were given a rude awakening by Odense in the first half-hour of the match. The Danes won a penalty after only three minutes – a clear example of a nervy Arsenal start. Fortunately for the Londoners, Thorup hit the post with the spot-kick. Their luck ran out in the eighteenth minute, however, when Keown deflected a shot past Seaman for an own-goal. Inevitably Ian Wright grabbed the equaliser after a superb through-ball from Paul Davis confused the Danish defence and, with Merson adding another in the second half, Arsenal seemed to have the tie sewn up.

The return fixture at Highbury also produced a scare for Arsenal as Odense grabbed a late equaliser to Campbell's headed goal (the cross was again supplied by the excellent Paul Davis). For four or five minutes it was shades of Benfica before Arsenal heaved a collective sigh of relief and marched into the next round.

The tie against Odense was a necessary hurdle for Arsenal to finally rid themselves of the Benfica hangover. For those looking for pointers to Arsenal's tactics in Europe, there were some revealing glimpses during this match. Paul Davis, no longer quite having the legs for the 100 mph of the Premiership, clearly revelled in the European scene where he had more time to play the ball, his cultured left foot responsible for two assists in this tie. At the back, Martin Keown was deployed as marker for the Cameroon danger-man Alphonse Tchami, a ploy which was repeated in later rounds.

With the European campaign kick-started, the domestic business of the Premiership, which was sandwiched between this tie, faltered badly at Old Trafford. Cantona's 38th-minute 'Exocet' free-kick was an unwanted present on David Seaman's 30th birthday, calling into question again his positioning at set-pieces, something which was to receive much greater attention in Rotterdam a month later. The Frenchman's strike proved the decider in a tense match with little goalmouth action, Arsenal being surprisingly unambitious given Graham's penchant for taking on the big northern clubs in their own citadels.

The few chances which came Arsenal's way fell to Campbell, but both were spurned. This time there were no heroics from Wright to save the day as Arsenal surrendered three points. With only a month of the season gone, Arsenal would not get as close to United again during the campaign. Their tilt at the Premiership was effectively dead on 19 September.

If it was merely a suspicion at the beginning of the season that George Graham was concentrating on Europe, it was now beyond doubt. For the Manchester City game immediately prior to the first leg of the next tie against Standard Liege, Graham 'rested' three key players – Keown, Jensen and Merson – claiming that 'I have to balance the team. The League is a nine-month race but two errors in Europe and you are out. I view Wednesday's game against Liege as far more important than today's.' Nobody could ever question George Graham's single-mindedness but long-suffering Highbury regulars could have been forgiven for asking 'where's the beef?' in the League campaign. Graham may have been concentrating on half-a-dozen games in Europe but Arsenal season-ticket holders had forked out up to £500 for 21 League fixtures as well. Were they all destined to be glorified practice games for Europe? This would not have been such an issue if the team had been performing well in the League but October brought a goal drought of Saharan proportions, with the League games in that month producing four 0-0 draws.

Also, at the time of the Manchester City game, Arsenal were only five points adrift of Manchester United – hardly an insurmountable gap, with three-quarters of the season to go. So why did Graham decide to concentrate almost exclusively on Europe at this point? Did he feel apprehension at trying to compete effectively on two demanding fronts, or was it a tacit admission that the Arsenal squad was not strong enough to challenge Manchester United for the Premiership? Perhaps it was simply Graham's sense of historic destiny, an urge to win a trophy in the one arena that had so far eluded him. As Alan Smith commented after Copenhagen, 'The lads sensed that the manager would like to win it [the Cup-Winners' Cup]. As the season progressed, it became obvious he was resting players before the European games. He wants to win all the trophies but this season Europe seemed to matter most.'

The home leg against Standard Liege on 20 October came a week after a sorry night for English football when the national side were beaten controversially in Rotterdam 2-0 by an ageing Dutch team, a defeat which effectively denied them World Cup qualification. If Ian Wright – used once again as substitute by Graham Taylor who preferred a clearly unfit Alan Shearer – was smarting from this setback, he soon made Liege pay with two sharply-taken goals either side of a beautiful Paul Merson strike from a free-kick. This type of goal was a rarity at Highbury. The Liege players tried to provoke Wright all night but for once he turned the other cheek: 'Don't get mad, get even, is my philosophy. Vengeance is the inspiration.'

Unfortunately, Wright picked up a yellow card, something which would have great significance later in the competition. Prior to the Odense tie, Graham had commented that 'you can pass and pass and pass and not go anywhere', a defensive reaction to critics of Arsenal's more direct style of play. After beating Liege 3-0, Graham was more sanguine, observing 'we outpassed the Continentals'.

Paul Davis, Arsenal's best passer of the ball, was not so highly praised in the dressing-room after the game. The coaching staff had thought Davis was pushing too far forward at the risk of leaving space behind him. At 3-0 this may seem a moot point but Graham, mindful of the chance, however remote, of an away goal, is ever the perfectionist. If any further evidence was needed of the hunger to win in Europe, this was it. With a three-goal cushion from the first leg at Highbury, the Gunners travelled in good spirits to Liege for the return leg on 3 November. Graham took the calculated decision to rest Ian Wright (who was on a yellow card) for this fixture, and for once the team hardly seemed to miss him.

Alan Smith opened the scoring in the second minute, scuppering any Liege thought of resistance, and soon a rout was on the cards. Selley and Adams added two more goals before Campbell (free from the shadow of Wright at last) collected his first just before half-time. It was 4-0 to Arsenal at the break. In the second half, Eddie McGoldrick came on as substitute and had his finest 45 minutes in an Arsenal shirt, making goals for Merson and Campbell. Saving the best till last, McGoldrick scored his first goal for the club, smashing the ball past Munaron from just inside the box, after a run from halfway. Wright, who had celebrated his 30th birthday the day before, was not missed as Arsenal cruised into the Quarter Finals of the competition in some style – 10-0 on aggregate.

Back in the League, Arsenal were still out of sorts, losing their third game of the season, this time at home to Aston Villa who came from behind to score an injury-time goal through Andy Townsend, another player who had been linked with the club. In truth, Arsenal should have won this game easily, but Wright failed to add to his goal in the 58th minute, missing a penalty and unusually spurning a number of chances. Arsenal's over-reliance on their main man was even beginning to get to

George Graham, who publicly voiced what many fans had been thinking for some time – namely that some of the players had an inferiority complex when it came to the goal-scoring *über* God. The defeat left Arsenal in sixth place in the Premiership after fourteen games, a massive fourteen points behind the leaders, Manchester United. The most telling statistic was in the goals for column, with Arsenal's thirteen paling by comparison with United's thirty. How Arsenal could have done with some of the goals that were flowing so freely in Europe.

At this stage in the season, Arsenal had also begun their defence of the Coca-Cola Cup, nonchalantly dispatching Huddersfield 6-1 on aggregate in the Second Round. Arsenal travelled to Carrow Road a week after the game in Liege for a Third Round replay against Norwich. This was Ian Wright's 100th game for Arsenal and he celebrated in some style with two audacious goals. The first, in which he outrageously chipped Bryan Gunn, was a goal of equal quality to that scored by Wright earlier in the season against Everton at Highbury, where he had flicked the ball over Matt Jackson with one foot before lobbing Southall from the edge of the box with the other. Norwich had no answer to Arsenal on a night like this. 'Probably our best display of the season,' mused Graham, with Smith, Merson and Limpar providing expert assistance to Wright whose two goals took his total to a remarkable 72 in 100 games with the club.

Arsenal's challenge for the title may have stalled early on but there were still plenty of intriguing fixtures in the League. None more so than the visit of Newcastle on 27 November to Highbury, which coincided with the re-opening of the Clock End and saw the ground transformed into an all-seater stadium with a capacity of 39,000. Arsenal sportingly turned the whole of the Clock End over to the travelling 'Toon Army' to create the best atmosphere at Highbury for two seasons, since the demise of the North Bank.

The real talking point of this match was the return of Andy Cole, the player with the shortest first-team career under George Graham (six minutes as sub). Inevitably, Cole's first game back at Highbury was billed as the Young Pretender (Cole) against the Master (Wright). It was no contest. Wright – fittingly featured on the front cover of the match programme with the legendary Ted Drake – scored in the fifteenth minute to cap a display of intelligent running and constant threat. Cole, on the other hand, ran aimlessly like a novice, doing little until he provided a telling ball to set up Beardsley's consolation goal, 2-1 to Arsenal. Everyone acknowledged that Wright had been the master on the day, with Newcastle manager Kevin Keegan admitting that, 'I told Andy he hadn't had his fairy tale after all.' In the next issue of *One-Nil Down, Two-One Up*, the Wright phenomenon was summed up as follows: 'They [the club] may have ruined Highbury, they may employ Jensen and McGoldrick, they may be greedy and insensitive but, in mitigation, they've given us Ian Wright. And watching Ian Wright might just mean you're watching the best football of your life.'

If the game against Newcastle had seen Arsenal close to their best, the Coca-Cola Fourth Round tie against Villa at Highbury the following Tuesday was probably the worst. Arsenal's unbeaten 25-game Cup run was destroyed by a solitary strike from the languid Dalian Atkinson in what was a lacklustre display by the Gunners.

Even the normally ultra-loyal *Gunflash*, the supporters' club magazine, was disappointed by the performance which led the editor, Mike Coppock, to reflect in his leader column that, 'It wasn't until the last ten minutes, when the players realised that they could be going out of the competition, that they came to life. A number of players had an off-day [night], but where was the passion and fight we had become accustomed to? We obviously had to lose a Cup game sooner or later, but when it happened I would have expected us to go down fighting.'

Graham commented that he had 'no complaints' – not a view shared by fans who had witnessed the ineptitude of a midfield comprising McGoldrick, Jensen and Morrow. Not the ideal way of relinquishing their hold on the League Cup.

However, the season's nadir was yet to come. After two more tedious games – a 1-0 defeat at Coventry (Quinn again!) and an uninspiring 1-1 draw against Tottenham at Highbury – Sheffield Wednesday arrived on 12 December for a match that was to test the patience of even the most hard-bitten Highbury devotee.

These two teams, over-familiar with each other after the three Wembley games in April and May, combined to produce the most sterile and mind-numbingly boring match of the season. Even Ian Wright's classic last-minute strike, after finally escaping the clutches of Des Walker, could not prevent Arsenal being booed off the pitch by their own supporters. Wednesday boss Trevor Francis said after the game, 'It's never a classic when we play Arsenal', which was a masterly understatement in relation to an abomination of a game.

Defeat at Elland Road six days later left Arsenal in fifth place, approaching Christmas Day eighteen points adrift of runaway leaders Manchester United. Over the traditional festive programme, however, the Gunners raised brief hopes, mostly among tabloid sports editors desperate for somebody to push United, who had enjoyed three convincing wins on the trot.

Away to Swindon on 27 December, Arsenal exploited Swindon's suicidal offside trap, winning 4-0 at the County Ground. Swindon's likeable manager John Gorman seemed shell-shocked after the game when interviewed by BBC Radio, commenting that 'we had not discussed playing offside at all. The players just took it upon themselves to play that way.'

This was further evidence, if any were needed, of the frustrating impotence of any manager once his charges take the field. At least Gorman had the good grace to concede that Arsenal had displayed 'the best performance against us by any team this season, including Manchester United.' Kevin Campbell scored a good hat-trick in this match, prompting George Graham to call him 'outstanding'. Whether this was a piece of kidology to psyche Campbell up is open to question. More cynical Arsenal fans simply noted that, once again, Campbell was scoring against the weaker teams without troubling the stronger defences. In a season that saw him score a career-best nineteen goals for the first team, ten came against Swindon, Sheffield United, Ipswich and Standard Liege.

Even with a hat-trick under his belt, Campbell was once more upstaged by the mercurial Wright who finished things off with a 35-yard chip over Swindon keeper Fraser Digby. It was his third outstanding goal of the season.

Two more 3-0 victories, first over Sheffield United, and then Wimbledon on New Year's Day, saw Arsenal back up to third place but still fourteen points behind United. Arsenal would not win again in the League until 26 February when a 1-0 victory at Highbury over high-flying Blackburn ended a run of five consecutive League draws. In a League season of might-have-beens, five victories at this stage (and in every game Arsenal were arguably the better team), would have put the Gunners within reach of United, with a game against them at Highbury to come. As it turned out, too many draws throughout the season ruined Arsenal's chances of pressuring the champions. By the season's end Arsenal finished with seventeen draws – a total surpassed by only Manchester City, who narrowly avoided relegation, and Sheffield United, who didn't.

During this five-match spell, Arsenal were once more busy in a Cup competition, this time beginning their defence of the FA Cup at Millwall on 10 January. The 'New Den', far from being the friendly community-based super-stadium of numerous PR handouts, proved to be as inhospitable as the old Den at Cold Blow Lane. The racial taunting of Arsenal's black players by a sizeable section of the Millwall crowd was disgusting, complementing the physical mauling which Keith 'Psycho' Stevens was giving Campbell and Wright on the pitch.

A dour game seemed destined for a replay at Highbury until the 90th minute, when Tony Adams bundled in Eddie McGoldrick's corner after a fumble by Millwall's American goalie Kasey Keller that would have graced the NFL. Shades of Andy Linighan at Wembley in May, as once more the big man up from the back at a set-piece sealed a last-gasp victory for the Gunners.

The fourth round saw Arsenal drawn away to FA Cup upset specialists, Bolton Wanderers, who had famously knocked Liverpool out of the same competition at Anfield the previous season and had already taken care of Everton in the Third Round this time round.

McAteer opened the scoring for Bolton on the half-hour after an uncharacteristic mix-up between Bould and Keown. Arsenal looked destined to follow Everton out of the competition as Campbell and Wright missed decent chances before the interval. However, with six minutes of the second half gone, Wright pounced on a deflection to score from 6 yards and within fifteen minutes Arsenal were ahead as Adams again got on the end of a well-placed free-kick, this time put over by Nigel Winterburn.

Once more, Campbell had good chances to sew the game up for the visitors, but missed them. Arsenal eventually paid for their continued profligacy when Coyle scored the equaliser in front of an ecstatic Burnden Park crowd with four minutes to go. The replay at Highbury 10 days later in front of a crowd of 33,863 saw the pattern of the first match repeated with McGinlay opening the scoring for Bolton in the 20th minute, only for Arsenal to equalise in the 36th with a goal from Alan Smith – his first since November. Shortly before Smith's goal, Arsenal's baby-faced midfielder David Hillier took a knock and was substituted by Martin Keown, a central defender, occasionally used to good effect in Europe as a man-to-man marker. However, with only Ray Parlour on the pitch as a recognised midfielder, Arsenal began to struggle to contain Bolton's lively midfield duo of Kelly and McAteer.

In the second half Arsenal had chances to win the tie but the best of them fell once more to Campbell, by now suffering a real crisis of confidence. George Graham had recently been exhorting the fans to get off Campbell's back, citing the fact that he was a 'confidence player' who needed all the encouragement he could get. Unfortunately, the club themselves did little to help Campbell on this occasion as the teams waited on the pitch for the beginning of extra-time.

One of the much heralded arrivals at Highbury early in the season were the Jumbotron screens in the corner of the ground which provided pre-match entertainment and half-time highlights. During the break before extra-time the Jumbotron displayed the full horror of Campbell's misses to groans from the North Stand while the player stood there on the pitch, no doubt hoping the ground would open up and swallow him. Some way to treat a 'confidence player'!

If Campbell's inability to convert an acceptable number of chances was a long-running theme at Highbury, so was Nigel Winterburn's reluctance to do anything with his right foot except stand on it. As the game went into extra-time this weakness was to prove Arsenal's undoing as a poor back-pass from Winterburn, created by his unwillingness to propel the ball back to Seaman with his right foot, led to Bolton's second goal. Coyle's shot rebounded off the post for the excellent McAteer to make it 2-1. With Ian Wright – Arsenal's saviour in the domestic Cups the previous season – off injured, Arsenal were unlikely to come back. Bolton rubbed salt into the wound when Andy Walker scored a third in front of their fans massed behind the Clock End goal.

Arsenal's second domestic Cup exit at home in the season highlighted a number of issues which many Arsenal fans felt to be at the heart of the 'problems' afflicting George Graham's teams in the past few seasons. Specific individual weaknesses – Winterburn's right foot, Seaman's flapping at free-kicks, Merson's laziness and general lack of fitness, and Campbell's profligacy – were all glaring faults which were augmented by structural weaknesses – a midfield of Parlour and Keown (which was hardly likely to strike terror in the opposition) and the over-reliance on Wright for goals.

Finally, when one goal behind in a Cup-tie at Highbury (Benfica, Villa, Bolton) to a team adept at breaking quickly from midfield, Arsenal seemed to have no answer. Fortunately, in Europe, Arsenal were never to be headed, apart from in the very first game of the campaign against Odense.

Out of the domestic Cups and with progress in the League stymied by too many draws, Arsenal's only chance of success now lay firmly in Europe with a visit to Turin on 2 March for the first leg of a Quarter-Final which was to provide Arsenal with their first tie against Italian opposition since they defeated Juventus in the Semi-Final of the same competition in 1980. It would also be the first time an English club side had played in Turin since the Heysel Stadium tragedy in 1985 where 39 fans from the city died. Prior to the game, George Graham took his players to one side at London Colney to run through the strengths and weaknesses of Torino.

Alan Smith takes up the story. 'Before we flew out to Turin he was really painting the Torino players as world-beaters. I got annoyed because from what I'd seen they were not as good as he was saying. He kept saying, "You've got to stick to him or he'll destroy you". In the event they did have good players but they didn't show a lot on the night and that surprised the gaffer afterwards.'

If ever a side was equipped to play the Italians at their own ultra-defensive, cautious game, Arsenal are that team. In the *Stadio delle Alpi*, where England fell to West Germany on penalties in the World Cup Semi-Final in 1990, Arsenal put up a typically resolute performance to gain a valuable 0-0 draw. Graham often likens European football to a game of chess but only hardcore Arsenal fans gained any enjoyment from this stalemate, as ITV struggled to find five minutes of highlights of this cat and mouse affair.

With Ian Wright omitted, it was left to Jensen and Hillier to perform a stopping role in front of the parsimonious Gunners' back four, which limited the Italians to two half-chances. However, at the other end Smith, as a lone front runner with occasional support from Campbell and Merson, fared little better.

Oblivious to the entertainment-value, Graham seemed pleased enough with what he had seen. 'I was happy with the performance, if not with the result. Sometimes we in England are in awe of the Italians. I told my players just to go out and express themselves.' This comment no doubt provoked some wry amusement at London Colney.

For the return leg, 34,678 fans packed Highbury to see Arsenal complete the job and they were not disappointed. On the night, Arsenal demonstrated how clearly they had learnt the lessons of the Benfica defeat in 1991. This time there was no gung-ho policy of attack, but instead a more patient approach, wary of the counter-attacking capabilities of the Italians and their Uruguayan striker Enzo Francescoli. The Arsenal back four was as solid as a rock, with excellent protection from the combative Jensen, Hillier (who only lasted sixteen minutes) and his replacement, Selley. Upfront, Smith and Wright worked tirelessly, creating space for Merson who was playing one of his best games of the season. The heroes once more for the Gunners were Tony Adams and Paul Davis, with one of their free-kick combinations which most teams can anticipate but few can do little to counter.

After a goalless first half, Arsenal gained a free-kick in the 66th minute which Davis stepped up to take. How often had the Highbury faithful seen this before? Paul Davis, the only man in the maligned Arsenal midfield with the creative ability to put the ball on a sixpence, floated the ball across the face of the Italian penalty area and there was Adams arriving to power the ball home in almost a carbon copy of the finish which defeated Spurs in the FA Cup Semi-Final the previous season. Arsenal were through to the Semi-Finals.

Amidst the excitement of Europe, the League campaign continued in low-key fashion with Arsenal still fourth in the table after the Torino fixture. The following Saturday, the Gunners travelled to Southampton, a happy hunting ground for Graham's teams, for a routine match enlivened by another Wright hat-trick which included his fourth outstanding goal of the season. Graham rested six of the heroes from the Torino second leg, which seemingly gave Anders Limpar another chance to stake his place in the first team. Instead, it proved to be his last game for the club; Graham was perhaps finally convinced, after victory against top-class Italian opposition, that the virtues of team-spirit, resilience and relentless organisation would always win out over fitful individual brilliance. At the Dell, Limpar did enough to give Arsenal fans a glimpse of what they were missing before being replaced by Alan Smith who had ended the career of England's Gary Lineker in similar fashion at the European Championships in 1992.

The £1.6 million which George Graham extracted from the new Everton manager, Mike Walker, is further evidence of the hard bargaining that the shrewd Scot employs when offloading players *he* clearly feels are past their Highbury sell-by date. As with so many others, Limpar failed to haunt Graham with peripheral displays in an Everton side that only escaped relegation on the last day of the season by coming from two goals down to beat Wimbledon 3-2 at Goodison Park. And that was after Limpar had conceded a bizarre first-half penalty to the Dons. Good business or not, though, many at Highbury were saddened by the Swede's departure, not because of Limpar himself – who had patently failed to deliver during his last two seasons – but because they sensed that they may not see his like again under a manager openly cynical of players who could not match flair with equal amounts of work-rate and commitment.

Others like Nick Hornby saw it differently, as he explained in *One-Nil Down, Two-One Up*: 'The sad history of Anders Limpar is, to some extent, the recent history of Arsenal. It isn't a choice between winning and playing good football but a choice between winning and not winning, and that's no choice at all.' The debate over Limpar – or perhaps more accurately the type of player he represents – still rages at Highbury. One thing is certain: Hillier, Selley, Jensen, Morrow and Parlour could spend a lifetime in first team football and never dream of replicating Limpar's audacious lob from the half-way line against Liverpool in 1992, one of the finest goals ever witnessed at Highbury. That's what made Limpar special, and the soul of the beautiful game at Highbury, if it ever existed, was poorer for his departure.

In the Semi-Final of the European Cup-Winners' Cup, Arsenal faced the mighty Paris Saint-Germain, a team which had outclassed Spanish giants Real Madrid in the previous round and were well on their way to comfortably winning the French title. Understandably the Gunners approached the first leg in front of 46,000 fanatical Frenchmen (give or take a few thousand travelling North Londoners) at Parc des Princes with some trepidation, for a game dubbed in the French sports paper *L'Equipe* as 'A night for men'.

Changing his tactics from the previous round, Graham unexpectedly included Ian Wright up-front in place of Campbell, who had been particularly ineffective in Turin. Once again Graham opted for the 'Christmas tree' 4-3-2-1 formation, with the trusty back four of Dixon, Winterburn, Adams and Bould, a midfield trio of Davis, Jensen and Selley, and Ian Wright and Paul Merson pulling wide, but tucking in behind Alan Smith, the lone spearhead.

The system worked, with Arsenal playing some of their best and most attractive football of the campaign to date. Jensen, of all people, almost opened the scoring in what was to be a fine all-round display by the Dane. In the 35th minute, Arsenal scored the crucial away goal they coveted when Davis angled one of his famous free-kicks across the penalty area for Wright to glance a header past PSG's goalkeeper Lama. It was the perfect riposte to the racist taunting of the PSG fans.

At half-time the French looked stunned but recovered their poise for an early second-half onslaught on the Arsenal goal, which culminated in an equaliser in the 50th minute when David Ginola nicked a near post header from a corner after some untypically bad marking by Arsenal from a set-piece. Ginola, the French Footballer of the Year, continued to be the main threat to Arsenal and was later described by Lee Dixon as 'a footballer who's got everything. I wouldn't like to play against him every week. I've never seen anyone who's got as much ability and strength and adaptability. There isn't anything he can't do. He's good in the air, strong, fast, two-footed. He can play on the wing, behind the front two. If it was a question of money, transfer-wise I would sign him up tomorrow if he was available.' (In the subsequent close season, Arsenal were to be linked with the extravagantly talented Frenchman, but once again another big fish slipped through the Highbury net.)

After Ginola's equaliser, Arsenal fought back to shade the second half and the match, with Smith passing up a late chance to seal a conclusive away victory.

Arsenal, however, were well-pleased with their night's work and now looked forward to the second leg at Highbury on 12 April. The return leg was a tense and nervous affair with the Arsenal team and fans remembering the home defeat against Benfica in the 1991 Champions' Cup, after returning from Portugal with a fine 1-1 draw in the first leg. Some of the tension was quickly relieved, however, when Kevin Campbell (in for Paul Merson as the only change from the first leg) opened the scoring in the fifth minute with a glancing header inside Lama's near post from a Lee Dixon cross. Tempers began to fray as the stakes rose but Arsenal kept a crucial grip on midfield by constantly raising the tempo of the game and closing down the talented French midfield before their creative players could do damage.

The Brazilian Valdo had escaped Jensen several times in Paris to set up dangerous attacks, but this time the Dane had him in his back pocket. The unsung hero of the Arsenal midfield was nineteen-year-old Ian Selley, a tireless worker wholly committed to the role allotted to him by George Graham, who ran himself almost to the point of exhaustion in this match. It was Ian Wright, however, who was to grab the headlines once more, this time for the wrong reasons.

Wright's game is based on playing on an emotional edge which inspires his striking genius but has its flipside too. In the 39th minute, PSG defender Alain Roche was chasing a ball back towards his own goal near the touchline in front of the East Stand. It was a non-threatening position for Arsenal and arguably a challenge was not necessary. With a rush of blood, Wright launched a reckless two-footed tackle from behind and the defender tumbled. Since his booking against Liege, George Graham knew he had been playing Russian roulette with Ian Wright but surely hadn't expected him to commit professional suicide in this way. (Five Arsenal players had gone into the game on a yellow card, including the hard-tackling Tony Adams, yet Wright was the only player cautioned.) Wright immediately knew what he had done and sank to his knees, only to rise tearfully in a manner reminiscent of Paul Gascoigne in the World Cup Semi-Final of 1990 (another hot-head booked for a needless tackle). Wright admits he was close to breaking-point at half-time. 'I just went into the dressing-room and felt completely crazy.' Fortunately Tony Adams was on hand to exert a soothing captain's influence.

On the pitch, Adams was a colossus, cajoling his men through a tortuous second half as Arsenal lived dangerously. PSG pushed for the equaliser but their best chance was spurned by David Ginola, for once eluding the limpet-like Lee Dixon but blasting wide in the 72nd minute. With Hillier on for a tired Davis, Arsenal held on to win 1-0, the relief and exhilaration plainly visible on the players' faces, the ghost of Benfica finally exorcised.

If Ian Wright was down in the dumps, it didn't show as after the match he bared his backside from a window to a delighted crowd thronging Avenell Road, before leading a rendition of 'Spurs are on their way to Wembley, aaaarghh!' and throwing his shorts to the adoring masses. Arsenal had done it. Next stop, Copenhagen.

With their sights now solely ranged on Europe, the Gunners understandably lost their focus on the League, although an unbeaten twenty-match run was only punctuated right at the end of the campaign with two defeats against West Ham and Newcastle, either side of the Cup-Winners' Cup Final.

While the European adventure was not to be underestimated in terms of significance, the true legacy at Highbury is League Championships and there was a residual degree of frustration amongst the club's supporters that Graham's team had failed to launch a credible League challenge for the third season in a row. These feelings were exacerbated by the poor quality of football at Highbury, the almost universal consensus being that you could count the number of decent League games at Highbury during 93/94 on the fingers of one hand. The rumblings of discontent provided their own tensions between players and supporters, with Ian Wright summing up the prevailing mood amongst the players regarding the Highbury crowd's lack of appreciation of their efforts: 'I love our fans but I think sometimes they're spoiled by success and take winning for granted. What they have to realise is that many teams come here just to defend by putting bodies behind the ball. All that booing just makes things worse and gives the opposition a lift.'

This rather patronising view was at odds with the oft-expressed statement of Arsenal vice-chairman David Dein to the effect that Arsenal were now in the entertainment business. With the best seats at Highbury costing up to £25, fans expected to be entertained *and* to see a winning team. After all, Manchester United had proved it could be done.

Visiting teams have always entered the Marble Halls with containment in mind and Arsenal fans were not booing the team per se, merely being critical of their inability to muster the wit and invention to prise open a packed defence. The inability of Arsenal to launch an effective title challenge also threw into doubt the strengths of Graham's much-vaunted squad system. The suspicion was that Graham had bought too many 'squad' players, such as McGoldrick, Keown, Carter, Lydersen in recent years, rather than quality first-team regulars. In fact it could be argued that Graham had not made a really top-quality signing since Ian Wright.

George Graham would no doubt reply that the squad was strong enough when pitted with the best in Europe. What's more, as long as Arsenal are

265

winning something each season, then momentum is being maintained. And certainly, for the majority of Arsenal fans, a trip to Copenhagen for the Cup-Winners' Cup Final was more than adequate compensation for the disappointments in the League.

Arsenal travelled to Denmark in sombre mood, their already difficult task against extravagantly talented opponents made seemingly impossible by the absence of: Ian Wright (suspended), John Jensen, Martin Keown (rumoured to have been earmarked for a man-to-man assignment on Parma danger-man Zola) and David Hillier, who were all injured. To cap this worrying list, David Seaman boarded the plane with a suspected cracked rib. It seemed a foregone conclusion that Arsenal would lose with the bookies' odds stacked 3-1 against the Gunners in a two-horse race. The odds, however, failed to take into account three crucial factors which were to tip the balance in the Londoners' favour. The first was the fantastic support Arsenal took to Copenhagen, the travelling North Bank teeming out of every corner of the city to descend on the Parken Stadium and outnumber their Italian counterparts four to one. Arsenal's stadium dominance was completed when their travelling DJ, Paul Burrell, hijacked the PA system to endlessly play the adopted theme tune of the season, The Pet Shop Boys' 'Go West', with the re-worked lyrics 'one-nil to the Ar-se-nal'.

The second factor in Arsenal's favour was the organisation, resilience and indomitable team-spirit of Graham's unit. There is no better example of this never-say-die attitude than Tony Adams, Graham's closest confidant amongst the players, who is nicknamed 'Captain Colossus'. Bob Wilson, the former Arsenal goalkeeper now turned BBC commentator, saw the Arsenal skipper come down for breakfast on the morning of the match and observed that he walked in like John Wayne. 'You could see him thinking: "This is the day of battle". He devotes himself to Arsenal and winning a game of football. In the dressing-room he is just extraordinary. It's the noise. He bellows at them. He is their rock.'

Allied to the rock-like qualities of Adams and fellow centre-half minimalist Steve Bould (many Arsenal fans' player of the season), was the adaptability of the Arsenal system which allowed Steve Morrow and Ian Selley to come into midfield in place of Jensen and Keown/Hillier without the team losing its shape. The years of hard work which George Graham had put in at London Colney, drilling players in the exact nature of their roles on the pitch, were about to bear fruit.

The third factor is a corollary to the team-spirit of Arsenal, who perfectly embody the fighting qualities of English League football. During the 70s and 80s, English club sides with less natural talent than their Continental peers plundered the European trophy cabinet, because of the will-to-win which was seemingly unique to the English club game.

After the match in Copenhagen, many Arsenal players commented on the impression that the Parma players did not seem to 'fancy it'. For all its quality, there is a view that Serie A is a league of over-paid prima donnas who only turn it on when a new contract needs to be negotiated. (AC Milan is an honourable exception to this generalisation.) After all, for many in the Parma side, the Cup-Winners' Cup Final was just another stepping stone to a platform on the world's greatest stage – USA 94. Significantly, no Arsenal player, apart from Eddie McGoldrick, was destined for the States and even 'Steady Eddie' knew there was only a bit-part waiting for him in Jack Charlton's sequel to Italia 90.

In front of a crowd of 33,765 on a chilly night in the Danish capital, Parma dominated the early stages of the Final. As early as the first minute, Bould was in action to deny the lively Asprilla, put through by the dangerous Brolin. Three minutes later Benarrivo, overlapping down the right flank, put in a cross which Brolin headed just over Seaman's bar, although the huge Yorkshireman seemed to have it covered.

Arsenal recovered to threaten with a couple of trade-mark Tony Adams headers from free-kicks just before Campbell, unfortunately with another trade-mark of the season, fluffed a good chance to get a shot on Bucci's goal. From the resulting clearance, Zola swept a diagonal pass crossfield into the path of Brolin. The Swede's shot beat Seaman, only to come back off the inside of the post, in front of the massed ranks of Gooners behind the goal. Arsenal were riding their luck. Five minutes later the apprehension of the Arsenal fans turned to ecstasy as Smith pounced on Minotti's miscued clearance. Displaying the goal-scoring instincts which had served Arsenal so well when under pressure over the last seven years, Smith volleyed the ball into the net off Bucci's left-hand post. Nineteen minutes gone, 1-0 to the Arsenal, and cue pandemonium in three-quarters of the stadium.

Parma replied by forcing two free-kicks in quick succession just outside the Arsenal box, but Zola failed to trouble Seaman with his set-piece attempts. By now Arsenal were beginning to look relatively comfortable, with the dependable and experienced back four providing the foundations for a famous victory.

Steve Morrow, in for the injured Jensen, performed the Dane's role of defensive shield in front of the back four. Although he had shown in the League Cup Final the previous year that he could move forward to score vital goals, he accepted his specific duties on this occasion with equanimity, admitting that he felt restricted, but accepting his role. 'I had to be very disciplined. It was a question of: do you want to be pretty or do you want to win things?' Not only did the quiet Northern Irishman bear a passing physical resemblance to his manager – he was even beginning to talk like him!

That Parma were starting to get frustrated toward the end of the first half was shown by the bookings of Crippa and Asprilla for reckless challenges. Arsenal were wearing their opponents down in classic fashion, and entered the dressing-room at half-time well-pleased. During the break, Graham warned his men that they were defending too deep, allowing Parma space to run at them. Another tactical change was to re-assign Paul Davis who had originally been charged with tracking Tomas Brolin, but did not have the legs to stay with the Swede.

In the second half Arsenal grimly stuck to the task of denying Parma. If anything, they began to defend deeper. 'It was the fear factor,' Morrow said. 'We just wanted to defend our lead.' As Parma piled on the pressure, Selley was booked for time-wasting, but Arsenal gradually came back into it and Dixon almost put Campbell clear through on goal in the 63rd minute. With the attacks floundering on the twin rocks of Arsenal's defence, Adams and Bould (the latter voted 'Man-of-the-match' by no less an authority than *World Soccer Magazine*), the Italians began to lose heart.

The Parma supporters vented *their* frustration by pelting Nigel Winterburn with coins as he lay injured in front of them with fifteen minutes to go. Winterburn was eventually helped from the pitch but quickly recovered.

With time running out, Parma surged forward in search of the equaliser, and Crippa volleyed over after good work by Asprilla.

In injury-time, Arsenal hearts almost stopped as a loose ball was bundled into the Gunners' net by Italian substitute Melli. The referee correctly ruled it offside. And that was it. In a masterly display of defensive organisation, Arsenal had beaten the Italians at their own game. George Graham summed up the prevailing mood when he said, 'The players showed tremendous character and once we went a goal ahead we knew we had a chance because our strength is keeping clean sheets.'

The Parma coach, Nevio Scala, muttered the word '*negativo*' at the Press conference, although the diplomatic translation of his post-match comments read that, 'Arsenal were the better side. They showed how to control our system of play and to me they are the least typical English team I have seen.'

Graham, in magnanimous mood, praised the Italians, saying, 'Parma looked much sharper. They have better technicians than we do in England.'

The final word, however, must go to the Arsenal hero of the night, Alan Smith, who, when asked how he felt having scored the winner in a major European Final, answered with masterly Brummie understatement that he was 'quite pleased'. Priceless. Arsenal's victory was built on the backbone of the old guard of Adams, Bould, Winterburn, Dixon, Davis and Smith, all present on the night of 26 May 1989 when Arsenal clinched the Championship at Anfield.

In Copenhagen, the back four made light of the absences further forward by easily snuffing out the threat of Asprilla, Brolin and Zola after a shaky first fifteen minutes. In midfield, Paul Davis was at his majestic best, rarely wasting a ball and always available, in space, for a simple pass from a less experienced colleague. Paul Davis never looks like he is doing a great deal but his reading of the game is so advanced that he can get away with half the running of a less perceptive player. For many of the Highbury *cognoscenti*, Davis had been *the* difference in the domestic Cup Finals the previous season. In Europe, with more time on the ball than he could expect in the hurly-burly of the Premiership, he stamped his authority on the campaign.

Up-front for Arsenal, the peerless Alan Smith was another link with the class of 89, proving once again that he has the composure to score the goals that really matter, an art not quite perfected by the mercurial Ian Wright despite the hyperbole surrounding him. This nucleus of six players who played a full part in the Championship-winning teams of 89 and 91 proved the key to Arsenal's success in Copenhagen. With so many thirtysomethings in the group, however, would this prove to be their last great hurrah?

Arsenal's victory in Europe was greeted with more enthusiasm by neutrals in England than their Cup successes of 92/93, although there were some dark mutterings in the Press about the entertainment value. In truth, Copenhagen was not a thriller but few media pundits gave Arsenal enough credit for a mighty achievement. After all, they were one of only two non-Italian club sides to lift a European trophy in the last two seasons.

European finals are often tedious affairs, though this game was not flattered by comparison with the Champions' Cup Final later in the month when AC Milan demolished Barcelona 4-0 by playing some exhilarating football.

After the match Graham tried to put the dour nature of the game down to 'the slog of the English season' but this is a slightly disingenuous excuse coming from the manager of a club which took its team half-way round the world to South Africa for some meaningless pre-season friendlies. A more cogent explanation of Arsenal's lack of flair could be gleaned by making some more comparisons with the class of 89. Missing from the current Arsenal set-up are the likes of a box-to-box midfielder, in the mould of Michael Thomas, with a knack for scoring vital goals. Thomas had no peer in Copenhagen.

Could anyone envisage Jensen, Morrow, Selley, Hillier or Parlour scoring *that* goal at Anfield? David Rocastle and Brian Marwood provided width, penetration and a service for Alan Smith which Eddie McGoldrick and Paul Merson could not hope to replicate. Merson was also present at Anfield on that night, but a cursory glance at the video highlights of the 1989 season serves only to confirm how far he has fallen from the consistent standards he set in those early years.

In Copenhagen the vertebrae of the wonder years held together to defeat Parma with the blend of experience, organisation and discipline, glued together by a unique team-spirit. George Graham should rightly take enormous credit for building that team and instilling those durable qualities in his players. If there is a criticism, however, it is that he has not replaced the other elements, in midfield and out wide, which made the Championship side of 89 so much more potent and exciting than the new model Arsenal.

Graham accepts that he will need to rebuild if Arsenal are to challenge for the elusive third Championship he obviously covets – as ever, he is in the market for 'quality players'. His ability to find those players and blend them into another effective unit will ultimately determine his final resting place in the club's history. Will he haul himself alongside Herbert Chapman or nestle in behind the legend, just ahead of Bertie Mee, Tom Whittaker and George Allison?

The victory in Copenhagen proved – not for the first time in the last few seasons – that where there's a will, there's Arsenal. But what a shame it would be if the talented and determined Scot is burdened with the final epitaph of 'the end justified the means'. George Graham is capable of more.

BY GEORGE . . .

'The fans keep on to me about a midfield player. They're telling me nothing I don't already know. I've been searching for one for three years now. There aren't many players who could improve our squad. I only want the best. Young players like Ray Parlour and Ian Selley are developing fast. I don't want to hold them back by making a signing for the sake of it. There was only one outstanding midfielder available this summer – Roy Keane – and he chose Manchester United.'

A new season begins but George is still on the same old tack (August 93).

'Winning isn't just about pretty football. It's about hunger – application.'
Ditto . . . August 93.

'The moment the media and others start feeling sorry for Arsenal I'm not doing my job properly. Let's get back to the "lucky Arsenal" tag as quickly as possible.'
After undeserved defeat at home to Aston Villa (6 November 1993).

'Our main strength is our mental approach to the game. In that we've more than surpassed anybody we've played against. It's a side of the game that English people don't understand. It's sad that the English media, especially the journalists, haven't got a clue what you're talking about. They just want action and incidents. But I think the Continental media and fans are more educated about football. They can discuss tactics. I've actually sat in on Press conferences in Europe and they talk about the game. The last thing they talk about in English Press conferences is football, and that's sad.'

'I give my lads a lot of credit for the way they've conducted themselves in these games. They've not got involved in any barneys or crowding around the referee. We've handled that very well this year and yet nobody's mentioned it. I think the lads have really enjoyed it, but not more than I have. I've loved the battle of wits, going to see teams and looking at their strengths and weaknesses.'
After Semi-Final victory over Paris Saint-Germain.

'There are a lot of quality players around but whether they can handle the pressure of playing for Arsenal is another matter. When you play for a big club there is pressure on you week-in, week-out. Playing and performing

271

in one out of three is not good enough. They have to perform three times a week for ten months.'

Just like Paul Merson?

'It was a magnificent performance because my players were so tired and we've had so many injuries in the last few weeks. That is down to the number of games we play in England and it's nice for me to be able to make that point when we've just won a match like this. In terms of techniques we can't compare with the Continentals, especially the Italians, and I was very impressed with Parma. They looked much stronger and fitter than us. My players did a great job and although it's personally satisfying to win my first European trophy, I'm pleased for my players most of all. It's not easy working for me. I drive them on all the time because I want to win things. I don't ask the impossible but I always want their maximum. Working for me is tremendously hard but they respond time and again.'

'Parma looked much sharper than us. They were able to bring their last League games forward to help their preparation. It was only our character and resilience that got us through. Even though we've just won a Cup I still think we've got it wrong. At this stage of the season our players aren't as fresh as the Continentals. We should look at the situation and maybe copy them and have a mid-season break to give our players a rest physically and mentally.'

Not that George would change a thing . . .

'People forget that the majority of games in countries like Spain, France and other countries, are a pain in the backside. The teams pass the ball to death, nobody has a shot, there's no physical contact, and the stadiums are empty. The great thing about the English game is the passion. Sure, we could always improve on technique, but are we going to sacrifice all the other things for technique?'

'I'd like us to play with more flair. We have a good defence, which all top teams need. Manchester United have it right. They have a strong defence, a midfield with flair and creativity up front.'

End of season musings.

'It got absolutely stupid last year. Every paper, every radio station, every TV station, was saying: "George needs to buy a midfield player." In fact, I actually had a T-shirt made up which said "I AM TRYING TO BUY A

MIDFIELD PLAYER"! I was thinking of wearing it after a Press conference after a game, but eventually thought better of it . . .

'It's OK people saying, "I love to see a classy through-ball", but my idol – and I don't mind admitting it – was a Tottenham player, Dave Mackay. He was a competitor, whose incredible skill was overlooked simply because he competed so hard. Stefan Schwarz isn't as gifted as Brady or Hoddle, but he's got a beautiful left foot, he can take control of dead-ball situations, and most importantly of all, he competes. If you're going to win the Championship, at least half your team must be good competitors.'

> *Absolutely the last word on that Bermuda triangle for midfield players they call Fortress Highbury.*

'Trevor Brooking doesn't know what the winning mentality is about. He doesn't know what it takes to win the Championship because he was never in a team that won it. I won it as a player and I've won it as a manager. It's OK to sit back and philosophise about passing the ball, but we're in the job of getting results, as well as entertaining.'

> *George answers the TV pundits at the end of the season.*

'The difference between them [Manchester United] and us is that their midfield players are better than ours. I still think Cantona will let you down at the very highest level. I think he let Leeds down last year against Rangers, twice, and in the big games, against Inter Milan or whoever, I think Cantona will go missing. He's a cry-baby when the going gets tough.'

> *Why Jensen is better than Cantona.*

'I admit that there are times when I lie to journalists. I'll lie rather than slag off my players.'

> *George in candid interview.*

FA CARLING PREMIERSHIP 93/94

Final League position: 4th
Average home gate: 30,563

Coventry City	(h)	0-3	
Tottenham Hotspur	(a)	1-0	Wright
Sheffield Wednesday	(a)	1-0	Wright
Leeds United	(h)	2-1	Merson, og
Everton	(h)	2-0	Wright 2
Blackburn Rovers	(a)	1-1	Campbell
Ipswich Town	(h)	4-0	Campbell 3, Wright
Manchester United	(a)	0-1	
Southampton	(h)	1-0	Merson
Liverpool	(a)	0-0	
Manchester City	(h)	0-0	
Oldham Athletic	(a)	0-0	
Norwich City	(h)	0-0	
Aston Villa	(h)	1-2	Wright
Chelsea	(a)	2-0	Smith, Wright (penalty)
West Ham United	(a)	0-0	
Newcastle United	(h)	2-1	Wright, Smith
Coventry City	(a)	0-1	
Tottenham Hotspur	(h)	1-1	Wright
Sheffield Wednesday	(h)	1-0	Wright
Leeds United	(a)	1-2	Campbell
Swindon Town	(a)	4-0	Campbell 3, Wright
Sheffield United	(h)	3-0	Campbell 2, Wright
Wimbledon	(a)	3-0	Campbell, Parlour, Wright
Queens Park Rangers	(h)	0-0	
Manchester City	(a)	0-0	
Oldham Athletic	(h)	1-1	Wright (penalty)
Norwich City	(a)	1-1	Campbell
Everton	(a)	1-1	Merson
Blackburn Rovers	(h)	1-0	Merson
Ipswich Town	(a)	5-1	Wright 3 (1 penalty), Parlour, og
Southampton	(a)	4-0	Wright 3 (1 penalty), Campbell
Manchester United	(h)	2-2	Merson, og
Liverpool	(h)	1-0	Merson
Swindon Town	(h)	1-1	Smith
Sheffield United	(a)	1-1	Campbell
Chelsea	(h)	1-0	Wright
Wimbledon	(h)	1-1	Bould
Aston Villa	(a)	2-1	Wright 2 (1 penalty)
Queens Park Rangers	(a)	1-1	Merson
West Ham United	(h)	0-2	
Newcastle United	(a)	0-2	

FA Cup 93/94

Third Round:			
Millwall	(h)	1-0	Adams
Fourth Round:			
Bolton Wanderers	(a)	2-2	Wright, Adams
Fourth Round replay:			
Bolton Wanderers	(h)	1-3	Smith (after extra time)

League Cup 93/94

Second Round:
Huddersfield Town (a) 5-0 Wright 3,
Campbell,
Merson

Huddersfield Town (h) 1-1 Smith
Third Round:
Norwich City (h) 1-1 Wright

Third Round replay:
Norwich City (a) 3-0 Wright 2,
Merson

Fourth Round:
Aston Villa (h) 0-1

European Cup-Winners' Cup

First Round 1st leg:
Odense (a) 2-1 Wright,
Merson

First Round 2nd leg:
Odense (h) 1-1 Campbell

Second Round 1st leg:
Standard Liege (h) 3-0 Wright 2,
Merson

Second Round 2nd leg:
Standard Liege (a) 7-0 Campbell
2, Smith,
Selley,
Adams,
Merson,
McGoldrick

Quarter-Final 1st leg:
Torino (a) 0-0
Quarter-Final 2nd leg:
Torino (h) 1-0 Adams
Semi-Final 1st leg:
Paris Saint-Germain (a) 1-1 Wright
Semi-Final 2nd leg:
Paris Saint-Germain (h) 1-0 Campbell
Final (Copenhagen)
Parma 1-0 Smith

Appearances

	League	FA Cup	League Cup	Europe	Total
David Seaman	39	3	5	9	56
Ian Wright	39	3	4	6	52
Nigel Winterburn	34	3	4	9	50
Tony Adams	35	3	2	8	48
Lee Dixon	32+1	3	4	8	47+1
John Jensen	27	0+1	5	8	40+1
Kevin Campbell	28+9	3	2+2	6+2	39+13
Paul Merson	24+9	2+1	4	8	38+10
Steve Bould	23+2	3	3	5+1	34+3
Alan Smith	21+4	1+1	4+1	7+2	33+8
Martin Keown	23+10	2+1	3	4+3	32+14
Eddie McGoldrick	23+3	1+1	4	3+2	31+6

275

GEORGE GRAHAM: THE WONDER YEARS

	League	FA Cup	League Cup	Europe	Total
Paul Davis	21+1	0	1+2	9	31+3
Ray Parlour	24+3	3	2	0	29+3
Andy Linighan	20+1	0	4	1+1	25+2
Ian Selley	16+2	0	1+1	5+2	22+5
David Hillier	11+4	3	0+1	2+1	16+6
Anders Limpar	9+1	0	2	0	11+1
Stephen Morrow	7+4	0	1	1	9+4
Mark Flatts	2+1	0	0	0	2+1
Alan Miller	3+1	0	0	0	3+1
Neil Heaney	1	0	0+1	0	1+1
Paul Dickov	0+1	0	0	0	0+1

Goal-scorers

	League	FA Cup	League Cup	Europe	Total
Ian Wright	23	1	6	4	34
Kevin Campbell	14	0	1	4	19
Paul Merson	7	0	2	3	12
Alan Smith	3	1	1	2	7
Tony Adams	0	2	0	2	4
Ray Parlour	2	0	0	0	2
Steve Bould	1	0	0	0	1
Eddie McGoldrick	0	0	0	1	1
Ian Selley	0	0	0	1	1

The Wonder Years Statistics

Arsenal by numbers 1986–94

Appearances

(includes League, FA Cup, League Cup and Europe)

	86/87	87/88	88/89	89/90	90/91	91/92	92/93	93/94	Total
Tony Adams	55	51	43	45*	37	43	50+2	48	372+2
Nigel Winterburn	0	24+1	45*	42	50*	48	44	50	303+1
Alan Smith	0	47+3	43	42+2	47+2	40+6	39+6	33+8	291+27
Lee Dixon	0	6	37+2	45*	50*	46	44	47+1	275+3
Paul Merson	5+2	8+9	35+8	24+11	48+1	49+1*	49+1	38+10	256+43
David Rocastle	48	52*	45*	34+6	15+3	44+3	0	0	238+12
Paul Davis	51	33+3	13+3	10+3	46+2	17	11	31+3	212+14
David Seaman	0	0	0	0	50*	50*	56	56	212
Steve Bould	0	0	32+4	22	50*	24+2	30	34+3	192+9
John Lukic	49	52*	45*	45*	0	0	0	0	191
David O'Leary	52	33	28	35+6	16+12	13+15	9+8	0	186+41
Michael Thomas	14+4	45+1	40+4	41+2	37+4	9+5	0	0	186+20
Kevin Campbell	0	0+1	0	8+7	19+13	29+9	41+12	39+13	136+55
Ian Wright	0	0	0	0	0	33	45+1	52	130+1
Perry Groves	25+9	38+8	7+18	24+11	20+20	6+15	0+1	0	120+82
Kevin Richardson	0	34+6	37+4	39+1	0	0	0	0	110+11
David Hillier	0	0	0	0	14+8	28	38+5	16+6	96+19
Anders Limpar	0	0	0	0	39+2	27+6	18+11	11+1	95+20
Kenny Sansom	48	46	0	0	0	0	0	0	94
Andy Linighan	0	0	0	0	10+4	18+3	30+2	25+2	83+11
Steve Williams	43+1	36	0	0	0	0	0	0	79+1
Martin Hayes	42÷5	23+13	3+18	10+4	0	0	0	0	78+40
John Jensen	0	0	0	0	0	0	36+3	40+1	76+4
Niall Quinn	48	8+8	2+1	9	0	0	0	0	67+9
Brian Marwood	0	4	38	18	0	0	0	0	60
Ray Parlour	0	0	0	0	0	2+4	23+6	29+3	54+13
Viv Anderson	52	0	0	0	0	0	0	0	52
Martin Keown	0	0	0	0	0	0	15+1	32+14	47+15
Charlie Nicholas	33+5	3	0	0	0	0	0	0	36+5
Ian Selley	0	0	0	0	0	0	13	22+5	35+5

GEORGE GRAHAM: THE WONDER YEARS

	86/87	87/88	88/89	89/90	90/91	91/92	92/93	93/94	Total
Eddie McGoldrick	0	0	0	0	0	0	0	31+6	31+6
Gus Caesar	7+10	19+6	2	0+3	0	0	0	0	28+19
Stephen Morrow	0	0	0	0	0	0+2	19+6	9+4	28+12
Graham Rix	14+6	10+4	0	0	0	0	0	0	24+10
Jimmy Carter	0	0	0	0	0	6+1	13+6	0	19+7
Colin Pates	0	0	0	0+1	0+1	13+2	2+5	0	15+9
Pal Lydersen	0	0	0	0	0	5+2	8+1	0	13+3
Mark Flatts	0	0	0	0	0	0	7+4	2+1	9+5
Ian Allison	8+13	0	0	0	0	0	0	0	8+13
Alan Miller	0	0	0	0	0	0	3+1	3+1	6+2
Rhys Wilmot	6	0	0	0	0	0	0	0	6
Stewart Robson	5	0	0	0	0	0	0	0	5
Neil Heaney	0	0	0	0	0	0+1	3+2	1+1	4+4
Siggi Jonsson	0	0	0	1+6	2	0	0	0	3+6
Scott Marshall	0	0	0	0	0	0	2	0	2
Paul Dickov	0	0	0	0	0	0	1+2	0+1	1+3
Kwame Ampadu	0	0	0	0+2	0	0	0	0	0+2
Gavin McGowan	0	0	0	0	0	0	0+2	0	0+2
Andrew Cole	0	0	0	0	0+1	0	0	0	0+1

*Ever-present

Supporters' Club
Player of the Year

1986	David Rocastle	1990	Tony Adams
1987	Tony Adams	1991	Steve Bould
1988	Michael Thomas	1992	Ian Wright
1989	Alan Smith	1993	Ian Wright

Goal-scorers
(includes League, FA Cup, League Cup and Europe)

	86/87	87/88	88/89	89/90	90/91	91/92	92/93	93/94	Total
Alan Smith	0	16	25	13	27	17	6	7	111
Ian Wright	0	0	0	0	0	26	30	34	90
Paul Merson	3	5	14	7	16	13	8	12	78
Kevin Campbell	0	0	0	2	10	14	9	19	54
David Rocastle	5	12	7	2	2	4	0	0	32
Martin Hayes	24	3	1	3	0	0	0	0	31
Michael Thomas	0	11	7	8	3	1	0	0	30
Tony Adams	6	2	4	5	4	2	2	4	29
Perry Groves	3	9	4	5	6	1	0	0	28
Anders Limpar	0	0	0	0	13	5	2	0	20
Niall Quinn	12	2	1	4	0	0	0	0	19
Paul Davis	7	5	1	1	3	0	0	0	17
Brian Marwood	0	1	10	6	0	0	0	0	17
Lee Dixon	0	0	1	5	6	4	0	0	16
Charlie Nicholas	11	0	0	0	0	0	0	0	11
Kevin Richardson	0	7	1	0	0	0	0	0	8
Nigel Winterburn	0	1	4	0	0	1	2	0	8
Viv Anderson	7	0	0	0	0	0	0	0	7
Andy Linighan	0	0	0	0	0	1	4	0	5
Ray Parlour	0	0	0	0	0	1	2	2	5
Steve Bould	0	0	2	0	0	1	0	1	4
Steve Williams	2	2	0	0	0	0	0	0	4
David O'Leary	0	1	0	1	1	0	0	0	3
Ian Allison	2	0	0	0	0	0	0	0	2
Jimmy Carter	0	0	0	0	0	0	2	0	2
Paul Dickov	0	0	0	0	0	0	2	0	2
David Hillier	0	0	0	0	0	1	1	0	2
Graham Rix	2	0	0	0	0	0	0	0	2
Siggi Jonsson	0	0	0	1	0	0	0	0	1
Eddie McGoldrick	0	0	0	0	0	0	0	0	1
Stephen Morrow	0	0	0	0	0	0	1	0	1
Colin Pates	0	0	0	0	0	1	0	0	1
Kenny Sansom	0	1	0	0	0	0	0	0	1
Ian Selley	0	0	0	0	0	0	0	1	1

Debuts by home-grown players
under Graham

Paul Merson	22 November 1986	Manchester City	(h)	League
Michael Thomas	8 February 1987	Tottenham Hotspur	(h)	League Cup*
Kevin Campbell	7 May 1988	Everton	(a)	League**
David Hillier	25 September 1990	Chester City	(a)	League Cup
Kwame Ampadu	24 March 1990	Derby County	(h)	League
Andrew Cole	29 December 1990	Sheffield United	(h)	League***
Ray Parlour	29 January 1992	Liverpool	(a)	League
Stephen Morrow	8 April 1992	Norwich City	(a)	League
Neil Heaney	18 April 1992	Sheffield United	(a)	League
Ian Selley	12 September 1992	Blackburn Rovers	(h)	League
Mark Flatts	19 September 1992	Sheffield United	(a)	League
Alan Miller	21 November 1992	Leeds United	(a)	League
Paul Dickov	20 March 1993	Southampton	(h)	League
Scott Marshall	6 May 1993	Sheffield Wednesday	(a)	League
Gavin McGowan	6 May 1993	Sheffield Wednesday	(a)	League

*Littlewoods Cup Semi-Final – 1st leg
**Campbell came on for just twelve minutes in what was the last game of the season. He didn't make his next appearance until November 1990.
***Andy Cole's Arsenal career lasted just six minutes as a substitute.

The following home-grown professionals were already on Arsenal's books when George Graham arrived:

David O'Leary – debut 1975	Gus Caesar – 1985
Graham Rix – 1977	Martin Hayes – 1985
Paul Davis – 1980	Martin Keown – 1985
Stewart Robson – 1981	Niall Quinn – 1985
Tony Adams – 1983	David Rocastle – 1985

George goes shopping

. . . IN

Perry Groves	£65,000	Colchester	September 1986
Alan Smith	£850,000	Leicester City	March 1987
Nigel Winterburn	£350,000	Wimbledon	May 1987
Kevin Richardson	£150,000	Watford	August 1987
Lee Dixon	£350,000	Stoke City	January 1988
Brian Marwood	£500,000	Sheffield Wednesday	March 1988
Steve Bould	£390,000	Stoke City	June 1988
Siggi Jonsson	£475,000	Sheffield Wednesday	July 1989
Craig McKernon	£200,000	Mansfield	December 1989
Colin Pates	£350,000	Charlton Athletic	January 1990

280

David Seaman	£1.3 million	Queens Park Rangers	May 1990
Andy Linighan	£1.2 million	Norwich City	July 1990
Anders Limpar	£1 million	Cremonese	August 1990
Ian Wright	£2.5 million	Crystal Palace	September 1991
Jimmy Carter	£500,000	Liverpool	October 1991
Pal Lydersen	£500,000	Start Kristiansand	November 1991
John Jensen	£1.1 million	Brondby	July 1992
Eddie McGoldrick	£1 million	Crystal Palace	June 1993

. . . OUT

Tony Woodcock	£150,000	Cologne	Summer 1986
Stewart Robson	£750,000	West Ham	January 1987
Viv Anderson	£150,000	Manchester United	Summer 1987
Charlie Nicholas	£500,000	Aberdeen	January 1988
Kenny Sansom	£300,000	Newcastle	December 1988
Steve Williams	£300,000	Luton	June 1988
Niall Quinn	£750,000	Manchester City	March 1990
Martin Hayes	£600,000	Celtic	July 1990
John Lukic	£1 million	Leeds United	Summer 1990
Kevin Richardson	£750,000	Real Sociedad	Summer 1990
Brian Marwood	£350,000	Sheffield United	September 1990
Pat Scully	£100,000	Southend	March 1991
Kwame Ampadu	£50,000	WBA	June 1991
Michael Thomas	£1.5 million	Liverpool	December 1991
Andy Cole	£500,000*	Bristol City	July 1992
Perry Groves	£750,000	Southampton	August 1992
David Rocastle	£2 million	Leeds United	August 1992
Neil Heaney	£300,000	Southampton	March 1994
Anders Limpar	£1.6 million	Everton	March 1994

*plus a percentage of the £900,000 which Newcastle subsequently paid to Bristol City.

. . . you shake it all about

| Martin Keown | £200,000 | to Aston Villa | Summer 1986 |
| Martin Keown | £2 million | from Everton | February 1993 |

As the figures above show, no one could ever accuse Graham of having spent his way to success; in his first eight trophy-laden years at Highbury the club's net outlay in transfers was barely £1 million.

Unbeaten runs in the League

86/87	17 games	from 4 October until 24 January
87/88	12 games	from 29 August until 21 November (including club record of 10 consecutive wins)
88/89	11 games	from 4 December until 21 February
89/90	7 games	from 22 August until 18 October
90/91	23 games	only one defeat all season, against Chelsea on 2 February
91/92	17 games	the last 17
92/93	7 games	from 19 September until 21 November
93/94	19 games	until the last two were lost either side of the Parma final

'Clean sheets' in the League

86/87	16 in 42 games		90/91	24 in 38 games
87/88	15 in 40 games		91/92	10 in 42 games
88/89	14 in 38 games		92/93	16 in 42 games
89/90	14 in 38 games		93/94	21 in 42 games

Pick that out of the net . . .

★ In 86/87 Arsenal were the 7th highest scorers and had the 2nd best defence.
★ In 87/88 Arsenal were equal 4th highest scorers and had the 4th best defence.
★ In 88/89 Arsenal were top scorers and had the second best defence.
★ In 89/90 Arsenal were 8th top scorers and had the equal 2nd best defence.
★ In 90/91 Arsenal were the 2nd highest scorers and had the best defence.
★ In 91/92 Arsenal were the top scorers and had the 5th best defence.
★ In 92/93 Arsenal were the lowest scorers and had the 2nd best defence.
★ In 93/94 Arsenal were the 11th highest scorers and had the best defence.

Arsenal's League record against major rivals under Graham

	pld	w	d	l	f	a
Liverpool	16	6	3	7	18	14
Manchester United	16	5	6	5	15	17
Tottenham Hotspur	16	8	5	3	19	12
Everton	16	9	4	3	22	14
Aston Villa	14	5	2	7	21	15
Chelsea	14	7	3	4	20	12
Nottingham Forest	14	5	5	4	20	15
Leeds United	8	2	4	2	10	11
Blackburn Rovers	4	1	1	2	2	3

Before . . .

	P	W	D	L	F	A	Final Position
78/79	42	17	14	11	61	48	7th
79/80	42	18	16	8	52	36	4th
80/81	42	19	15	8	61	45	3rd
81/82	42	20	11	11	48	37	5th
82/83	42	16	10	16	58	56	10th
83/84	42	18	9	15	74	60	6th
84/85	42	19	9	14	61	49	7th
85/86	42	20	9	13	49	47	7th
Total	336	147	93	96	464	378	

. . . and after George

	P	W	D	L	F	A	Final Position
86/87	42	20	10	12	58	35	4th
87/88	40	18	12	10	58	39	6th
88/89	38	22	10	6	73	36	Champions!
89/90	38	18	8	12	54	38	4th
90/91	38	24	13	1	74	18	Champions!
91/92	42	19	15	8	81	46	4th
92/93	42	15	11	16	40	38	10th
93/94	42	18	17	7	53	28	4th
Total	322	154	96	72	491	278	

For the train-spotters amongst you, the above proves conclusively that under Graham, Arsenal score more goals and concede less:

average score BG . . . Arsenal 1.38 A. N. Other 1.12

average score AG . . . Arsenal 1.52 A. N. Other 0.86

Bring on the noise . . . the Highbury crowds*

86/87	
86/87	29,056 average gate – fourth-best in the League
Best crowd	47,777 against Liverpool on 10 March
Spurs' average	25,906
87/88	29,902 average gate – third-best
Best crowd	54,703 against Liverpool on 15 August
Spurs' average	25,921
88/89	35,593 average gate – third-best
Best crowd	45,129 against Tottenham on 2 January
Spurs' average	24,467
89/90	33,672 average gate – third-best
Best crowd	46,132 against Tottenham on 20 January
Spurs' average	26,484

90/91	36,878 – second-best	
Best crowd	42,393 against Queens Parks Rangers on 23 April	
Spurs' average	30,632	
91/92	31,914 – third-best	
Best crowd	41,703 against Manchester United on 1 February	
Spurs' average	27,809	
92/93	24,403 – eighth-best	
Best crowd	29,739 against Manchester United on 28 November	
Spurs' average	27,740	
93/94	30,563 – fifth-best	
Best crowd	36,203 against Manchester United on 22 March	
Spurs' average	27,160	

*League only

Arsenal's England Internationals (86/87–93/94)

Tony Adams	31 caps		David Seaman	11 caps
Lee Dixon	21		Viv Anderson	6
Kenny Sansom	15		Steve Bould	2
Paul Merson	14		Martin Keown	2
David Rocastle	14		Michael Thomas	2
Ian Wright	14		Nigel Winterburn	2
Alan Smith	13		Brian Marwood	1

Given Arsenal's practically unbroken success story under George Graham, his players have been surprisingly peripheral to England's fortunes. The forwards made even less impact than a cursory glance at the figures suggests – both Merson and Wright made eight of their appearances as a substitute while Smith (top scorer in two Championship-winning campaigns, remember) only started seven games; Marwood's England career lasted just nine minutes. Not that the defenders fared much better; Bould and Winterburn – two of the stalwarts of the League's most parsimonious defence – made only four appearances between them (both of Winterburn's as a sub. and Bould's at the eleventh-hour under Terry Venables). Even Tony Adams has not been that assiduous a selection if you consider that his 31 appearances were spread over eight seasons. In major tournaments, Arsenal's contribution has been even more spartan: only one of Graham's players made the plane to the 1990 World Cup Finals in Italy (David Seaman, who joined the club one month before the World Cup, but who was injured training in Italy, never played and was replaced by Chelsea's

Dave Beasant), and only Adams and Sansom took part in the 1988 European Championship Finals in Germany; in the 1992 edition in Sweden, Merson and Smith started just one game apiece.

Afterword: Gods and Tomatoes

by Al Fresco

In history there's often a 'little man' who gets forgotten as another charismatic figure grabs the glory. It was an Egyptian water boy who discovered the steps leading to Tutankhamun's tomb, although Howard Carter took all the credit. Similarly with George Graham – a Dave Cusack penalty at Colchester in 1983 saved Millwall from the dreaded drop into the then Fourth Division. Had they been relegated George would undoubtedly have been sacked and would certainly never have moved from managing the Lions to the glorious Gunners.

As I write, George has been in charge at Arsenal for just over eight seasons, during which time he has won six trophies. It is hard to remember the so-called 'song and dance' team of the early 1980s and harder still to imagine anybody else in charge in the foreseeable future. George has steeped himself in Arsenal traditions and from the outset declared his intention of founding a dynasty. His avowed model is the Shankly/Paisley/Fagan era at Liverpool and before that the Chapman/Allison/Whittaker Arsenal of the 30s–50s.

The comparison with the legendary Herbert Chapman is both appropriate and deserved as well as being a yardstick that George aspires to. A visit to the Arsenal Museum shows not only the difference between old and new but invites us to compare George and Herb's training methods; George and Herb's tactical awareness; and so on. George Graham has contextualised himself with the demi-god of Highbury folklore. Maybe we don't realise it now because we're too close to events, but the future may paint the years 1986–94 and beyond as Arsenal's golden age. The Georgian Era.

George Graham has in football terms delivered the goods. There are those who maintain reservations about his style of management, transfer dealings, apparent aloofness and adoption of a tactical approach where '1-0 to the Arsenal' seems the most likely outcome of every game. Comments such as, 'I learned nothing from the World Cup' (1990) and 'I'm not interested in crowd-pleasers' (1994) say something about his personality

286

but 'I'm only interested in winners' says something else. And what winners! Anfield, 26 May 1989: Michael Thomas wins the League for Arsenal with a last-gasp shot, perhaps the finest-ever moment in English League football. The 1990–91 champions lose only ONE game all season. A banner unfurled at the Clock End during the celebratory win over Manchester United says simply, 'George knows'. 1993: the unique double of the FA Cup and League (Coca-Cola) Cup. 1994: nine games in the European Cup-Winners' Cup, only three goals conceded, culminating in an unforgettable night in Copenhagen as George Graham wins the sort of trophy which Chapman and his ilk were never able to compete for. Dream on, all you Tottenham fans!

These past several years have witnessed major changes to the very character of football in this country. The Taylor Report into the Hillsborough Disaster of 1989 has led directly to the requirement for all-seater, smaller capacity stadia and the heart-breaking dismantling of favoured ends such as the Liverpool Kop and our very own North Bank. The insidious influence of television, particularly BSkyB, has meant games can kick off at 12 o'clock in a heatwave or 4 pm on a Sunday. Admission prices have soared. The top clubs now make most of their money from spin-offs such as sponsorship, videos and the *de rigueur* fashion item of the 1990s – the replica shirts. The ordinary supporter seems dwarfed – one might even say sidelined – by all these shenanigans. But we're still here and we're making ourselves heard because, by a curious coincidence, George's reign as Arsenal manager is almost exactly contemporaneous with the rise of the football fanzine. Some, of course, are mostly pub talk or student rag-mag-style humour; others show up the bias and inadequacies of Britain's most celebrated football journalists and pundits such as David Lacey and Jimmy Hill. *One-Nil Down, Two-One Up* is most certainly in this latter group. First appearing in December 1987, this glossy, appealing publication has its finger firmly on the true pulse of events at Highbury. When somebody comes to write the Arsenal Double Centenary book in 2086 it will be *One-Nil Down, Two-One Up*, *Fever Pitch* and indeed this book which they will refer to in order to get the *real* story.

Fanzines exist not because we're frustrated novelists and journalists (we are! we are!) but to enable the football follower to read an honest, discriminating view on the game. We are removed from the sycophancy of club and kiddie publications. Nor do we indulge in the build-you-up-to-knock-you-down, 'gods and tomatoes' approach of the tabloids. Many football books are shamelessly lowbrow but I'm certain that this book has given you plenty to think about. What more could you want? Then again, to borrow and misuse somebody's quote, maybe writing about football is like dancing about architecture.

George knows.